the

hen
party
handbook

BATH SPA
MEDIA

the hen party *handbook*

The No. 1 guide to planning an
unforgettable last night of freedom

BATH SPA MEDIA

Published by

CUTTING EDGE GUIDES

an imprint of
Bath Spa Media Ltd
The Tramshed, Beehive Yard,
Walcot Street, Bath BA1 5BB
email: guides@bathspamedia.com
www.bathspamedia.com

Also by Bath Spa Media Ltd
www.HenNightDirect.com and www.StagNightDirect.com

Creative Director Zoë Hughes Gough
Sales Director Lola Dali-Kemmery
Words by Rosie Gordon and Zoë Hughes Gough
Cover design by Clare Barber (www.cb-design.co.uk)
Book design by Lisa Hext (www.merrickspublishing.com)

Printed by Butler Tanner & Dennis Ltd
Caxton Road, Frome BA11 1NF
email: info@butlertanneranddennis.com
www.butlertanneranddennis.com

ISBN 978-0-9564368-0-1
A CIP record for this book is available from the British Library.

Distribution by MMC Ltd
Octagon House, White Hart Meadows
Ripley, Woking GU23 6HR
Tel: 01483 211222
email: enquiries@mmcltd.co.uk
www.mmcextranet.co.uk

contents

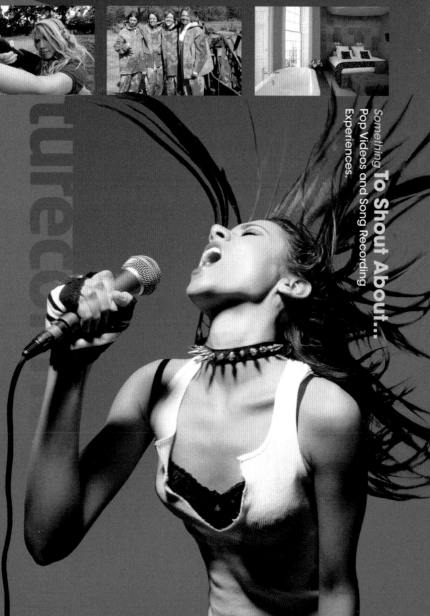

Luxury Hen Parties **For The Girls...**
You need to give your Hen a celebration to remember.
We know the devil's in the detail and the details in the planning.

Something **To Shout About...**
Pop Videos and Song Recording
Experiences.

introduction

There are few occasions in life where self-indulgence is the name of the game. But let's be clear on this. Your hen party is one. It's your party and you can do what you want to. You'll be surrounded by ladies whose sole aim in life is to launch you into married life in style. Our advice? Milk it.

This is the first guide of its kind: a UK-only, ladies-only book of inspiration and perfect plans. Find out which cities rock your world, and take your pick from top clubs, karaoke bars, restaurants, fancy dress, entertainers, DJs and many more venues and services to help you make it a party that's talked about for years to come.

The problem for brides-to-be is this. You often have to organise your hen party yourself. While obviously this means you won't end up in venues, outfits and activities that make your toes curl, on the other hand it's tough enough organising a wedding, without worrying about a hen do on top. That's probably why stag parties are often more extravagant – a best man has both the time and the inclination to organise a lavish send-off for the groom. We can't let this sexual inequality continue though, can we?

Your hen night is an opportunity to take on a new challenge, log on to exhilaration.co.uk for ideas.

So, what to do? Nominating a head bridesmaid to do all the legwork for you is a great plan. Or get the girls over for a few glasses of wine and a brainstorm – find out how much people want to spend, the dates you can all do, the food you all like and fun stuff like themes, fancy dress and entertainment. Use the guide for inspiration – you'll be truly amazed at some of the activities available – from foreplay lessons (no, we're not joking!) through to white-water rafting, there are hundreds of weird and wonderful thrills to be had, day and night. We've included ideas for all budgets, including DIY tips for brilliant parties at home.

If you're too busy, too indecisive, or too hung over after a girls' night of 'discussion' to remember what's what, then worry not. There are many hen party organisers out there who will take one look at your budget and produce a fantastic, tailor-made event for you in the city of your choice.

So, ladies, enjoy your last maiden voyage. Whether your sailing in champagne-bucketloads of style or cobbling together your own raft, we hope you reach married shores safely and with fond (if hazy) memories of a truly legendary Hen Party.

how to plan an unforgettable party

afternoon **tea** amazing *awesome* bars **best-ever** brilliant bubbly **bungee jump** bunny **girls** camp **casino** celebration **champagne** *cocktails* comedy cool cracking crazy **dancing** **queen** *delight* disco drinking eating enjoy entertainment excitement **extraordinary** fabulous *fancy dress* fantastic food friends fun girls **gorgeous** group *happy* hens

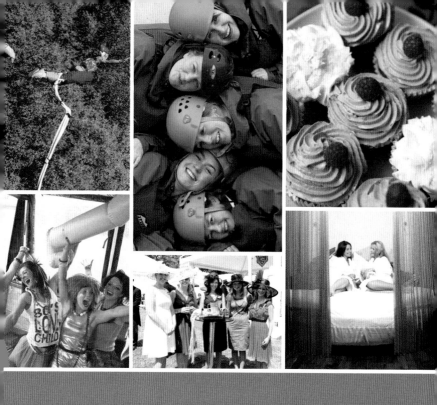

high spirits **hilarious** *ideas*
immense jollity **last night of freedom**
laughter limousine luxury marvelous
massage *music* naked **nightlife** *outrageous*
pamper party people pleasure pole
dancing quirky *racy* sensational
shopping sexy smiling spa stripper
stupendous ***superb*** theatre underwear *VIP*
wild women x-rated zany

who, what, when, where…

The wedding is approaching. Your dress is nearly finished, the invitations have been sent, the cake is on order, the hymns have been picked. Now for the important bit… THE HEN NIGHT!

why?

A married friend who didn't have a hen party says, 'I thought I would, but when the time came I just couldn't be bothered with the hassle of who might get on with who and picking a night out they'd all enjoy. I was so stressed out with organising the wedding that I just decided to give the hen party a miss.' And does she regret it? 'Definitely. I should have set aside the time and money to do something for myself. As it was, I hardly enjoyed any of the run up to the wedding.'

Ah, what a tragic tale! So, the advice from Lady Hindsight is this: 'Make time, make yourself a priority, invite who *you* want to – not who you *should* or *shouldn't* – and remember, getting married is supposed to be enjoyable!'

Of course you could hand the whole thing over to your best mate – that's what bridesmaids are for isn't it?

when to book?

If you've just got engaged and you're already scheming for a hen do, fantastic. You can budget for something truly unforgettable, book your friends early and bag those popular venues before they get booked up. But if you're all last minute – don't panic! Pick a date (about two–four weeks before the wedding, unless you want to go to an event with a fixed date of course). Make sure the people you actually want to be there can make it. That's the crucial stuff done. Now get your budget into shape. The rest is mere detail…

if budget is no object then why not book into a sophisticated spa hotel, like Swinton Park in Yorkshire.

what's on offer?

Working out the detail is the fun part. Will you make your own cocktails or have fizz served by naked waiters? Picnic in the park or upmarket dinner? Dancing or comedy? Club dress or fancy dress? Theme, decor, dance class, DJ, boat trip, spa hotel or B&B? Or all of the above? If you want to bring in caterers or entertainers, then book them up as soon as you can. When it comes to theme, decoration and fancy dress, well they can wait until the last minute if they have to. For now, get the nuts and bolts in place, then relax and enjoy dreaming up your ideal party.

If your style is more canvas than caviar, how about a camping trip – Smugglers Haven, Newquay perhaps.

We've heard people get married just to try out one of our Weekends!

www.GoBananas.co.uk

0871 789 6200

how much?!

OK, so you've constructed your ideal party in your head: the unique theme, the shiny happy people, the gorgeous male models serving you canapés, your bespoke outfit and the world-class venue…the pages in *Hello!* It's genius. Now how are you going to get this legendary event off the ground? Well, whether you're skinted or minted, it's all down to budgeting. Dull, maybe. Essential? Yes.

get it down

If you're super organised, you can factor the hen (and stag) do into your grand wedding budget and have it all on a nicely controlled simmer from word go. If you want to keep it separate, well, that makes life easy too. Your other half won't be able to interrogate you about every stripper or other *perfectly legitimate* expense you clock up. You need to set up a proper spreadsheet and factor in travel, venue hire, meals, drinks, licences for bar or music hire, entertainers, hotels…and whatever else your heart desires. Be very, very thorough at this stage and there won't be any nasty surprises down the line. If you can't afford something, use this guide to research cheaper alternatives or just cross it out and move on.

delegation, that's what you need

It's all very well talking about budgets. But what if you just don't do figures? Well, be very careful. The solution here is not *necessarily* open season on credit cards. It might work better for you to delegate the hen party to an organised and resourceful bridesmaid. Or it might make sense to hire the services of a party planner. There are many planners out there ready to take the sting out of the whole operation for you, at a price.

They will tailor-make packages for budgets big and small, ensuring you get the best rates (because they negotiate with the hotels, clubs etc) and that you don't spend wildly beyond your means.

the art of illusion

The other great thing about hiring a professional is that he or she might amaze you with theme and entertainment ideas that can be done on your budget. With their contacts, suddenly theatrical props, look-alikes, waiting staff, glamorous or bizarre venues and more will be available for your event, making a small spend look like a million dollars.

top tips

Mark Scott of Go Bananas says, 'Travel is expensive – book early to get much, much cheaper deals. Also, as soon as you know who wants to be involved, get deposits from everyone. Aim for low season and avoid special events, such as Edinburgh festival.' But his biggest tip? 'If you're partying, get a cheap hotel. As long as it's a safe place to put your bag and get a couple of hours kip, it's fine.' Go Bananas can do an Edinburgh hen weekend from just £49, so the man knows what he's talking about.

themes and schemes

A well-thought out theme can turn a good party into a great party, whatever budget you're juggling. It's time to get creative.

cheap and cheerful

Show me the woman who won't adopt a comedy persona when presented with a wig and assortment of 'fancy dress' from Oxfam and I'll show you my grandmother, who will just ask me what the hell I've been doing in her bedroom. My gran aside, at the very cheapest level, a box full of bad second-hand clothes in a room full of girls is the basis of a hilarious 'bad taste' party. Complete the theme with cheesy music, naff party food and games of Twister and you're on to a winner.

A colour theme for clothes (and hair!) will really make your hen party stand out.

theme your drinks

Scarlet harlots – Kir Royale
Pour a half shot of crème de cassis into a champagne flute and top up with fizz.

Latin ladies – Margarita
Shake a double shot of tequila, a shot of triple sec and shot of lime juice with ice. Wet the rim of a Margarita glass and dip into salt. Strain the cocktail into the glass.

Garishly gorgeous – Pina Colada
Blend ice with a double shot of white rum, double shot of coconut cream and three double shots of pineapple juice. When smooth and thick, pour into a chilled glass and garnish with the tackiest plastic stuff you can find.

Class acts – Cosmopolitan
Shake one and a half shots of vodka, one shot of Cointreau, one shot of cranberry juice and a dash of lime juice with cracked ice. Strain into a chilled flute or cocktail glass and garnish with a slice of lime.

the pink parade

All over the UK, every weekend, are broods of hens wearing short dresses and pink cowboy hats, carrying inflatable penises. They're usually having fun, so don't knock it…but if you want to be a bit different, tweaking basic outfits with personal touches is a simple and effective way to go. For example, if the bride's blonde, then give everyone blonde wigs. If you're at a seaside resort you all wear snorkels…and so on. Why not get your friends together over a glass of wine to mull over some ideas?

risqué business

If you're staying in, an Ann Summers party might make things a little edgier than the more predictable dinner and drinks. Or how about asking your guests to a sexy red-themed dinner party? Serve pink Kir Royales and hire a handsome butler to serve you. Butlers in the Buff and Cheeky Butlers will meet your needs.

If you're going out, there are plenty of edgy, sassy or downright dirty venues to make you feel satisfying close to crossing the nice girl/naughty girl line – just this once.

the big night in

As Dorothy so wisely noted after her house crushed the Wicked Witch of the West, 'there's no place like home'. Whether it's childcare, logistics, budget or pure love of the place, many hens have good reasons to choose home sweet home for their party.

get a man in

Inviting a performer to schmooze and amuse your guests means you're able to get on with enjoying yourself and feeling you've laid on something a little bit special. Choose from dancers, strippers, magicians, and cocktail 'mixologists' – there are performers in every region of the UK who will come to your home and wow your guests.

If the girls are unimpressed by such hi-jinks but you have kids running around, a balloon modeller or clown would be a good way of keeping them happy while you get on with the serious business of eating and drinking.

lights, canapés, action

If you're theming, decor is key. Turning up to a Halloween party as Morticia from the Addams family only to find the beige scatter cushions and tasteful lily arrangements still in situ is just embarrassing, after all.

If it's a summer garden do, little tables scattered around and covered with white cloths and posies of flowers look very dainty. Plates of pretty cupcakes and elegant sandwiches or canapés laid out under strings of bunting will complete the 'garden party' scene. For a sophisticated winter bash, architectural displays of berried twigs and pussy willow can look stunning, as do twinkling white fairy lights and plenty of candles dotted around. The aroma of wine a-mulling is another winner. And colour themes work well to set a scene and make the atmosphere less 'homey' and more 'party'.

larging up the lounge

If you're going for an all-out rave (and perhaps you've chosen to stay in because you have no neighbours to disturb), then disco lights, karaoke machines, glitter balls and good DJs are all available for hire, as are mobile bars and smoke or bubble machines. With all your favourite people, a clean loo, hand-picked music (why not subscribe to spotify.com for the night) and no queue for the bar, home is scoring high.

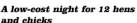

Ideal Home Show

A low-cost night for 12 hens and chicks

5pm Kiddy entertainer arrives. Serve Pimms for the ladies.

Lay out a fabulous picnic tea – delivery of pizza for the kids, yummy deli goodies for the grownups, pretty cupcakes and a few bottles of fizz.

7pm Have a session with the children on the karaoke machine before their sleepover.

9pm Mixologist arrives for private cocktail lessons. Get the spotify going, hand out the canapés and get the party started.

10.30pm Now you're all cocktail experts, it's time for silly games, laughs and more karaoke…

the ultimate girls night in!

get the experts in!

Experts in etiquette, charming and gorgeous, 'Butlers in the Buff', offer a tasteful yet cheeky way to make hen parties unforgettable! Don't let the hen run around getting her own drinks – let the butler take the stress out of hosting for you.

The butlers can serve you and your guests champagne and nibbles, help with hen party games and look gorgeous wherever you chose to hold your hen party. What's more they do it wearing only a collar, bowtie, cuffs and a bottom revealing apron!

One hour is simply not enough so make sure you book your butler for at least two hours. He can take care of everything from opening doors, serving guests, pouring champagne and even hosting your very own 'Mr & Mrs' quiz.

"I would just like to thank you all for providing the gorgeous butlers for Angie's hen party – they really were the icing on the cake!

The whole evening was brilliant; we haven't stopped talking about it yet!

We're so glad we booked Butlers in the Buff and will definitely be using you again for another hen later this year!"

dressed for it

If you have a particular theme for the hen party, the Butlers can even be dressed to suit the occasion. So if you would prefer them to wear something other than their pinny, you can tailor their outfit to match the party's theme. How about a topless Butler in trousers, or even a kilt?! Or something a little more fancy – cowboy chaps or builders belt and helmet! Everyone loves a workman!

top 5 reasons to hire a butler in the buff

• Have a quizmaster for the night to host a 'Mr & Mrs' style quiz.

• Champagne on tap…just make sure you've stocked up on the chilled bubbly then your Butler can serve the guests without them having to lift a finger.

• On any good hen night breakages are to be expected, so sit back and relax whilst your Butler takes care of any mishaps.

• We hear that Butlers in the Buff Butlers are not only gorgeous but have outstanding cocktail-making skills to boot, so why not let them mix up a mojito, a cosmopolitan or anything that takes your fancy?

• Butlers in the Buff cost from £60 per hour so split between a few friends that's less than a tenner each!

grand days out

Too early for karaoke? You're right, there's a time and a place for everything. And in the daylight hours of your hen party day or weekend, there are some truly fantastic treats to be had, whatever the British weather throws at you.

the big chill

If high polish is your thing, and you have a set of girlfriends with a little cash to splash, how about a day spa or even a full-on pamper weekend? You know it will all make sense when you're wrapped in that fluffy robe with a glass of bubbly in your manicured paw. Ooh, yes. You can't beat the UK for gorgeous, ivy-clad hotels and elegant day spas with fine dining, free-flowing champagne and luxurious treatments. And if your taste is more bountiful than your bank balance, there are mobile therapists in your area to pamper you at home. A few scented candles, music and a well-stocked fridge are the only trimmings you need.

great escapes

For those of us who don't know why an emery board has two surfaces and prefer tramping through mud to slapping it on our faces, think the Great Outdoors.

There are lots of choices, and don't be afraid to exclude some hens from your daytime group – you can always catch up with them in the evening. Clay pigeon shooting, sailing and go-karting are just a few of the events you'll find here. Horse riding also makes for a fantastic short break in the countryside. Your kit is transferred between lovely B&Bs while you and Dobbin (and the rest of your group, we hope!) trot there at leisure.

let them eat cake

Why not indulge your inner Nigella with a sumptuous, home-based tea party, complete with a delivery of cupcakes and fizz? Or for something more hands-on, cookery lessons are available at many venues, specialising in anything from Moroccan spice to classic Italian, and chocolate desserts to ice-cream. They make a delicious daytime treat for a small group of friends. Go on, bring out the domestic goddess in you.

Chill out in a hot tub like this oasis of calm at Swinton Park spa, Ripon, Yorkshire. Book with Leisure Vouchers.

Clay pigeon shooting is available at outdoor activity centres around the UK with Virgin Experience Days.

No hen party is complete without a well chilled bottle of bubbly, so pop that cork and enjoy!

If white knuckle rides are your thing, there are plenty of UK theme parks to thrill you.

simple pleasures

Shopping, a long lunch and a little more shopping? Perfect. Some of the listed bars in Part Two are great for dim sum or elegant lunches in funky surroundings while you take the weight off. Tuck yourselves into a quiet booth with champagne on ice, or spread out on a sunny terrace with a cocktail, before heading back out into retail therapy. It's a hard life, isn't it?

three-ring circus

Real life can be such a bore. Yet, if you are contemplating the mechanics of a home-based do with a random selection of friends, kids and family, do not despair. Circus Whiz can nip down to your garden and erect an inflatable circus ring, and extroverts and kids can join in with various acrobatic antics. You can hire a face painter too, which the kids will love – allowing you to get on with the serious business of kicking back with a glass of Pimms. If you wake up under the trampoline painted up like Bobo the Clown, then it's been a good party. And for those of us who love a good old-fashioned fete – and who

doesn't – well Sidestalls.net can set you up with a coconut shy, hoopla, hook-a-duck and other retro delights. Go as large as you like with this theme – get your hens to dress up, hire a Victorian carousel – the sky's the limit. Candyfloss, balloons or home-made party loot bags would make the perfect finishing touches.

fairground attractions

If you're in search of thrills, there's no need to go on a pricey snowboarding break or fling yourself out of an aeroplane – what could be better than screaming your way through a rollercoaster ride? The 'official photographs' taken as you descend the deadliest loop are guaranteed to supply laughs for the night ahead. Not enough thrills for you? Perhaps you need a whole weekend at Alton Towers, complete with fairytale hotel accommodation and enough rides to guarantee you'll have screamed and giggled your vocal chords dry by the end. For smaller groups of strong-stomached friends the theme park is a winner – affordable and wicked fun.

Surfing lessons in the South West are a fun hen party activity, especially at englishsurfschool.com.

parties with splash

Fancy surfing lessons with a few friends down in Cornwall? Slides, spa and cycling at Centerparcs? How about sailing, rowing boats on a lazy river, jet-ski races or a River Thames cruise? Water babies will find lots of suggestions in this guide to whet their whistles and to suit all pockets. Cruises and row boats are great for groups where some friends are pregnant or you have a big age range. Conversation will flow, and quieter guests will love the freedom of being able to enjoy a glass of something cool as they take in the wonderful views. We're not pretending that Britain is the warmest, driest destination for watery activities, but who cares? There's something magical about partying on the water, rain or shine.

high kicks

Pole, street and belly dancing lessons have become an affordable and fun hen party staple. And now, Burlesque dance lessons are gaining huge popularity, thanks to the likes of Immodesty Blaize, who has helped bring this risqué art form back into the spotlight. For a price, you can hire Immodesty Blaize, Marianne Cheesecake or other circuit Burlesque beauties to appear at your private party. Polestars, the nationwide chain, offer lessons in ten dance styles at venues across the country. But if you want a room full of screaming ladies, it has to be The Devil – a strip act that will make your knees go weak. Save that for later!

go wild

If you're a bit of a petrol head, how about Castle Coombe – a beautiful, picture-postcard Wiltshire village with a deadly secret – a race track that you can take your car to (or perhaps more wisely hire a car), and drive as fast as possible. Outdoorsy types might opt for a sportier extreme thrill with white-water rafting breaks in Wales, or a good old-fashioned bit of bungee jumping at venues countrywide. And it might not be glamorous, but that grin you'll have all over your face after a day's zorbing (doing somersaults inside a big clear plastic ball) will make it a hen party to remember. Just be careful whom you invite – your mum probably won't enjoy it!

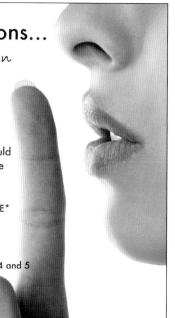

goodnight ladies

When the sun sets on your day of pampering, wild fun or mellow treats, the hen party can really rev up a gear. No matter how loud, outrageous, elegant or memorable you want your night to be, if there's one thing that we Brits are good at, it's partying the night away.

follow that cab

Choosing how to get to your venue is crucial. Is everyone getting there under their own steam and if so, have you checked that there will be night buses, trains or cabs around to get them home again? Why not dispense with such tiresome nitty gritty by hiring yourself a chauffeur, darling? Whether it's a discreet Mercedes, a Club Class Party Bus in Manchester, the Scooby Doo mystery machine from Cardiff Limos or a flower-strewn Karma Cab in London you can arrive in style, or at least in stitches.

To get the innuendoes flowing early, hens in the London area can even travel by converted fire engine courtesy of Hot Hire. There's champagne on board and a fire bucket full of 'naughty goodies' to set the tone, as well as a fireman's helmet for each hen. Hose and helmet jokes at the ready…

The bright lights of the Big City are an intoxicating draw to any group of hens.

food – fuel up for a fun night

If you've a large group then there's a lot of sense in booking a seasoned party venue with food that everyone likes, such as gourmet pizza and pasta gem La Vittoria on The Bridge in Edinburgh. The staff won't fall over in shock at the sight of a troupe of lairy women, and your dining neighbours are more likely to join in than complain.

But don't assume a corner of TGI Fridays or another 'party restaurant' is the only option. Low budgeteers should consider a barbecue or riverside picnic for long summer nights – leaving funds free for hiring some entertainment, or perhaps for a spot of clubbing afterwards. If you book early, out of season or using all your charms, you can often get bars to hire you their private room at very reasonable rates (or even free). A thrifty tip is to opt for City or financial district bars, which tend to be both good quality and often empty at weekends, so will gladly cater for you. A private room gives you all sorts of advantages – including no competing for the waiters' attention, playing your own music and decorating the place in the theme of your choice.

As for those on user-friendly budgets, the world's your freshly-shucked oyster. Whether you want to hire an entire restaurant, have sumptuous sushi served from the very flesh of a semi-naked man, courtesy of Playtime Platters (yes, really); the purple van from Lola's on Ice to turn up with ice creams and alcoholic sorbets, or a chef to hide away in your kitchen and conjure culinary magic while you take the credit. Nothing need limit you, except your imagination.

the art of 'boozology'

There's more than one way to get a skinful. While the end result may be similar – wobbling in front of a mirror with your best mate going 'Look, it's us', followed by getting your stiletto stuck in a drain cover, an unfortunate rendition of 'Sisters are doing it for themselves', then waking up with half a kebab stuck to your face – you could at least *start* the night with a bit of originality. Cocktail-making lessons are fantastic fun. Either book them at a good cocktail bar or hire a mixologist to bring the tools of their evil trade to your home or hired room. You

Whether you're hiring a mixologist or camping out in a cocktail bar, alcoholic concoctions are always a winner.

A drag show, such as the infamous Madame JoJo's in Soho, is quality entertainment for a brood of hens.

and the girls can craft cocktails, Tom Cruise stylie, under the watchful eye of a seasoned pro. Mine's a Cosmopolitan!

If you're starting out with drinks at home, a Spritzer (white wine and soda) or a Buck's Fizz (Champagne and orange juice) is easy to whip up and sets a less scary pace than liberally sloshing out huge glasses of Sauvignon. Fragrant mulled wine or spiced cider for winter parties raise the spirits nicely, too.

Out and about, choose from big, brash party bars, Pimms-on-the-terrace hotels, elegant wine tastings, chic cocktail bars or perfect winter pubs with open fires…. Check the listings for something that seems to ring your bell, get on the phone and book it.

belly laughs

There is no better endorsement of a hen party than everyone in fits of giggles. Booking into a comedy club (preferably a major one like Jongleurs, to guarantee class acts) makes sense on many levels. Not only will the entertainment be live and hilarious, but you and your mates will be served food and drinks at your table all night. Add to this the fabulous facts that you'll be only one of many fun-loving groups there, that there's usually a disco afterwards, and that the cocktails and beers are served in pitchers and you're laughing.

stage fright

Fancy taking in a show, you say? How very cultural. Ohh, *that* kind of show. You'll find acts such as The Adonis Cabaret Show at Bournemouth's Lava Ignite. With top male strippers, drag queens and comedians, games, cocktails and three rooms of dancing on the agenda, it's like Butlin's and Soho on a one-night stand. Not for the faint-hearted, but definitely fun. Of course there's always the legendary Madame JoJo's in the heart of Soho where Lily Savage walked the boards!

For those who really do like a bit of the old culture, well it won't be hard to track down theatrical and musical events in your city of choice. All you need to do is sandwich the event between an early supper and a hotel with a decent bar for relaxed chats and late night drinkies. It's a classy night that you can book very cheaply with numerous agencies or tailor-make yourself.

Become a pop star for a day at studios across the country, such as 'Pop Stars' in Edinburgh.

crowd of people with their fingers in their ears, karaoke might be killing music but we girls just love it. The real mystery is when are those talent spotters going to make contact? Alternatively you could hire a recording studio and cut your own CD. Studios up and down the country are gearing up to welcome hen parties and make it an experience to remember. We think Pop Stars just outside Edinburgh offer a fantastic deal at £20 a head including bubbly, snacks and a copy of your very own CD!

dance 'til you drop

If you fancy clubbing, you probably already know the type of clubs you like. Check the city listings to see what's on offer, and always try to book your group in. Not only will this give fair warning to the club about a descending hen party, it will also give you a chance to queue jump and get access to any special deals. Many clubs can offer a cosy little VIP lounge with waiter service and other luxuries to retreat to when you need a break from the dance floor…or somewhere to lie down!

killer tunes

Behind sound-proofed doors, all over the nation, terrible things are happening. Whether it's a small room of mates head-banging through 'Bohemian Rhapsody' with inflatable guitars, or Stacey caterwauling 'I will always love you' to a

Brighton spice
A mid-budget night for eight cool chickens

Saturday, 2pm: Check in to 3 star Kings Hotel on the seafront.

4–6pm: Salsa lessons with Cubashe.

Back to the hotel to change.

8pm: Early evening cocktails at smart Duke Street bar Havana.

9pm: Dinner booked at El Mexicano – top-notch Latino food.

10.30pm: Head back to the Lanes to the stylish Water Margin for all night DJs or live bands, cocktails and dancing…reserved to be on the safe side!

A short walk back to the hotel and sleeeep…

Sunday: Brunch on the beach or a legendary Brighton pub roast.

hen party destination guide

belfast birmingham **blackpool**
bournemouth brighton
bristol & bath **cardiff**

edinburgh **glasgow** leeds
london *manchester* newcastle
newquay **oxford** york

london

Short of blowing your wedding fund on shipping your hens off to New York or Paris – tempting as it may be – there is no destination that can beat London for glamour, fun and sheer entertainment value. You'll find something from our listings to suit your budget and please any group, whether you're quiet, genteel ladies or eardrum-shattering banshees!

Big Ben (top), black cab (middle), London Eye (bottom).

what to do

Before you land at Paddington station clutching your little case and chewing nervously on a marmalade sandwich, have a good, hard stare at this guide. London is full of surprises, and it will only take a little imagination and planning to make this a hen party to remember.

If you live in London and want to base your party at home, or you're booking a room at a London bar, you have the pick of the country's finest DJs, entertainers, therapists, cooks and mixologists to bring a touch of luxury to your party. There's even Choc Star's van (chocstar.co.uk) to deliver cocoa-based delights, for heaven's sake. If you're going out, well, you're going out in style. Gigs, shows, sport, comedy, food, cocktails, cabaret, clubbing, shopping, dancing, karaoke, markets…it's all happening here in London town.

But decisions, decisions…how – when it's hard enough to decide from a restaurant menu, lest you miss the best thing – are you going to work this one out? Hopefully our 'sounds of the city' will whittle it down for you a little. After that, practical considerations such as travelling in heels, Chantal's table manners, and your cousin's tequila-induced party stunts, will no doubt come into play. We didn't say it was easy…but we're here to help.

If you really can't decide, and it's all a bit much – you need to call on your friends. Your friends the professional party organisers, that is. They'll negotiate good deals for clubs, activities and hotels, so that you end up with something that feels like a long weekend on a Friday night budget. Or if you've managed to get your mitts on the fun-finance that most hens only dream of, they'll let their imaginations run riot and make your fantasy come true.

10 reasons...

1. the UK's best shows
2. tea at Claridges
3. the London Eye
4. Thames cruises
5. top nightclubs
6. free art galleries
7. Carnaby Street
8. Selfridges shoe department
9. Camden Stables
10. chilling on the South Bank

sounds of the city

With so much to do by day and by night in the capital we can't possibly include everything here, but hopefully these suggestions will give you some foundations to build your ideal hen party upon.

i want to break free

The frazzled bride-to-be who is, in common parlance, doing her nut, should take this opportunity for indulgence and serious relaxation: The Sanctuary, Covent Garden. Ahhh. There you see, it's already working. Book in on a Friday evening to use the spa pools, sleep retreat and heat and steam rooms. Choose from a range of treatments, from manicure to calming floatation. Enjoy a mouth-watering supper and a glass of champagne before drifting out at 10pm to join the rest of the girls at The Langley nearby, a cool, unpretentious little bar where you can drink and dance in stylish surrounds but keep that new found serenity intact.

Failing that, perhaps some physical exertion and fresh air will put the roses back in the bride's cheeks. A DIY school sports day with sack racing, egg and spoon etc, followed by a picnic on Hampstead Heath is inexpensive and blissfully simple. Dress up in gym kit for authenticity! Alternatively, for warm summer evenings, choose well chilled champagne, divine deli food and live music at Kenwood House, you just can't go wrong. Check out the English Heritage website or picnicconcerts.com for 2010 listings.

Relax at The Sanctuary.

the one that i want

For posing Pink Ladies and tomboys alike, a few games of bowling can't fail. Posher poulets (that's 'chickens' in French!) head for All Star Lanes in Holborn, Brick Lane or Bayswater. Here, large groups of 25 or so can book a stylish two-lane private room with a DJ and cocktail bar all to yourselves. They will even bring you canapés to nibble on while you contemplate a strike. For a slightly less upmarket but seriously authentic vibe – and the added bonus of lane-side karaoke rooms – book in at Bloomsbury Bowling. American food and hard-hitting milkshakes are on the menu, naturally. The fifties theme is readymade and you won't have to decamp to another venue for your evening entertainment – strike!

HEN tastic
Specialists in
Hen Party
Merchandise
Free delivey
on all UK
orders
Visit our Online Shop at:
www.hentastic.com

yodelay he hoooo!

When nothing will ring your bell quite as loudly as a man in leather shorts, it's time to book in to the Tiroler Hut in Notting Hill. Be warned, he'll literally ring it, as there's a cowbell show (and audience participation) whilst you tuck into steins of beer, hearty mountain fare and lashings of cheesy fun, served by Austrian wenches and goatherders. The family von Trapp would love it, and so will you. Good night, good night, good ni—ight!

Ah, hark, The Sound of Music. Yes, it's time to cut up your granny's curtains and skip over to the Prince Charles Cinema for some wimple-wobbling, lederhosen-tastic fun courtesy of Sing-a-Long-a-Sound of Music. Around four hours of dressed up, singing and heckling fun can't be bad for £15 (it all comes back to dough, right?) and there's a complementary bottle of champagne for hen groups of ten or more. Check out princecharlescinema.com for screening dates and times. Cheer for Julie, hiss for the horrid countess and of course, scoop the prize in the fancy dress competition…brilliant! And if lederhosen doesn't float your boat, but loincloths do, then why not sing-a-long-a Joseph?

Sing-a-long-a-Sound of Music at the Prince Charles cinema near Leicester Square.

don't cry for me, marg and tina

Oh, you're *singing*…sorry. Thought you were upset about something. You see it's best to keep these things well contained with a few people who understand you. And that, my lusty-lunged lovelies, is where Karaoke Box comes in. The Smithfield venue has sixteen private karaoke rooms of various sizes, with wireless mikes, flat-screen TVs, easy-touch selection screens and thousands of tracks, leather sofas, waitress service (there's a truly impressive cocktail list, plus sumptuous sushi and posh pizza) and surround sound. Youch. If you must escape, don't go too far. The bar is very cool indeed and you can dance the night away while the DJ spins your favourite tracks.

Sing your hearts out at Karaoke Box.

who let the dogs out?

Dorgs and *'orses* have been staples for London fun for many a decade and are still the ticket for a great fun day or in fact a whole night's entertainment.

Wimbledon Greyhound Stadium's Star Attraction restaurant serves up reasonably priced food and drinks to up-for-it party groups as they watch the mutts in action. There are three packages – trackside with fast food and pitchers of booze, sit down meal with pitchers of booze and a VIP option with a lovely buffet and, you guessed it, pitchers of booze. It's a piss up with live entertainment, basically, and you can't say fairer than that.

she's a lady

If you're more interested in the hats and champers end of things, a day's horseracing at Kempton Park in Sunbury is great fun. Hampton Court is just up the road – with the palace and its lovely gardens and maze, and a smattering of pubs and shops there's time for a spot of mooching in this gorgeous riverside location before you hop on a Thames cruiser and head into Putney for your night out in west London.

But Ascot, of course, is the crème de la crème for the gee gees. The racecourse to the rich and famous runs hen packages throughout the season to include grandstand admission, a race card, a £2 flutter and 2 glasses of wine, or you can opt for champagne and strawberries on the Plaza Lawn. Place your bets and remember, if Audrey Hepburn can scream it and still look knockout in that hat, so can you…'Move yer bloomin' arse!'

i like you better when you're naked

Why not invite Simon over to your place, or book a private room in a restaurant (Le Piaf in Wimbledon is an option), for a little 'tasteful male nudity without the strip' – perhaps as a diet-friendly option after a boozy supper?

Don a hat for Royal Ascot.

Find your artistic side with Simon Lloyd!

Here's how you serve him up. Tell the ladies you've got a game where they all have to draw something. Set them up with pencils and paper and a bit of still life – perhaps some artfully arranged fruit. Make sure everyone is drinking plenty. Then bring in a rather more interesting subject – the charismatic nude model.

Simon says 'The funniest bit is waiting to go in to a party where they are not expecting me. As soon as my boxers are off the giggles start. I'm totally game for a laugh.' As his website malelifephotographicmodel.com will show you, he's prepared to flaunt what he's got, which is more than most, and make the party go with a 'schwing'.

Simon's beautiful body is a pleasure to behold and he has a lovely manner to help you get past the 'elephant in the room' and on with the job in hand. (These puns are enough to make your eyes water, aren't they?) 'I regularly do parties for professional ladies in their 20s and 30s' he says, adding, 'the teachers are the worst – they definitely do the naughtiest drawings.'

pour some sugar on me

With the currant (d'ohh) trend for all things cupcake, this is the tastiest little piece of zeitgeist going. After a champagne river cruise or London Eye flight, whisk your yummy mates off to utterly fab cake shop Bea of Bloomsbury for tea, or cocktails and canapés, and sit around health-consciously picking the icing off the delectable, almost-too-good-to-eat cupcakes and then eating it anyway. Alternatively, book in for a baking lesson and bring out the domestic goddess lurking within.

At Cookhouse, hens will be split into two groups, one making cocktails and the other crafting canapés, under the guidance of professionals of course. The groups then swap. It's a social event and lesson rolled into one, where you'll have time to mingle and catch up with your mates as well as learning how to make delicious bite-sized delights. Go to cook-house.co.uk for more information.

Less filling but just as sweet for creative ladies are Create Boutique's 2–4 hour workshops. You'll learn how to unleash your inner creativity, and can choose from producing your own gorgeous pashminas, making Burlesque-style nipple tassels, mixing and packaging a beauty cream, or learning how to design accessories and jewellery to echo the latest catwalk trends. Visit create-boutique.co.uk to see which tickles your fancy.

Make unique gifts at Create Boutique.

born to be wild

Here's a bit of motorized fun that will both please the greens and thrill the grease monkeys – Revolution Karting is based in Mile End Park, in the city's only floodlit track. This is the site of the proposed solar dome, which will supply electricity to the local area as well as supplying buzz to your hen party. With 700 metres of straights and chicanes and London's fastest karts, you'll be hitting speeds of up to 50mph. Keep the driving theme by scooting up to Barrio North near Angel and booking into the funky caravan booth for nachos, cocktails and tequila slammers. Watch the trash without trailers partying down from your comfy perch, or join in the fun.

If you fancy an evening with a little more splash, try The Carwash at London's only club with a pool, Club Aquarium in Shoreditch. It gives you the perfect excuse to dress up and make a watery theme of the whole hen weekend.

Revolution Karting.

if i could turn back time

If you seek a night as sweet, familiar and potentially unhealthy as jam roly poly, it has to be School Disco. Every

School Disco.

Saturday night at the Portland Girl's School in the West End, grown men and women are dressed up to the Year Nines, snogging, breakdancing and misbehaving the night away. Uniform is compulsory, naturally. And don't be late, or you'll be straight to the headmasters office.

holding out for a hero

Where have all the good men gone? And where are all the gods? Ah, if only Bonnie Tyler knew what we know. Which is that strip show pros The Dream Men and Dreamboys have all got together for some regular Saturday sing 'n' strip soirees at Sound Night Club in the West End. They're lovely chaps who's only mission in life is to display their mouth-watering muscles – and you don't get an offer like that everyday, except at the fishmonger's (ha ha!).

Along with topless hosts and waiters, dinner and a drink, VIP nightclub entry after the show and more goodies, it's certainly a crowd-pleasing package.

SwayMe Swayze Weekend

Sway Me Swayze Hen Weekend
in London includes:

- 1 Night at the NEW Grange
- 5 Star Luxury Hotel
- Dirty Dancing Theatre Tickets
- VIP Nightclub Entrance
- Dirty Dancing Experience

The main event of this weekend is the Dirty Dancing themed workshop where the hunky choreographer will teach you some steps so you can put together your own routine from the movie! Not only will you learn the routine but you will also record your favourite song from the film. You can wow your friends and family at the wedding with your very own CD and dance routine!

ONLY £139*

LIMITED AVAILABILITY! Call us **NOW** FREE

0800 634 7569

*Limited availability for low season price. Typical RRP £315

 The world's favourite Hen & Stag company
redseven

where to stay

Looking for a place to rest your weary bones in the UK's capital can be a daunting prospect. There are thousands of places all claiming to offer you the best value in town. Well we've sorted out the 'men' from the 'boys' and checked what's on offer from hospitality to hairdryers!

hotels and hostels

Best Western Mostyn Hotel £££

4 Bryanston St, Marble Arch,
London W1H 7BY
Tel. no 020 7935 2361
www.mostynhotel.co.uk
info@mostynhotel.co.uk

Situated just a 1-minute walk from Oxford Street and Marble Arch for shopping and close to Paddington station, this hotel has a prime location for hens. The comfortable, well-furnished rooms with ensuite facilities (and good power showers) feature satellite TV and all the amenities you'd expect in a three-star nationwide chain. There is a magnificent Georgian staircase and ornate ceilings in the public areas; and the Mostyn boasts two restaurants and a champagne bar.

Generator Hostel £

37 Tavistock Place, London WC1H 9SE
Tel. no 020 7388 7666
www.generatorhostels.com
london@generatorhostels.com

This great value hostel is the largest in London. Situated in Russell Square, it is well located for sightseeing and the West End. With a popular bar and nightclub there is always a party atmosphere here. Unlike many London hostels an 'all you can eat' breakfast and bed linen are included. Choose between dorms (up to 12 people in bunks) and private rooms (up to six people), mixed or female only. All rooms have a wash basin and lockers or a hanging unit. Spotless showers are available on every floor, but don't expect ensuite facilities here.

Grange Holborn Hotel £££

50–60 Southampton Row, London WC1B 4AR
Tel. no 020 7242 1800
www.grangehotels.com
holborn@grangehotels.com

If you're seeking to celebrate in style then the hen party package on offer here (or at Grange City) might be just what you're looking for. On offer is one night's accommodation in a superior room, breakfast, full use of the five-star health club, a 30-minute beauty treatment of your choice, plus a complimentary glass of champagne, sandwich platter and free nightclub pass. The rooms are en-suite with all the amenities you could wish for and if you mention it's your hen night, you might get a good luck cake too!

Grange Holborn Hotel.

Haymarket Hotel £££

1 Suffolk Place, London SW1Y 4BP
Tel. no 020 7470 4000
www.firmdale.com
haymarket@firmdale.com

In the heart of theatreland, this hotel is 'jaw droppingly beautiful' according to a recent guest. The stunning interior design is complemented by top quality amenities, including a gym, beauty treatment rooms and an inviting pool. You can have a pamper hen party in one of the rooms off the pool area, or enjoy a civilised afternoon tea in the hotel's fabulous restaurant, Brumus. If you like a bit of luxury and something a bit different, this is the hotel for you.

The funky pool at the Haymarket Hotel.

the hotel staff could not have done more to make this a memorable occasion

Haymarket Hotel.

Hoxton Hotel £££

81 Great Eastern St, London EC2A 3HU
Tel. no 020 7550 1000
www.hoxtonhotels.com
info@hoxtonhotels.com

In the heart of The City, this uber-cool hotel is well located for Liverpool Street station and good if you are visiting City bars and clubs on your hen night. The Hoxton boasts a lively bar open 'til late and Grille, which is excellent if a little pricey. The funky rooms are small but perfectly formed with luxurious linen on the comfortable beds and excellent bathrooms complete with Aveda toiletries and decent hairdryers. Book early to get a good price.

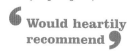

Would heartily recommend

Imperial Hotel ££

Russell Square, London WC1 5BB
Tel. no 020 7837 3655
www.imperialhotels.co.uk
info@imperialhotels.co.uk

This three-star hotel is clean and fresh, although a little dated in style. It's in a great location close to Russell Square tube, 10 minutes walk to Oxford Street or Covent Garden for retail therapy. It makes a good base for theatre going or casino – 24-hour one around the corner!

Cool rooms at the Haymarket Hotel.

A luxury room at K West Hotel.

Jurys Inn ££

60 Pentonville Road, Islington,
London N1 9LA
Tel. no 020 7282 5500
www.jurysinns.com
islington_reservations@jurysinns.com

Modern rooms with large comfortable beds
and all the amenities you could want make
this a great value-for-money choice. Just
across the road from Angel tube and one
stop away from King's Cross main line, this is
an excellent spot whether you plan to eat out
in trendy Upper Street or head into the West
End. You can book a three-bed room here,
which makes it a very economical choice. The
self-service breakfast goes on until 11am and
check out is at noon, which is very civilised for
the morning after the night before.

K West Hotel and Spa ££

Richmond Way, London W14 0AX
Tel. no 020 8008 6600
www.k-west.co.uk
info@k-west.co.uk

K West is handy for the new Westfield
Shopping Centre; it's also walking distance to
Notting Hill and Kensington High Street for
shopping or eating out. The modern large
bedrooms feature plasma screens, waffle
robes and hand-made mattresses. The
sophisticated contemporary design is
modern, but not completely minimalistic. Go
for a Spa package, or alternatively for the
'Rock'n'roll' package and get a three-hour
recording session in boutique studio around
the corner. The bar is buzzing on a Friday and
Saturday night with DJs playing until 2am.

❛ staff were very efficient ❜

Indulge at the K West Hotel spa.

Popular with the music & entertainment industry, 4 star deluxe design hotel K West Hotel & Spa is the place to stay in London

Boasting London's new premier health spa, the K Spa offers over 80 holistic treatments, as well as a Hydrotherapy pool, sauna, sanarium, nail bar and state-of-the-art gym.
The spa also features London's first Snow Paradise.

The unique Kanteen restaurant serves fresh, casual contemporary cuisine and the trendy K Lounge bar is the place for an informal bite or grooving 'til dawn with a resident DJ playing on Fridays and Saturdays.

K West Hotel & Spa Richmond Way London, W14 0AX
T: +44 (0) 20 8008 6600   F: +44 (0) 20 8008 6650
www.k-west.co.uk   &   bookit@k-west.co.uk

Park Inn London, Russell Square Hotel ££

92 Southampton Row,
Bloomsbury WC1B 4BH
Tel. no 020 7242 2828
www.rezidorparkinn.com
info.russellsquare@rezidorparkinn.com

With good access to King's Cross, St Pancras and Euston Stations and walking distance to Covent Garden, the West End and Oxford Street, this hotel has a prime location. Recently renovated, the rooms are comfortable and well equipped (the standard rooms even have an iron and ironing board!), the bathrooms are not huge though. The hot and cold buffet breakfast is really impressive for a hotel of this standard – that will sort the hangover out! All in all it's very good value for a four-star hotel in a central London location.

Sidney Hotel ££

68–76 Belgrave Road, Victoria,
London SW1V 2BP
Tel. no 020 7834 2738
www.sidneyhotel.com
info@sidneyhotel.com

This recently refurbished hotel is modern and stylish. The rooms are clean and well appointed, some are on the small side however, perhaps why it has a two-star rating. Very well located if you are arriving in London at either Victoria train or coach station and it's just a short walk to Sloane Square for a bit of retail therapy. The staff are friendly and helpful and our researchers gave the thumbs up to the showers and comfy beds. Check their website for offers – group bookings of five plus rooms get a discount.

St Christopher's Inn £

48–50 Camden High Street,
London NW1 0JH
Tel. no 020 7388 1012
www.st-christophers.co.uk
bookings@st-christophers.co.uk

If you're young at heart and want the slumber party experience, hostel accommodation is for you. This no-frills accommodation is clean and tidy; you can choose between mixed and female only dorms in rooms of six or eight. On the spot for clubbing at the legendary KOKOs (formerly Camden Palace), St Christopher's is close to the six Camden markets and the Lock. You're guaranteed

fresh linen and a locker in the room, but you might have to fight over the mirror. Breakfast is included in the price, so it's great value for money.

St Giles Hotel £££

Bedford Avenue, London WC1B 3GH
Tel. no 020 7300 3000
www.stgiles.com
frontoffice@stgiles.com

Location-wise the hotel is a short walk from Oxford Street, one tube-stop from Leicester Square and a good base for most of the main attractions, especially theatreland. St Giles offers an excellent room rate for a three-star central London hotel, it has decent sized rooms with ensuite shower rooms and basic but clean facilities, providing a comfortable night's stay. It has a great after-hours bar and the breakfast is plentiful and varied.

❝ **exceptional concierge service** ❞

discount deals

There are plenty of bargains to be had on the many hotel booking websites. We have listed a few that hens have found useful in the past:

www.bookdirectrooms.com

www.booking.com

www.expedia.co.uk

www.hoteldirect.co.uk – this website features a 'hidden gem' deal where you get a fantastic deal, but they only tell you the star rating and the location of the hotel.

www.hotels.co.uk

www.lastminute.com

www.laterooms.com

www.travelrepublic.co.uk

self-catering

Get the slumber party experience by renting an apartment in the capital. It may not be quite as central as some of the hotels, but is still a really good option. You can all get ready together (even friends who aren't staying) and have a few glasses of bubbly before hitting the town! There are loads of places to choose from. We suggest you try one of these online booking agents to find the ideal pad for your party.

Central London Apartments ££
Tel no. 0845 6442714
www.central-london-apartments.com
info@central-london-apartments.com

With over 180 apartments based in all areas of London, from Chelsea to the City and Bayswater to Victoria, they have something to suit everyone. There are plenty of one-night rentals available in all types of accommodation from studios to three-bed apartments in bronze, silver and gold categories starting at around £60 a night for a studio apartment for two.

Coach House London Vacation Rentals £–£££
Tel no. 020 8133 8332
www.rentals.chslondon.com
rentals@chslondon.com

This family run business has about 70 apartments on its books. Almost all of its self-catering rentals are the central London apartments and houses of residents temporarily away from the city. You have the informality, warmth and convenience of a real home in a London property, at prices to suit most pockets.

London Serviced Apartments ££
Tel no. 020 8923 0918
www.londonservicedapartments.co.uk
roy@londonservicedapartments.co.uk

Promising you the best rates on serviced apartments in London, this company has hundreds to offer. Arranged in luxury, mid-range and economy categories, you'll find something to suit every budget starting at £30 per person per night.

London School of Economics £
Tel no. 020 7955 7575
www.lsevacations.co.uk
vacations@lse.ac.uk

This award-winning, great value central London accommodation is available in University holidays only. The London School of Economics opens up its seven residencies, located around the West End all within reach of London's top attractions, to visitors with no link to the University. Ideal for groups and great for those on a budget, the rooms on offer are singles, twins and triples. B&B is also available.

Quality London Apartments ££
Tel no. 020 7476 8963
www.qualitylondonapartments.co.uk
sales@qualitylondonapartments.co.uk

This letting agent claims to have the best quality aparthotels in London. Offering apartments in three price brackets it covers all sectors of the market.

Serviced Lets Design Apartments ££
Tel no. 0871 226 1902
www.servicedlets.com

Serviced Lets specialise in modern city centre apartment homes. What makes them different to other serviced apartment agencies is that they exclusively lease all their own apartments, furnished and managed by them, guaranteeing a consistency of quality and service. Take a look at their award-winning conversion of the former Westminster Hospital – it's world class. This company also has serviced apartments for rent in Bristol and Cardiff.

Unilet Vacations £
Tel no. 020 7911 5181
www.westminster.ac.uk/vacations
summeraccommodation@
westminster.ac.uk

Unilet offers accommodation in university residences located in the West End, Victoria, the South Bank, the City and Harrow-on-the-Hill with single and twin rooms available during the summer vacation. There are also a limited number of self-catering apartments on offer.

where to eat and drink

London bars, especially the hip and trendy ones, are always choc full, so make sure you call ahead and reserve some space for your group. Some restaurants aren't keen on large groups, so you may not get your first choice of eatery. We have listed some here that happily cater for hen parties.

bars

B@1

20 Great Windmill Street, Soho,
London W1D 7LA
Tel no. 020 7479 7626
www.beatone.co.uk

With nine cocktail bars across the capital, Be At One is something of a London institution. These are genuine old-school bars and definitely a pretension-free zone! The Soho branch is the flagship, but you'll find outlets from the City to Clapham. It's free to reserve an area here for your party and the helpful bar staff will make sure your bash goes without a hitch. With a buy-one-get-one-free cocktail happy hour every day, B@1 is guaranteed to make you smile.

Barrio North

45 Essex Road, Islington,
London N1 2SF
Tel no. 020 7688 2882
www.barrionorth.com
shout@barrionorth.com

This ghetto fabulous bar, with its eccentric latino decor featuring real caravans as booths, always offers a warm welcome, however cold outside. The outstanding hand-crafted cocktails, the scintillating selection of rums and tequilas, the 'street food', together with their service with a personal touch, makes this the perfect venue if you're in the Islington area. At the weekend there's a vibrant party atmosphere as top DJs play cool tunes for the friendly up-for-it crowd.

Boundary Rooftop

2–4 Boundary Street, Shoreditch,
London E2 7DD
Tel. no 020 7729 1051
www.theboundary.co.uk/rooftop
info@theboundary.co.uk

Imagine a sun-drenched island bar then put it in the East End...you have the Boundary Rooftop! Part of Terence Conran's Boundary project, it includes a large bar with seating around an open fireplace, a 48-seat grill restaurant, served by its own kitchen, and a designer garden. There are stunning 360-degree views from Canary Wharf to the City's Gherkin and Barbican to the rooftops and spires of East London. The space is replete with a large sail-like canopy, heating, festoon lighting and Welsh blankets (for when it gets chilly). If you want a hen night with a view, get the lift to the roof!

The Boundary Rooftop bar.

Buddha Bar.

Buddha Bar
8 Victoria Embankment,
London WC2R 2AB
Tel. no 020 3371 7777
www.buddhabar-london.com
enquiry@buddhabar-london.com

On the north bank of the river, just below Waterloo Bridge, this opulent bar exudes Asian exoticism. Cocktails are sophisticated and well mixed, and the pan-Asian food is exquisite, if a little on the expensive side. The lounge bar area is an elegant and impressive mezzanine overlooking the impressive ground floor dining area, all themed with Asian decor and moody lighting creating a warm and inviting ambience. The laid-back atmosphere early in the evening gets livelier as the evening progresses and the music picks up.

'been there...'

My reason for choosing London was that I live there and I'm lazy! We booked a big table at Pizza Express near Shaftesbury Avenue, then went and saw La Clique at the Hippodrome, which was the best cabaret show I've ever seen. We'd all dressed the part, so we went to this little club called Storm afterwards. It was a great night, not too mad, and we definitely picked the right show.

Cellar Door
Zero Aldwych, Covent Garden,
London W2E 7DN
Tel. no 020 7240 8848
www.cellardoor.biz
open@cellardoor.biz

If you're looking for a sexy speakeasy vibe with a very intimate atmosphere, then this could be the bar for you and your chicks. Live acts entertain from 9pm each evening (and some afternoons) serving up a range of events from seductive swing to bawdy cabaret. Indulge in their exclusive signature cocktails or try a pinch of snuff! At Cellar Door you can expect the unexpected...

Dirty Martini
11/12 Russell Street, Covent Garden,
London WC2B 5HZ
Tel. no 0207 632 2317
www.dirtymartini.uk.com
events@cgrestaurants.com

Right on the famous Covent Garden piazza beneath the cosmopolitan London restaurant, Tuttons Brasserie, Dirty Martini is a great place for a hen party, whether it's for pre-dinner drinks or for late-night dancing. The intimate vaulted underground bar offers stunning cocktails, delicious bar food, laid back atmosphere & funky bar vibes making it a stylish and sexy late night venue. Book a luxurious leather seating booth for you and your hens.

Dirty Martini.

Loungelover

1 Whitby Street, London E1 6JU
Tel. no 020 7012 1234
www.lestroisgarcons.com
info@loungelover.co.uk

This glamorous bar with its themed 'areas'
operates on a booking system so you will
need to pick up the phone to make sure you
have a space even if you just want to come
for a drink. Japanese-inspired food is
available in the form of small plates for
sharing. Book an area to yourself if you've
got a large group, choose from the luscious
Red Area with its Deco furniture or the classic
Baroque Area with a floor to ceiling tapestry
enough to set off any hen party!

Mark's Bar

(Downstairs bar in Mark Hix's
Soho restaurant)
66–70 Brewer Street, Soho,
London W1F 9UP
Tel. no 020 7292 3518
www.hixsoho.co.uk

Open from noon–12.30am, this New York
style bar is cool and funky. With an
impressive team of London's leading cocktail
shakers (and movers), the cocktail list is
legendary. But if cocktails don't float your
boat, then don't worry there is a huge wine
list and enlightened beer menu. Part of the
deal is that you order some food, but with
fabulous bar snacks, like sloe gin jelly, that's
easy! You can even book a private room for
up to 12 people.

On Anon

London Pavillion, Piccadilly Circus,
London W1V 9LA
Tel. no 020 7287 8008
www.onanon.co.uk
info@onanon.co.uk

Overlooking Piccadilly Circus, On Anon is a
great multi-room venue with a room to suit
every mood, from the relaxed Studio Bar to
the feisty Glam bar and the retro Lodge to
the lively Club! On four floors and with nine
beautifully designed individual bars there's
bound to be one that captures your
imagination. Choose from an extensive range
of cocktails, wines and premium draught
beers, perfect place anytime: for lunch, to get
the evening started or for full on clubbing.

On Anon in Piccadilly Circus.

The Moose Bar

31 Duke Street, Mayfair,
London, W1U 1LG
Tel. no 020 7644 1426

If you dream snow-capped mountains all
year round, then you'll love the Moose Bar.
With cowhide upholstery and panoramic
mountain scenes painted on the walls it is
just the right side of kitsch. Could be a good
place to go before you Sing-a-long-a-Sound
of Music! And with a very happy 'happy hour'
this is an excellent place to start your night.
There's a large basement space for some
après-drinks dancing till 3am.

The Langley

5 Langley Street, Covent Garden,
London WC2H 9JA
Tel. no 020 7836 5005
www.thelangley.co.uk
info@thelangley.co.uk

Covent Garden media and fashion types
know a good thing when they see one. That's
why The Langley remains a design classic –
complete with menus to match. Go kitsch at
its retro Geneva bar or retire cosily
underground in The Vault. Whatever your
bag, you're bound to enjoy The Langley's
fantastic wines and cocktails, go for a platter
to share or choose 3 dishes for £10. There's
a great choice of private rooms and booths
that can be reserved for your hen party. And
when it's time to get on down, there's
absolutely no shortage of funky beats.

restaurants

**2 courses
+ half a bottle
of wine**

£ under £20
££ £20–£35
£££ over £35

Barrica ££–£££

62 Goodge St, Fitzrovia, W1T 4NE
Tel. no 020 7436 9448
www.barrica.co.uk
info@barrica.co.uk

Typically Iberian in style, this classic Spanish tapas bar has a really fantastic selection of great wines, such as the trendy white, Albariño from Galicia. The Spanish waiting staff are all very helpful and will help you choose a good combination of dishes, from the jamón ibérico de bellota to the Padrón peppers – deep-fried and salted they're delish, but be warned that one in ten retains a fierce spiciness that brings tears to the eyes. For pudding, indulge in the tarta santiago, a dense almond cake that is unsurpassable. A great party restaurant.

Café des Amis ££

11–14 Hanover Place,
London WC2E 9JP
Tel. no 020 7379 3444A
www.cafedesamis.co.uk

Situated in the heart of theatreland, this is the ideal venue for pre- or post-show food. The fantastic French cuisine served in elegant surroundings has all the chic of Paris without the Eurostar fiasco! Start your decadent night with cocktails in the Wine & Champagne bar and continue your celebration in the Long Acre private dining room. For a special ladies lunch or a 'Sex in the City' evening say 'au revoir' to singledom at Café des Amis…

Los Locos ££

24–26 Russell Street, Covent Garden,
London WC2B 5HF
Tel. no 020 7379 0220
www.los-locos.co.uk
info@los-locos.co.uk

This Tex-Mex party restaurant in Covent Garden has seen more than a few hen parties and they know how to make it a memorable night. There are three different party menus for groups of eight or more, each with plenty of choice from latino favourites, plus the hen gets a free sharing cocktail and souvenir t-shirt and everyone else gets shooters! 'Special entertainment' is even allowed if arranged in advance. Los Locos is restaurant, bar and club all under one roof, why go anywhere else?

Smollensky's Bar and Grill ££

105 The Strand,
London WC2R 0AA
Tel. no 020 7497 2101
www.smollenskys.com

Smollensky's on The Strand is a bright and spacious restaurant with a large and buzzing bar area. The restaurant at Smollensky's on The Strand is a cosmopolitan dining area with a distinct 'New York' feel, offering stunning modern American cuisine with some interesting twists. Choose the party menu for your hen night; there's something for everyone on there at a set price. Book the VIP stage area and let your hen night begin in this party central restaurant.

Tiroler Hut £–££

Westbourne Grove, Bayswater,
London W2
Tel. no 020 7727 3981
www.tirolerhut.co.uk
reservations@tirolerhut.co.uk

After 40 plus years of providing food and entertainment, Joseph your host knows a thing or two about throwing a party. This crazy Austrian restaurant, with staff dressed in traditional Alpine regalia and playing everything from accordion to cow bells offers you a night to remember. Vast platters of sausages, smoked meats, fried potatoes, sauerkraut and other Tirolean delights will be served up. Grab yourself a stein of beer and yodel the night away.

TGI Friday's ££

25–29 Coventry Street, London W1D 7A
Tel. no 0844 372 7914
www.tgifridays.co.uk
leicestersquare@tgifridays.co.uk

This nationwide bar and grill needs no introduction, there's one in every city and large town in the UK, but sometimes the familiar is comforting and the food is always good. So if you love all things American, the TGI's staff will dazzle you with their smiles and service making this a night to remember. All your favourites make an appearance on the menu: potato skins, nachos, burgers, salmon and tuna steaks, so order a Long Island Ice Tea and let Friday's do the rest.

where to party

The capital of choice, London has such a variety of places to party that one night may not be enough. Whether you want shows or cabaret, karaoke or clubbing, you'll find something here for everyone. So get the bling on and apply that lip gloss, it's time to party!

Club Aquarium
256–264 Old Street, London EC1V 9DD
Tel no. 020 7251 6136
www.clubaquarium.co.uk
info@clubaquarium.co.uk

The only club in London with its own swimming pool, Club Aquarium in Shoreditch encourages you to party in swimwear 'Tropicana style'. If you're prepared to get wet, then you can recline in the Jacuzzi sipping cocktails. When you've dried off, head to the dancefloor: on Saturdays the music ranges from 70s and 80s Carwash to the super-camp, hen party favourite Adonis Cabaret.

Fabric
77a Charterhouse Street, London EC1M 3HN
Tel no. 020 7336 8898
www.fabriclondon.com

This superclub serves up a line-up of superstar DJs pumping out heavy drum'n'bass and hip hop beats with the bass cranked up to the max. If you're a serious clubber, you're going love Fabric and especially lounging on its comfy beds. Make sure you're suitably attired, Saturday night is a seriously glamorous affair.

Jewel
29–30 Maiden Lane, London WC2E 7JS
Tel no. 020 7845 9980
www.jewelbar.com
info@jewelcoventgarden.co.uk

If you delve into the back streets of Covent Garden, just behind the Piazza, you'll find the hidden gem. Jewel Covent Garden and its

sister bar in Piccadilly have a little more sparkle than some of their jaded competitors. With plenty of drinks offers early on, it's a great place to start the evening off. The menu here is truly international so there's bound to be something to whet your appetite. Then after you've eaten immerse yourself in a world of distinctive global house music and high class style on Saturdays until 1am.

Jewel bar in Covent Garden.

Singstar at Karaoke Box Smithfield.

Karaoke Box Smithfield

12 Smithfield Street, London EC1A 9LA
Tel no. 020 7329 9991
www.karaokebox.co.uk
smithfield@karaokebox.co.uk

This is the perfect partnership between karaoke and bar-club and it's all about having fun. Whether you just come for a drink and a dance or if you book one of the 16 luxurious private rooms for your own exclusive karaoke session, this is going to be a night to remember. You can order stone-baked pizza, platters of sushi, champagne or cocktails all at the push of a button and they will be delivered direct to your room for your enjoyment.

KOKO

1a Camden High Street,
London NW1 7JE
Tel no. 0870 432 5527
www.koko.uk.com

One time theatre and infamously The Camden Palace until 2004, this venue is known throughout the world. It was where Madonna played her first UK gig and was 'home' to many New Romantic bands and local boys, Madness. Now after a multi million pound refurb KOKO has risen from the ashes once again providing quality live entertainment and club nights to North London.

Madame JoJo's

8–10 Brewer Street, London W1F 0SE
Tel no. 020 7734 3040
www.madamejojos.com
paris@madamejojos.com

Saturday nights at Madame JoJo's means the world famous Kitsch Cabaret: an evening of feathers, glitz and dazzling live music. It's sparkling with a million sequins and it's just waiting for you and your hen night. A blend of old-school music hall and Las Vegas floorshow, classic revue with a modern twist; you will enjoy a unique theatrical experience: drinks, supper and dancing, top notch cabaret with live singing, magic, comedy, high-kicking glamour and belting showstoppers. Check the website for other cabaret nights.

Medieval Banquet

St Katherine Dock, London E1W 1BP
Tel no. 020 7480 5353
www.medievalbanquet.com
info@medievalbanquet.com

Eat, drink and be merry. What more is there to a hen party? Well at Medieval Banquet there are fighting knights, strolling players and dancing wenches providing a magical medieval pageant for your delight, while you quaff mead (wine or beer actually), cry wassail and feast on medieval fare. After the show, there is music and dancing until late. All for one very reasonable rate.

Pacha

Terminus Place, Victoria,
London SW1
Tel no. 020 7833 3139
www.pachalondon.com
info@pachalondon.com

A little slice of the Ibiza club scene in London, Pacha is for you if you love uplifting house but can't afford a trip to the Balearic Islands. An all new state-of-the-art sound and light system along with refreshed decor and a luxe private VIP room for 20 people. In 2010 the club promises a new roof terrace offering an al fresco clubbing experience like no other venue in London. Check the website for more details.

Storm

28a Leicester Square,
London WC2H 7LE
Tel no. 020 7839 2633
www.stormlondon.co.uk
info@stormlondon.co.uk

This ever-popular intimate little club is right in the centre of the West End. At the weekend you'll find a range of music including RnB, funky house, old school garage and hip hop. If you're up for all night dancing, Storm takes you right through to 5am.

Supperclub

12 Acklam Road, London W10 5QZ
Tel no. 020 8964 6600
www.supperclub.com

Brand new on the London scene this avant garde club incorporates many of the provocative elements of its big sister in Amsterdam. Situated at the funky end of Portobello Road, this edgy club offers an exciting and memorable night out. Start off in Bar Rouge with drinks and live performances, move on to Salle Neige for an fine dining experience with a difference – a reclining one! Yes, you eat on beds. Later the room transforms into a nightclub for dancing. A totally unique night out.

The Ministry of Sound

103 Gaunt Street, London SE1 6DP
Tel no. 020 7378 6528/0870 060 0010
www.ministryofsound.com

Needing no introductions, this is the club that shot to fame in the 90s and has now become a household name. The concept was simple excellent house music blasting out through an unsurpassable sound system complemented by a great light show and uber cool design. Still drawing huge crowds to sample their special brand of clubbing The Ministry is a serious clubber's choice.

The Salle de Neige at Supperclub.

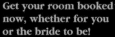

belfast

City Hall (top), Ferris Wheel (middle), River Lagan at night (bottom).

Ireland's buzzing capital is increasingly being recognised as one of the world's greatest city break destinations. With its long and varied musical heritage, Belfast has always been a place to enjoy the 'craic' – that's Irish for 'good time'. Rich in historic charm and modern wow-factor, it's a hen party destination with real class.

what to do

Our research has led to several key discoveries about Belfast. With limited space in which to publish these findings, a catch-all statement must suffice: it's brilliant!

Think of Northern Ireland's capital and the chances are that those old 80s news images of war-scarred streets will come to mind. But those days are past, and modern Belfast is an absolutely superb venue for a city break. The people are famously friendly, and the place is loved for being unpretentious and vibrant.

If you want to name two things the Irish are famous for, it's boozing and music. Therefore, you shouldn't be surprised to find that the capital is humming with a great party vibe.

For the more adventurous and outdoorsy among you, the landscape around Belfast is largely unspoilt and utterly stunning. The view from volcanic crag Scrabo is a 19-mile panorama including the Isle of Man, the Mourne Mountains and Scotland's coast. If you're into walking, riding or more extreme outdoor pursuits, it's pretty much paradise.

Strangford Lough is the place for craziness such as rock hopping. Dotted around the countryside are various hostelries where you can enjoy some good, old-fashioned Irish hospitality.

Taking a well-earned break from shopping!

10 good reasons

1. superb shopping
2. attractive city centre
3. extreme water sports
4. great live music scene
5. excellent clubs
6. chic, not pretentious
7. hospitable and lively
8. the botanic gardens
9. stunning scenery
10. horse riding nearby

Botanical Gardens.

sounds of the city

Gotta get away Northern Ireland is.breathtakingly beautiful. If you've never been before, try to get out of the city and have a look around. Contact the Northern Walking Partnership (northernwalking.com) or Ulster Rambles (ulsterrambles.com) to get onto organised walks, or get in touch with one of Belfast's riding clubs, such as Lagan Valley Equestrian Centre (www.ridingclubs.org), to arrange a fabulous, scenic hack.

Let me entertain you Ireland has an incredibly rich heritage of music and song. From Boyzone to the Boomtown Rats, the average karaoke menu will feature hits aplenty from the land of the leprechauns. Rude not to hammer out a few local faves after a couple of pints of strawberry daiquiri, surely? The best spots for karaoke are The Globe in Queen's Quarter, the stylish but fun Union Street in the Cathedral Quarter and The Galleon in Antrim.

Ice, ice baby For a rather more thrilling spectator sport than watching your mates swaying to Wind Beneath My Wings at the 'kroaky', check out the Odyssey Arena's ice hockey team, LBM Belfast Giants. Rough play, clashing sticks and a bloodthirsty crowd make this a really great night out with a difference. The Arena also hosts shows from the likes of Russell Brand, The Backstreet Boys and the Arctic Monkeys, so check the website www.odysseyarena.com to find out what's on when you hit town.

King of the swingers From the Havana Nights Social Club, with Latin tunes and dance lessons, to The Empire Laughs Back comedy club featuring stars such as Ardal O'Hanlon and Michael McIntyre, The Belfast Empire always has something really good going on. Tribute and covers bands are often playing, and themed club nights are classy and inspired.

Dancing in the city If your hens like to strut their stuff try some dance classes. Tony and Carolina at Latin Salsa will provide an unforgettable party offering beginners Salsa, Merengue, Cha Cha Cha and more. Or let your inhibitions go and burn some calories with Polercise – the latest dance craze.

Sample a Spanish themed night with Latin Salsa.

Bring me sunshine If there's a lingering disappointment that you're not all flying off to Ibiza for a week, don't fret. The Bambu Beach Club has all the beach-ready bar staff, games and promotions you could possibly need to pretend you're on the white isle, not the emerald one. This is the option for the ultimate, dress up and party night.

The real thing So you're after the authentic Belfast vibe? A properly organised crawl around the city's oldest pubs is one of the best ways to explore the city and get to know the locals. Belfast is stuffed with gorgeous old drinkeries. Expect live folk bands, a good mix of people and a non-poseur vibe along the way. We suggest that you include the likes of Crown Liquor Saloon, McHugh's, The Front Page, and Bittle's Bar.

Didn't we almost have it all? Bar Twelve is a classy bar on Botanic Avenue where you'll be able to grab a sofa and down a few champagne cocktails while you listen to the DJ. On site is the Metro Brasserie for good food, and maybe you'll treat yourself to a night of boutique hotel heaven at the Crescent Townhouse. Always nice to find one venue that has everything so that you don't have to walk far in those fabulous four-inch heels.

'been there...'

We'd heard loads of good things about Belfast and there were some cheap flights going, so we all headed over there for a joint hen and stag weekend. The boys stayed in a different hotel but we all met up in the daytime before splitting up in the evenings. Loved the Crown Bar, saw a great band at the Empire, loved the zoo! Shops were pretty good too.

If you're looking to settle into one venue for quite a few hours, then AM:PM is perfect. The Botanic Avenue bar has an events suite if you want want private space and your own bar. At the Arthur Street AM:PM things are a little funkier – cosy into this bijou venue for a champagne lunch followed by several atmospheric hours in the company of some of Belfast's finest DJs.

Learn some sassy pole-dance moves with a Polercise party.

where to stay

This cosmopolitan city is now a popular destination for weekend breaks and, as a result, has a large number of hotels and serviced apartments at excellent rates.

hotels

Benedicts Hotel ££
7–21 Bradbury Place/
Shaftesbury Square, Belfast BT7 1RQ
Tel. no 028 9059 1999
www.benedictshotel.co.uk
info@benedictshotel.co.uk

On the spot for great pubs and restaurants, this friendly hotel is modern with a traditional twist. The ensuite rooms offer excellent amenities with a luxurious feel, representing fabulous value for money. There's a well-renowned restaurant on the first floor and a lively bar downstairs, so you don't even have to step outside to start the celebrations.

Crescent Townhouse ££
13 Lower Crescent, Belfast BT7 1NR
Tel. no 028 9032 3349
www.crescenttownhouse.com
info@crescenttownhouse.com

In the heart of Queen's Quarter, this is Belfast's original boutique hotel. Elegant and intimate the Crescent presents superb accommodation behind a stunning 19th-century facade. Beautifully appointed en-suite rooms offer fantastic value and with the Metro Brasserie and Bar Twelve on site this is a gem. Rooms are limited so don't wait.

Lagan Backpackers Hostel £
121 Fitzroy Avenue, Belfast BT7 1HU
Tel. no 028 9033 9965
www.laganhostel.com
stay@laganhostel.com

Located close to Botanic Avenue and the buzzing nightlife in Belfast, the idea at Lagan is a simple one. You get a comfortable bed

**shared room
without
breakfast**

**£ under £30
££ £30–£60
£££ over £60
pppn**

and good cooked breakfast and friendly service for an excellent price. Like most hostels, there's a choice of dorms with three–six bunk beds or private rooms, clean linen is included, but there are no en-suite facilities and you need to bring a towel. However, with prices from £13 per night what have you got to complain about?

Park Inn ££
4 Clarence Street West,
Belfast BT2 7GP
Tel. no 028 9067 7700
www.belfast.parkinn.com
info.belfast@rezidorparkinn.com

This large three-star hotel is located near the ferris wheel and city hall just two minutes from the bus and train station, so it's right in the heart of the city. It's clean, modern, with a very bold colour scheme, and provides all the amenities you'd expect in a chain hotel. Friendly and professional staff will make your stay a pleasant one. Park Inn offers on site parking at a reasonable rate and the grill breakfast is excellent.

Relax in the warm environment at Park Inn, Belfast.

Tara Lodge ££

36 Cromwell Rd, Belfast BT7 1JW
Tel. no 028 9059 0900
www.taralodge.com
info@taralodge.com

Located once again in Queen's Quarter, on Botanic Avenue, this luxury B&B is the perfect spot for partygoers. It's just a few minutes walk from bars and restaurants to suit all tastes and budgets. With a four-star AA rating Tara lodge exudes style; it has all the facilites you could want in the rooms. Book early.

self-catering

Brookhill Luxury Serviced Apartments ££

41 Eglantine Avenue, Belfast, BT9 6EW
Tel. no 07751 240 654
www.brookhillapartments.co.uk
brookhillapartments@hotmail.com

These luxury four-star apartments are bright and spacious with modern decor and excellent facilities. Situated in a quiet tree-lined avenue close to Lisburn Road, Queen's, for nightlife, these apartments are well located. Fully furnished, the two-bedroom apartments tend to feature two double beds.

✳ **shared room
without
breakfast**

**£ under £30
££ £30–£60
£££ over £60
pppn**

Cordia Serviced Apartments ££

355–367 Lisburn Road Belfast, BT9 7EP
Tel. no 028 9087 8782
www.servicedapartmentsbelfast.net
mail@cordiaapartments.com

These stylish apartments are only 2 minutes from Great Victoria Street bus and railway station and the city centre. Belfast's fashionable boutiques, restaurants, cafés, and bars are within walking distance and there's a supermarket next door to stock up on beers. A generous welcome pack provides all the essentials and free parking is available in an underground car park.

Corporate Apartments ££

Ormeau Avenue, Belfast BT2 8HB
Tel. no 075 2566 4068
www.corporate-apartments.co.uk
info@corporate-apartments.co.uk

The Lucas Building is an uber cool base for any hen party. The two-bedroom apartments are spacious and well equipped with sophiscated decor. There is free parking and a welcome pack of groceries on arrival. Also available are Great Victoria Street Apartments.

Malone Grove Apartments ££

60 Eglantine Avenue, Malone Road, Belfast BT9 6DY
Tel. no 028 9038 8060
www.malonelodgehotelbelfast.com
info@malonelodgehotel.com

These five-star apartments feature one, two and three bedrooms and cater for up to six guests. Adjacent to one of Belfast's boutique hotels, as a guest here you'll benefit from all the hotel facilities, including free parking and fitness suite. A breakfast pack is provided.

Pearl Court Apartments £

11 Malone Road, Belfast BT9 6RT
Tel. no 028 9066 6145
www.pearlcourt.com
info@pearlcourt.com

Located in the Queen's Quarter, luxurious and spacious self-contained apartments. The four-bedroom duplex apartment is especialy good value for groups of up to seven people.

Titanic Apartments £

66 Lisburn Rd, Belfast BT1
Tel. no 028 9033 3367

These brand new luxury two-bedroom apartments, sleeping up to five people (with one fold-up bed) are in downtown Queen's Quarter. On-street parking, linen and towels included. Great value.

> ❛ **We wanted something a bit more flexible than a bog standard B&B or hotel and serviced apartments were a great alternative. We all got dressed and had a glass of bubbly before hitting the town.** ❜

where to eat and drink

pubs and bars

Bar Twelve
13 Lower Crescent, Belfast BT7 1NR
Tel. no 028 9032 3349
www.crescenttownhouse.com
info@crescenttownhouse.com

The cosy sofas and warm ambience of this bar, located in the Crescent Townhouse Hotel, make it the perfect place to kick back and have a good chat.

Bittles Bar
Victoria Square, Belfast BT1 4QA
Tel. no 02890 311088

Beautiful old bar in a narrow building off Victoria Square. As the night wears on trendy types pile in as a DJ plays disco until dawn. Try a sweet-hot whisky with lemon and cloves.

McHugh's
29–31 Queen's Square, Belfast BT1 3FG
Tel. no 028 9050 9999
www.mchughsbar.com
info@mchughsbar.com
Open: all day every day

This atmospheric bar/gastropub is in Belfast's oldest building. There's live music and DJs in the basement bar and a large restaurant serving traditional food with a twist.

The Crown Liquor Saloon
46 Great Victoria Street, Belfast BT2 7BA
Tel. no 028 9024 3187
www.crownbar.com
info@crownbar.com

Dubbed Belfast's most beautiful bar, there's a lot more to The Crown than stunning wood panelling. There's a wide selection of wines and beers and an extensive menu.

McHugh's bar in Queen's Square.

The Globe
36 University Road, Belfast BT9 1NH
Tel. no 028 9050 9840
www.theglobebar.com
info@theglobebar.com

This popular bar in the University Quarter has a buzzing atmosphere with karaoke and DJs on every night. The friendly staff will make sure you have a good time, and with drinks offers and meal deals we know you will.

The Front Page
106–110 Donegall Street, Belfast BT1 2GX
Tel. no 01232 324 924
www.thefrontpagebar.com
info@thefrontpagebar.com

This family owned pub is renowned for live music and showcases the best of the local Irish talent. It still retains much of its fantastic Victorian panelling and stained glass.

The Galleon
18 High Street, Antrim, BT41 4AN
Tel. no 028 94467748

Join the locals for a few bevvies and a spot of karaoke at this lively pub situated in Antrim.

restaurants

AM:PM ££–£££
67–69 Botanic Avenue, Belfast
BT7 1JL
Tel. no 028 9023 9443 and
38–42 Upper Arthur
Street, Belfast BT1 4GJ
Tel 028 9024 9009
www.ampmbelfast.com
info@ampmbelfast.com

2 courses + half a bottle of wine
£ under £20
££ £20–£35
£££ over £35

Whether in Queen's Quarter or
the city centre, AM:PM has your
needs covered with great menus at both
locations. Sample live jazz at Botanic Ave or
cool DJs at Arthur Street on Saturday nights.

Cafe Vaudeville ££
25–39 Arthur Street, Belfast BT1 4GQ
Tel. no 028 9043 9160
www.cafevaudeville.com
info@cafevaudeville.com
Open: 11.30am–1am (bar); 12pm–3pm
and 5pm–9pm (restaurant)

With a burlesque music hall theme, this 'luxe
bar and dining establishment' is truly a
showstopper on a grand scale. At the city
centre end of the Golden Mile, this is a
popular haunt with hen and stag parties. The
food is a clever mix of French with Irish/
American. Wash it down with plenty of
Champagne – tres bien!

Irene & Nan's ££
12 Brunswick Street, Belfast BT2 7GG
Tel. no 028 9023 9123
www.ireneandnans.com
info@ireneandnans.com
Open: 11am–1am (bar); 12pm–9pm
(restaurant)

This retro-kitsch brasserie is slap bang in the
middle of the famed Golden Mile. A bar as
well as a bistro, there's a good selection of
bar food, a lunch menu and a dinner menu. If
you choose it for the main event, start off with
the mussels and follow it with an 8oz Irish Rib
Eye Steak for a taste of the Emerald Isle.

Metro Brasserie ££
13 Lower Crescent, Belfast BT7 1NR
Tel. no 028 9032 3349

www.crescenttownhouse.com
info@crescenttownhouse.com
If you love your food, the Metro
serves up an excellent choice of
dishes all using locally sourced
ingredients. Also has a very
good vegetarian menu.

RBG ££
4 Clarence Street West,
Belfast BT2 7GP
Tel. no 028 9067 7700
www.belfast.parkinn.com
info.belfast@rezidorparkinn.com
Open: from 6.30am (last orders
9pm–10pm)

This New York style bar and grill in the Park
Inn Hotel won't disappoint when it comes to
steaks and classic burgers. The laid back
atmosphere is perfect for a chilled start to
your hen night, sample a few cocktails mixed
by their well trained and experienced bar
staff and you're set up for a great night on
the town.

Tedfords Restaurant ££
5 Donegall Quay, Belfast BT1 3EF
Tel. no 02890 434000
www.tedfordsrestaurant.com
info@tedfordsrestaurant.com
Close to The Odyssey complex, come and
sample the gorgeous local seafood (and
stunning desserts) in its fabulous dining
room and bar with views of the River Lagan.

RGB Grill and Steak House at the Park Inn.

where to party

Music is central to Irish culture so, not surprisingly, there is a plethora of live music venues and clubs of all descriptions to be found in Northern Ireland's first city.

The bar at Bambu Beach Club.

Bambu Beach Club

Unit 3, Odyssey Pavilion, 2 Queen's Quay, Belfast BT3 9QQ
Tel. no 028 9046 0011
www.bambubeachclub.com
bbclub@ultimateleisure.com

This is the ultimate fun party venue. With the bar staff in shorts or bikinis and sexy dancers on stage every half hour, the surf is most definitely up here!

Club Mono

96–100 Ann Street, Belfast BT1 3HH
Tel. no 028 9027 8886
www.monobelfast.co.uk
clubmono@btinternet.com

Close to the city centre, Mono is a favourtie for dance music fans playing great funky house tunes. The stylish interior is cool and trendy and the place attracts some seriously big name DJs.

Club Thompson's

3 Patterson's Place, Belfast BT1 4HW
Tel. no 028 9032 3762
www.clubthompsons.com
info@clubthompsons.com

A Belfast clubbing institution, Thompsons hosts numerous nights catering for the various styles from hip hop to house. On Saturdays you'll find stunning club decor and funky, uplifting house music.

Stiff Kitten

1 Bankmore Square, Belfast BT7 1DH
Tel. no 028 9023 8700
www.thestiffkitten.com
enquiries@thestiffkitten.com

This funky contemporary club is one for the committed clubbers. Attracting some big name DJs, the dancefloor is always packed with a music conscious crowd. You're more than likely to bump into a stag party too.

Go Bananas

London
Edinburgh
Brighton
Newcastle
Cardiff   Loads More..

We've heard people get married just to try out one of our Weekends!

www.GoBananas.co.uk

0871 789 6200

The Bot (Botanic Inn)

23–27 Malone Road, Belfast
BT9 6RU
Tel. no 028 9050 9740
www.thebotanicinn.com
info@thebotanicinn.com

Belfast's top live entertainment venue and
sports bar, this is top spot for action. With live
sport on big plasma screens it's a bloke
magnet. As night falls the DJs move in and
turn this into a kicking club for all to enjoy.

The Empire

42 Botanic Avenue, Belfast BT7 1JQ
Tel. no 028 9024 9276
www.thebelfastempire.com
info@thebelfastempire.com

This old church has had new life breathed
into it as a music hall with a full programme
of live music and comedy. The underground
bar is atmospheric and with three more floors
of entertainment this place is legendary.

Union Street

8–14 Union Street, Belfast BT1 2JF
Tel. no 028 9031 6060
www.unionstreetpub.com
info@unionstreetpub.com

This trendy award-winning gay bar is a
bar/restaurant/club all wrapped into one
highly camp bundle. Here, deep in Cathedral
Quarter, hens can enjoy a fun night out
without the cattle market factor. Try the
Saturday afternoon 'Sing or Die Karaoke'
with Tina Leggs Tantrum, oozing with glitz
and glamour, for new and seasoned singers
alike starting at 4pm. From 8pm join
Kenny K for the latest in chart, commercial
and high camp.

A night out in Belfast can be full of glitz and glamour, so don't forget your lippy!

THE CHEAPEST WAY TO THE BEST STAG AND HEN PARTIES IN EUROPE

BUDAPEST   **KAUNAS**
PRAGUE   **RIGA**
GDANSK   **KRAKOW**
POZNAN   **WROCLAW**

Aberdeen
GLASGOW   EDINBURGH
Derry
BELFAST   Newcastle
Teeside
Manchester   LEEDS
LIVERPOOL   Doncaster
EAST MIDLANDS
BRISTOL   BIRMINGHAM
Newquay   LUTON   STANSTED
Gatwick
BOURNEMOUTH

FLIGHTS FROM SELECTED UK AIRPORT

RYANAIR

birmingham

'More canal mileage than Venice' – so say the guidebooks. Come on, there's much more to Birmingham than ducks and barges. It's our most culturally rich city, slap bang in the middle of the country, and it's got soul.

Council House (top), Brindley Place (middle), Broad Street (bottom).

what to do

Ask not what you can do in Birmingham, but what can Birmingham do for you. Retail therapy, a great club scene, waterside bars, fabulous restaurants, skiing...

It doesn't matter if you're a dyed in the cashmere Harvey Nicks gal or a stout-drinking quasar addict, Birmingham has got it all. That's because it's our glorious Second City and it's got a duty to compete bitchily with London.

While it can't quite muster the charm of our dear old capital, it's certainly easier to navigate, and that makes it ideal for a weekend break. Simply hop off the train at New Street and you're right in the fabulous shopping action of the New Bullring, the Markets and the Mailbox.

Then there's the very convenient situation of the most buzzing nightlife being around Broad Street. By the time you've got these essentials on your radar it's just a question of dropping in the details.

Brum is a town with atmosphere, and not just from the balti fumes. With a huge young, cosmopolitan population it's not surprising that the city's pulse can be clearly felt, day and night.

10 good reasons

1. Tamworth Snow Dome
2. Selfridges sans London
3. Cadbury World, mmmnn
4. dressed-to-kill club scene
5. The Glee Club for comedy
6. canal-side picnics
7. best curries in the UK
8. two local dog tracks
9. BYOB restaurants
10. Selfridges Food Hall

The iconic Selfridges store, the centrepiece of Birmingham's famous shopping centre – the Bullring.

sounds of the city

Relax The Living Room is a rather chic affair for Broad Street, but that doesn't mean it's not for your party. Or for the first bit of it, at least, before things get messy. There's a gorgeous private room with chandeliers, beautiful fabrics and great city views, where up to 16 can sit down to lunch or dinner. The modern British/European food and sophisticated cocktails are very serious matters at The Living Room, and the whole vibe is good if you're looking for a bit of wow factor and class for your party. You could also book an entertainer to come along – from a magician to a cabaret artist – and make full use of your VIP enclave. Once the cocktails have started to work their magic, you've only to totter out of the front door and you're on one of Birmingham's most vibrant streets.

Don't cha wish your girlfriend was hot like me? For those whose very selfless focus is on being a stunning sight for all to behold, Serenity Spa in the city centre buffs up your face for a night out, gives make up lessons for fretting brides-to-be and offers a wide range of therapeutic and beauty treatments. How divine, darling, after a morning's hard shopping at The Mailbox – home to the likes of Armani, Harvey Nicks and Jesire. And after all that effort, it can only be Liberty's in Hagley Road for dinner, champagne cocktails and dancing with the other beautiful people. Although obviously, you're the best. Mwa, mwa.

Dancing queen Hitting the dance floor with your mates and some cheesy old choons is hen party gold, and Birmingham caters for your needs with clubs such as Reflex (80s) and Flares (70s), both on Broad Street. Nearby, The Works has club classics and charty stuff on a Friday, and club anthems on a Saturday.

Killing me softly Cake and coffee stops are an all-important part of any decent trip round town, and we'd rather eschew chainstore swank for old-school charm any day. The Floating Coffee Company is a barge moored just off Bridleyplace that will serve up your hot chocolate and sweet or savoury pick-me-ups as the water gently rocks you. Artery clogging bliss.

Indulge yourself in a relaxing massage before your big night out.

There's mountains of fun to be had at Snow Dome in Tamworth.

We will rock you You're never too old for a natural high and Creation, the biggest indoor climbing arena in the Midlands, is the place to get one. If you're complete beginners, don't worry, you can book an hour and a half taster session for two–six people. And if that doesn't grab you, the fact that climbers consume mountains of cake between climbs will. Make sure you take plenty of the spongey sweet stuff along.

Lady ice Hen party skiing doesn't need to be confined to groups with more money and time off than the Queen. You can have real, guaranteed snow all year round at the Snow Dome at Leisure Island. The three slopes are set up for boarding, skiing, tobogganing or adrenalin tubing (high speed, spinning downhill descent on an inner tube). And once you're tired and soaked through you can stop and go to a funky city centre bar. You can't get that half way up a mountain now, can you?

Going underground An underground bar is great when you need to ignore the fact that it's still daylight outside as you order your first drink. An underground bar is particularly great if it's Bacchus. This is one gorgeous little hideout, complete with ornate carved stonework, velvet drapes, art and pleasantly creaky antiques. Quirky rooms include a library and four poster bedroom which simply whisper to you, stay, stay my pretty. Resting happily in the seductive lap of the God of pleasure (that's Bacchus), sip a martini and just let all those daytime worries slide away. If you've managed to book rooms at the Burlington Hotel above, then the living is easy.

'been there...'

My mates and I are in our late thirties so we decided not to go for the full-on night out around Broad Street. The six of us headed over to the Arcadian area, which is all lovely bars and shops. We ended up at Sence. It's like a funky bar mixed with a nightclub. Quite elegant but with a good atmosphere. We could chat and have a good catch up as well as dance.

where to stay

From the original splendour of Victorian railway hotels to the modern and innovative chic of city centre accommodation, Brum has it all and in abundance.

hotels

Birmingham Central Backpackers £

The Eastside Tavern,
58 Coventry Street, Digbeth,
Birmingham B5 5NH
Tel. no 0121 643 0033
birminghamcentralbackpackers.com
info@birminghamcentralbackpackers.com

This family-run independent hostel is unique. From the warm welcome to the free nightly snack buffet, your hosts can't do enough to ensure you have a great time here. The usual range of single, twin and dorm rooms are all decorated in fun and funky colours.

✳ shared room without breakfast

**£ under £30
££ £30–£60
£££ over £60
pppn**

Burlington Hotel £££

Burlington Arcade, 126
New Street, Birmingham B2 4JQ
Tel. no 0121 643 9191
www.macdonaldhotels.co.uk
reservations.burlington@macdonaldhotels.co.uk

The historic Burlington hotel is situated close to the Mailbox, Selfridges and the Bullring for all your shopping needs, and Broad Street for nightlife and entertainment. The classic styling of the rooms suits the original Victorian splendour with all the facilities for a comfortable stay.

Eaton Hotel ££

279 Hagley Road, Edgbaston,
Birmingham B16 9NB
Tel. no 0121 454 3311
www.eatonhotel.co.uk
info@eatonhotel.co.uk

This beautifully styled independent hotel has all the modern facilities you need for a relaxing and luxurious stay in Brum. The hotel is located within 2 miles of the city centre so provides easy access to all the highligts. Why not have dinner in the top-class restaurant serving quality British fare?

NiteNite Birmingham £

18 Holliday Street,
Birmingham B1 1TB
Tel. no 0121 454 3311
www.nitenite.com
book@nitenite.com

This chic yet comfort-conscious hotel says 'no' to 'no frills' and gives you free Wi-Fi, blockbuster movies and bottled water all at a great price. The avant-garde design combined with the quality fittings makes this a cutting edge choice, complete with 42-inch plasma screens showing live views to the outside in lieu of a window. That's got to be a unique feature! This is a new take on affordable luxury.

❝ We were really surprised by the chic shops and stylish bars. Birmingham has so much more than we expected. ❞

self-catering

Burne Jones House ££

11–12 Bennetts Hill, Birmingham
B2 5RS
Tel. no 0845 080 5104
www.cityquarters.co.uk

Burne Jones House is a development of 29
fully furnished serviced apartments in the
shopping centre of Birmingham. The Grade II
listed building has been converted into a
range of unique apartments fully
equipped with all mod cons
including Wi-Fi. With a 24-hour
check-in system you can just
pick up the keys and chill
out. The historic building
even has a private roof
terrace!

City-Nites £

Arena View, Edward Street,
Birmingham
B1 2RX
Tel. no 0121 233 1155
www.city-nites.com
reservations@city-nites.com

A fabulous alternative to a hotel room.
Situated directly opposite the NIA and
Brindleyplace, these elegant apartments are
ideally located for all the city's clubs, bars
and restaurants. With a mixture of one- and
two-bedroom apartments sleeping two–four
adults, City-Nites is ideal for Hen Parties. If
you're booking as a group then simply
request adjacent apartments.

Postbox by Bridgestreet ££

120 Upper Marshall Street, Birmingham
B1 1LJ
Tel. no 0845 080 5104
www.bridgestreet.co.uk
info@bridgestreet.com

The PostBox is stylish city living at its most
desirable. The complex offers 50
contemporary one- and two-bedroom
apartments set right in the heart of
Birmingham's most fashionable
neighbourhood. A number of apartments
offer balconies and the development
provides the convenience of having a parking
space right in the centre of the city. All
apartments have freeview TV and DVD player.

SACO @ Livingbase ££

3 Brunswick Square, Brindleyplace,
Birmingham B1 2HR
Tel. no 0845 099 9092
birmingham.sacoapartments.co.uk
livingbase@sacoapartments.co.uk

Livingbase is home to 35 luxury serviced
apartments, all with spectacular views over
the city and are decorated to the highest
standard. The accommodation ranges
from studios through to double
height duplex suites. Each
apartment consists of fully fitted
kitchen, spacious living/dining
areas and bedrooms with
separate bathroom. Each
apartment features a range of
Molton Brown toiletries – oooo!

*shared room
without
breakfast*

£ under £30
££ £30–£60
£££ over £60
pppn

Staying Cool @ Rotunda ££

The Rotunda, 150 New Street,
Birmingham B2 4PA
Tel. no 0121 643 0815
www.stayingcool.com
hello@stayingcool.com

Hip hotel meets boutique serviced
apartment. Stay in one of the exclusive
apartments on the top two floors of the iconic
and beautifully refurbished 60s Rotunda in
Birmingham. Each Staying Cool apartment
has floor-to-ceiling windows offering a
breathtaking panorama of the city. Special
features include free Wi-Fi, an Apple Mac
entertainment system, a Bose iPod player
and a Poggenpohl kitchen with cool
appliances. Wow!

Sleep easy in this exquisite City-Nites bedroom.

chillisauce
www.chillisauce.co.uk
0845 4508269

Carnaby Street

*The first name in Hen Weekends -
Over 100 locations and 50,000
satisfied customers a year.
Find out why...*

Perfect Weekends for the Happiest Hens

where to eat and drink

bars & pubs

Bacchus

Burlington Arcade, 126 New Street,
Birmingham B2 4JQ
Tel. no 0121 632 5445
www.macdonaldhotels.co.uk

This quirky basement bar located under the Burlington Hotel is quite impressive. It has a sumptuous and elegant classical style – all velvet curtains, ornate plasterwork and antique furniture. It brings together the ancient civilisations of Rome, Egypt and Greece in one big orgy of excess!

The O Bar

264 Broad Street, Birmingham B1 2DS
Tel. no 0121 643 0712
www.obarbirmingham.com
trancef1@yahoo.co.uk

Slap bang in the middle of the nightlife is this super sexy 'style bar'. It serves some pretty fine cocktails and has a large selection of champagne. if you venture 'below' you'll find some lively beats down there and a great party atmosphere.

Malmaison

1 Wharfside Street, Birmingham B1 1RD
Tel. no 0121 246 5000
www.malmaison.com

Part of the Malmaison Hotel in The Mailbox, this light and airy, double-height bar and brasserie is stunning. With plenty of well selected wines and champagnes, chosen by their world class sommelier, and dangerously good cocktails, The Mal is a great place to kick off your evening in Birmingham.

Cocktails at Malmaison Bar.

Revolution

Five Ways, Broad Street, Birmingham
B15 2HF
Tel. no 0121 665 6508
www.revolution-bars.co.uk/birmingham

Set right in the heart of Brum's nightlife, this atmospheric bar can take you from early evening cocktails in comfy leather chairs to cool club atmosphere with late night DJ and there's plenty of fun to be had in between. Why not find out about their cocktail masterclasses for a little taste of mixology. There are over ten private party areas, so call to book one and discuss what other party packages they have on offer.

restaurants

Adil Balti and Tandoori £

148–150 Stoney Lane, Sparkbrook,
Birmingham B12 8AJ
Tel. no 0121 449 0335
www.adilbalti.co.uk

Renowned for some of the best curries in Birmingham, Adil's still manages to keep the price down. With a Bring Your Own (BYO) policy and an off-licence next door, this is guaranteed good value for money. They were undergoing refurbishment and had moved into temporary alternative premises as we went to press, so call to check the address and book beforehand.

Ha Ha Bar and Grill ££

178–180 Wharfside Street, Mailbox,
Birmingham B1 1RN
Tel. no 0121 632 1250
www.hahaonline.co.uk
haha.birmingham@
bayrestaurantgroup.com

With a fabulous view over the Gas Street canal basin, Ha Ha has an enviable location.

A night of carousing requires serious sustenance.

And with a 90-seater terrace, there's no better place to start your night off than with a few cocktails in the early evening sunshine. The food here is varied, but with a strong focus on British-sourced produce.

Las Iguanas ££

Arcadian Centre, Hurst Street,
Birmingham B5 4TD
Tel. no 0121 622 4466
www.iguanas.co.uk

Famed for its Caipirinhas and its buzzing funky Latino ambience, Las Iguanas is perfect for a party. If you love Mexican, Brazilian and Cuban flavours, you'll love it here. Whether Fajitas are your fave or you crave Chimichangas, you're going to find something to tantalise your tastebuds and tickle your fancy here. With cocktails served by the pitcher, your party is definitely going to swing.

Strada ££

109–111 Wharfside Street, The Mailbox,
Birmingham B1 1XL
Tel. no 0121 643 7279
www.strada.co.uk

If you love Italian food, you'll love Strada. The cuisine is authentic and the surroundings relaxed and contemporary. On the menu you'll find hand-stretched pizzas, fresh pastas, risottos as well as a selection of grilled meat and fish.

'real life'

We had lunch at The Floating Coffee Company, a barge at The Water's Edge in Brindley Place, then shopping at The Mailbox and dinner at Ha Ha's. A real girlie day!

Ha Ha Bar and Grill at The Mailbox.

where to party

Birmingham is literally brimming with canalside bars and restaurants together with city centre clubs and pubs. Going out here is...well, the new 'going out'.

If you need help, check out the 'fire officers' at the Pleasure Ladies Night at Oceana.

Flares

55 Broad Street, Birmingham B1 2HJ
Tel. no 0121 616 2957
www.flaresbars.co.uk
info@flaresbars.co.uk

No prizes for guessing this one...Flares is a 70s club and proud to be the grooviest disco around! If you love all those disco dancing floor fillers (and let's face who doesn't), Flares is the party destination for you. They will organise a personalised party package for you with your favourite funky 70s tracks, a free bottle of bubbly, 'Q Jump' tickets and a party pack with heaps of 70s bling. Groovy!

O2 Academy Birmingham

16–18 Horsefair, Bristol Street, B1 1DB
Tel. no 0121 622 8250
www.o2academybirmingham.co.uk
mail@o2academybirmingham.co.uk

The giant of the Birmingham music scene, this is where you'll find all the top gigs.

Current charting acts such as N-Dubz, Scouting for Girls and Paloma Faith are all featured in the line-up for 2010. With three separate venues rooms hosting different kinds of artists, this is *the* live music venue in Brum.

Oceana

1–5 Hurst Street, Birmingham B5 4EH
Tel. no 0845 4025390
www.oceanaclubs.com
birmingham@oceanaclubs.com

On the edge of Chinatown, this vast superclub has seven themed rooms to choose from. Book a private booth or suite, complete with champagne reception to add that extra layer of decadence to your nightclubbing experience. The resident DJs roll out a blend of dance music, commercial pop, R'n'B, hip hop and drum & bass mixed in with cheesy and party classics to lighten things up. Pleasure Ladies Nights male revue show is resident here on a Saturday night.

Reflex

36–37 Broad Street, Birmingham B1 2DY
Tel. no 0121 643 0444
www.reflexbars.co.uk/reflexbroadstreet

If the cheesy choons of the 80s are more your thang, then book yourselves a Reflex party night. Whether it's Wham!, Duran Duran or Spandau Ballet who float your boat, all the classics will be pumping out here, so get that New Romantic clobber on and backcomb your hair within an inch of its life. Make sure you book a party package here and get all the necessary accessories to make your 80s party rock.

Sence

70 Hurst Street, The Arcadian,
Birmingham B5 4TD
Tel. no 0121 622 4442
www.sencebirmingham.co.uk
info@sencebirmingham.co.uk

This self-confessed 'senceational' nightclub experience has arrived in Birmingham. It has the ambience of a glamorous bar, combined with the edginess of a nightclub to create an unbeatable atmosphere. At Sence the UK's top DJs unleash themselves on the state-of-the-art sound and lighting system. Book yourself into the luxurious VIP area for a truly memorable night. Don't worry, you won't even have to queue at the bar as it's all waitress service.

The Jam House

No.1 St. Pauls Square, Birmingham
Tel. no 0121 200 3030
www.thejamhouse.com
info@thejamhouse.com

A slightly more grown-up live music venue, The Jam House welcomes over 21s only. Located in the heart of the Jewellery Quarter of Birmingham the venue occupies an historic Georgian building. With seating spread over three stylish floors, the atmosphere is relaxed and infomal. Opened by R'n'B maestro, Mr Jools Holland, The Jam House has a similarly cool vibe. For dinner book a table on the top floor and sample some of the freshly cooked international cuisine, alternatively for a larger group you can arrange a buffet.

The Works

182 Broad Street, Birmingham B15 1DA
Tel. no 0121 633 1520
fivewaysleisure.com/the-works.htm

If you love your club classics and dance anthems with a few chart favourites thrown in for good measure, then head to The Works for a monster mash up. There are three rooms each with a different musical 'flava', so get dressed fresh and funky and check out the sounds.

The 'senceational' Sence nightclub.

Everything for your Hen Night!

Hen Night HQ

www.HenNightHQ.co.uk

- **ORGANISE** your Hen Night with our free Hen Party Planner

- **DESIGN** your own personalised Hen Night T-shirts

- **BUY** Hen Night dares, games, outfits, boppers and much more!

SHOP ONLINE NOW
FREE DELIVERY ON EVERYTHING!

Find us on Facebook or Google us!
Search for: Hen Night HQ

www.HenNightHQ.co.uk

blackpool

Beach and Tower (top), carousel (middle), trams (bottom).

England's answer to Las Vegas is a dizzying and rather delightful feast of fairground thrills, beach, clubs, arcades and illuminations, and she's ready to welcome you with wide-open arms. And a tequila slammer.

what to do

As we're pretty sure you must know the kind of thing that goes on in Blackpool, maybe we should tell you what doesn't go on? Snobbery, long faces, low-key tastefulness, early rising, boredom and work are all pretty low down the agenda. Sounds like a pretty good set up for a few days of mayhem with your best mates, doesn't it?

So how did one town on the north-west coast gain such a distinctive culture? Well, leisure isn't just an optional extra in Blackpool. The city was established as somewhere to 'take the cure' – that is bathe in the sea – in the 18th century, and bowling greens, archery ranges and holiday cottages were soon built. By 1893 the three piers (OTT and proud) were in place and hosting 19th century rave ups, such as tea dances and vaudeville theatre. The place was built for partying, day and night, and that has to be a good reason to go, doesn't it?

It's soooo tacky, you say? Well, maybe. But imagine a tasteful Blackpool. Zzzzzz...

We say, sort out some fancy dress, organise an itinerary and paint the town the loudest shade of red you can.

Thrill-seekers' paradise.

✳ 10 good reasons

1. **sandy beaches**
2. **candy floss highs**
3. **winning Daytona races**
4. **party atmosphere**
5. **the illuminations...ahhh**
6. **the rides**
7. **cheap accommodation**
8. **good value clubs and bars**
9. **compulsory fun 24:7**
10. **cycling along the prom**

sounds of the city

Killer queen Murder mystery nights and weekends have been popular in the UK for a good 20 years now. You turn up and get to dress up, eat, drink and be entertained by actors and a dubious, but usually hilarious, plot. You'll know your character and what to wear from an invite sent to you beforehand. It's brilliant fun and it's going on in Blackpool. Lots of party organisers offer sleuthing nights, but we suggest you check out ukgirlthing.com for more details.

Crazy Book in with sudden-impact.co.uk for MAD – multi activity days, that is. Here, you can wreak revenge on that cow who's beaten you to be chief bridesmaid by pumping paint bullets into her. If you fear such attacks from others, make it laser tag, which doesn't hurt but still involves running around shrieking a lot. Team that up with relatively relaxing archery, quad biking or air rifle shooting. Call the team, who are based on a farm just outside Blackpool, on 01253 767279.

You make it easy Contact blackpoolhenparties.co.uk and get a two night package wrapped up by people in the know. You can choose from a list of activities including paintballing, burlesque cabaret dancing and pampering. In the evening you'll be hitting The Syndicate nightclub or enjoying a little risqué cabaret, as well as getting free entry to various bars. Hotel B&B is arranged, and you can tag all sorts of extras on. Weekend prices start from just £59 per person.

I want to ride my bicycle Calling all fitness freaks – step away from the candyfloss and get on your bikes to explore the coastal areas, such as the pleasant nine-miler from Blackpool North Pier to Fleetwood. You can hire bikes to get around Blackpool itself, it being a leader of the national push to get people cycling, or escape into the mercifully flat lands of Fylde and Wyre. Here, miles of safe country roads are punctuated with teashops and pubs. Visitlancashire.com has a useful list of timed/ability rated cycle routes in the beautiful county of Lancashire, so you can get out and cycle 'til you're worn out, rest up in a country pub, then head back to the bright lights later on.

Blackpool Pier.

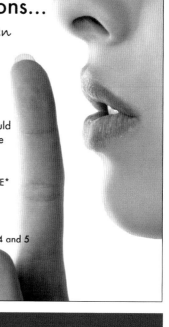

You spin me round Pleasure Beach Blackpool is Britain's most popular theme park, with 6.5m visitors per year. It was originally conceived as a place to 'make adults feel like children again and to inspire gaiety of a primarily innocent character'. Bless.

Sing when you're winning Take a ride on the 32m-high ferris wheel on Central Pier to warm up your vocal cords. Then, make some real noise at Nellie Dean's karaoke bar on the Promenade.

Meanwhile, at Club Sanuk, there's something altogether easier on the senses, with the Adonis Cabaret Show. The club itself is a party haven, with seven bars, five rooms and four music styles. Your hen party package will include friendly hospitality, a buffet and cocktail, games, prizes and comedy.

You're so vain If you think you'll need an afternoon away from the bright lights and partying, seek out the loveliness of the Imperial. This stunning Barcelo hotel on North Promenade is a city landmark and, more importantly, has a gorgeous pool and leisure suite, with spa and beauty therapists just dying to meet you and make you feel amazing.

Later, as you're looking so fine, maybe you should head for Rumours – one of Blackpool's newest and most sophisticated clubs. Drinks promotions ensure that it's still pretty good value for money, so you can dance and drink the night away without blowing your hen party budget.

Book into a leather-clad VIP booth, with private dance floor and reserved area of the bar, if you fancy upgrading yourself. Honey, you're so worth it.

Fairground rides are plentiful in Blackpool.

'been there...'

My hen party was in July, so I wanted to head for the beach. It was hot and sunny, so we got loads of time on the beach and drinking al fresco! The club was a bit naff, but you go for the holiday atmosphere – loads of people having a brilliant time. On the Saturday we spent the afternoon doing laser tag and quad bikes at Whyndyke Farm, which was a laugh.

❝ **We spent a day at the Pleasure Beach reliving our childhood, which was such a blast. We all screamed like banshees on the Infusion ride – what a laugh!** ❞

where to stay

b&bs & hotels

Ash Lodge £

131 Hornby Road, Blackpool FY1 4JG
Tel. no 01253 627637
www.ashlodgehotel.co.uk
admin@ashlodgehotel.co.uk

This cosy B&B is set in a residential area just a short walk from the Hounds Hill Shopping Centre, Blackpool Tower, the beach and the promenade. Proprietors Mary and Margaret will give you a warm welcome and there's even free parking.

Barceló Blackpool Imperial Hotel £££

North Promenade,
Blackpool FY12HB
Tel. no 01253 623971
www.barcelo-hotels.co.uk
stay@barcelo-hotels.co.uk

Victorian grandeur at its most impressive, the Imperial is a landmark on the North Promenade. You can walk to all the attractions from here or hop on the tram that stops across the road. All the facilities you'd expect from a four-star hotel, including a health club with swimming pool, are here.

Chequers Plaza Hotel ££

24 Queens Promenade, North Shore
Blackpool FY2 9RN
Tel. no 0800 0273107
www.chequersplaza.com
enquiries@chequersplaza.com

Having recently undergone a major facelift, this three-star hotel is the perfect place for peace and quiet. Set a little way away from the nightlife, but with fabulous views of the Irish Sea, it's a relaxing haven. Yet it's only ten minutes walk to the town centre.

Number One St Luke's ££

1 St Lukes Road, Blackpool FY4 2EL
Tel. no 01253 343901
www.numberoneblackpool.com
info@numberoneblackpool.com

Voted Britain's best B&B in 2007, this is no ordinary B&B. With elegantly styled rooms and luxury fittings it is more of a small boutique hotel. Even the beautifully appointed bathrooms have LCD TVs and speakers! You can have a continental breakfast brought to your room or indulge downstairs.

* shared room without breakfast

£ under £30
££ £30–£60
£££ over £60
pppn

Party Inn £

The Lark Inn, 41–43 Banks
Street, Blackpool FY1 2AR
Tel. no 0845 2575025 (local rate)
www.partyinn.co.uk

As the name suggests, this B&B accommodation welcomes party groups and offers several packages with VIP entry to all of Blackpool's top nightspots. Located in the centre of town, Party Inn is close to all the clubs, as well as the beach and train station.

Elegant bedrooms at Number One St Luke's.

The Lawton ££

58–66 Charnley Road,
Blackpool FY1 4PF
Tel. no 01253 753471
www.thelawtonhotel.co.uk
thelawtonhotel@gmail.com

The Lawton is dedicated to helping you have a great time in Blackpool. There's a large well stocked bar with wide screen TV to help you relax and prepare for the night ahead and multiple occupancy rooms to choose from.

Fantastic bathrooms at Number One St Luke's.

self-catering

Berkswell Holiday Apartments £

10 Withnell Road, Blackpool FY4 1HF
Tel. no 01253 342434
www.berkswellflats.co.uk
sheila.reception@tiscali.co.uk

With five apartments sleeping two–four people, the Berkswell can accommodate a group of up to eighteen. The apartments are well furnished with everything you need for a comfortable stay and your hosts, Jim and Sheila, will ensure you have a fantastic stay.

**✳ shared room
without
breakfast
£ under £30
££ £30–£60
£££ over £60
pppn**

Jade Holiday Apartments ££

10 Clifton Drive, Blackpool FY4 1NX
Tel. no 01253 341500
www.jadeapartments.com
jade-southshore@hotmail.co.uk

Overlooking the Pleasure Beach and just 1 minute's walk to South Promenade, these well appointed apartments are very well located. They're also close to transport links. The apartments are all one- or two-bedroomed and fully furnished.

Marton Mere Holiday Park ££

Mythop Road, Blackpool FY4 4XN
Tel. no 0871 4680494
www.caravancamping.co.uk

If you want to get away from the nightlife and enjoy the absolutely beautiful scenery and coastline just outside Blackpool, then camping is a great option. This Haven park is close to Midland Riding School, where you can enjoy wonderful hacks, or you can rent bikes at the Park and discover the true Lancashire yourselves.

The Beach House £

204 Queens Promenade, Blackpool
FY2 9JS
Tel. no 01253 352699
www.thebeachhouseblackpool.co.uk

These luxurious five-star apartments were regional best self-catering winners in 2008/9 and you can see why. With an gorgeous views over sea and sandy beaches, the seaside theme continues inside with a cool contemporary feel. The seven apartments in the complex sleep between two and five people, so you can all be together. Each apartment has a dedicated parking bay and the trams stop just across the road.

Blackpool Tower.

where to eat and drink

From fish and chips to fine dining, Blackpool has it all and plenty of it. However, you can't come to Blackpool and not try a big stick of fluffy pink candy floss – it's the law!

bars & pubs

Brannigans

35 Market Street, Blackpool FY1 1EZ
Tel. no 01253 752277
www.brannigansbars.com

With cocktails, shooters and drinks promos galore, Brannigans offer the best party night in Blackpool. On a Saturday, DJ Damo plays all the latest chart and party tunes from 8pm guaranteed to get you dancing. You can book your hen party here on the website.

Brannigans in Market Street.

Flagship Bar

Coral Island, Promenade, Blackpool FY1 5DW
Tel. no 01253 627250
www.theflagshipbar.com
info@theflagshipbar.com

There's always a party at the 'Flaggie' and it's alway free. So why pay to go anywhere else? During the day, sports are showing on eight giant plasma TVs and by night resident DJ Ian Bradshaw plays party choons, runs party games and gives away loads of stuff. Friday night is theme night so find out what's on and get dressed up!

Nellie Dean's Karaoke Bar

150–152 Promenade, Blackpool FY1 1RE
Tel. no 01253 623737

If you fancy yourselves as X factor stars and you want the microphone in your hand on your hen night, then Nellie Dean's Karaoke Bar is the place for you. Even if you just want to sit back and let the others make fools of themselves, this is a very entertaining night out. Open 'til 4am the atmosphere here is pumping all night long with all the best cheesy tunes.

Roxy's Fun Bar

23 Queen Street, Blackpool FY1 1NL
Tel. no 01253 622573
www.roxysonline.co.uk

In true Chicago style Roxy Hart and her friends will entertain you with fabulous drag acts. As well as the main stage, there's Velma Kelly's bar, Billy Flynn's bar and Mama Morton's. If you love Chicago, you'll love Roxy's. DJ Matty keeps the party going with cheesy choons 'til the small hours.

Walkabout

1–9 Queen Street, Blackpool FY1 1NL
Tel. no 01253 749132
www.walkabout.eu.com

The classic Aussie bar brings the spirit of Australia, through awesome food, beer and authentic Aussie staff. The atmosphere is second to none. With permanent amazing drinks promotions and hen and stag party packages, they'll make your party one to remember Aussie style. Check out the free Bucking Bronco on Saturday afternoons for the 2010 season. Try and beat your mates, you may even win a prize.

cafés & restaurants

2 courses + half a bottle of wine

£ under £20
££ £20–£35
£££ over £35

Baci £

37–39 Talbot Road, Blackpool FY1 1LL
Tel. no 01253 296688
www.baciitalianrestaurant.co.uk
info@baciitalianrestaurant.co.uk

Just round the corner from the famous Funny Girls is this funky Italian restaurant serving delicious pasta, mouthwatering steaks and fresh fish. Italian for 'kisses', Baci offers a great hen party option – the Italian Feast, where you can enjoy a selection of starters and main course dishes hand-picked for you by the chef.

Seniors £

106 Normoss Road, Blackpool FY3 8QP
Tel. no 01253 393529
www.thinkseniors.com
normoss@thinkseniors.com

A traditional fish and chip shop, but with a contemporary twist. The restaurant is modern and vibrant and fish comes fresh from Fleetwood each day. There's always something a bit different on the 'catch of the day' board, so why not give it a whirl?

'real life'

We had a real laugh at Nellie Dean's Karaoke Bar. It's a totally unpretentious place, you can just let your hair down and have a good time without any worries.

X factor hopefuls apply here.

West Coast Rock Cafe.

Toast ££

28 Corporation Street, Blackpool FY1 1EJ
Tel. no 01253 749777
www.toast-cafe-bar.co.uk
info@toast-cafe-bar.co.uk

New on the scene in Blackpool, Toast is dedicated to serving fresh locally sourced produce presented beautifully. Inside the double-height ceiling with mezzanine level gives it a feeling of city chic. Tapas is served all day and there's a great value early bird menu, but for the day-after-the-night-before we recommend the traditional Sunday Roast.

West Coast Rock Cafe ££

5–7 Abingdon Street, Blackpool FY1 1DG
Tel. no 01253 751283
www.westcoastrock.co.uk
westcoastrock@blueyonder.co.uk

A legend in Blackpool eateries, the West Coast has been serving Mexican food for 20 years and won the local Best Restaurant of the Year in 2009. You can also get juicy 100% beef burgers, the best steaks in town, succulent Barbecued Ribs, Chicken, Pizza, Pasta and loads more. Big parties are their speciality and you can party 'til late in the 'Club Above' upstairs.

where to party

In the season, Blackpool is totally buzzing with a party vibe. If you're thinking of heading here in the winter, check with venues for opening information first.

Club Sanuk

168–170, North Promenade, Blackpool
FY1 1RE
Tel. no 01253 292900
www.clubsanuk.co.uk
info@clubsanuk.co.uk

With six different rooms of pure entertainment, Sanuk is a great place for your hen night. They have a fab hen party package that can be booked online including free entry before midnight, Q Jump and a free bottle of bubbly to start your night.

Flares

124–130 Promenade, Blackpool FY1 1RA
Tel. no 01253 299688
www.flaresbars.co.uk

No prizes for guessing this one...Flares is a 70s club and proud to be the grooviest disco around! If you love all those disco dancing floor fillers (and let's face who doesn't?), Flares is the party destination for you. They will organise a personalised party package for you with your favourite funky 70s tracks, a free bottle of bubbly, Q Jump tickets and a party pack with heaps of 70s bling. Groovy!

Fun at Flares – the grooviest disco around.

Betty Legs Diamond puts on a spectacular show at the Green Parrot Bar.

Funny Girls

5 Dickson Rd, Blackpool FY1 2AX
Tel. no 0844 2473866
www.funnygirlsonline.co.uk
funnygirls@itpleisure.com

Funny Girls isn't just a club night it's more of a Blackpool institution. Now housed in the old Odeon cinema this is an utterly unique night of top quality live transvestite acts.

Green Parrot

22–28 Clifton Street, Blackpool FY1 1JP
Tel. no 01253 620906
www.greenparrotblackpool.co.uk
info@greenparrotleisure.com

During the day you can relax and chat over coffee and cake or a glass of wine and light lunch with background music and clips of iconic movies and dances for you to enjoy. At night the mood slowly changes to create a party atmosphere. Now with the infamous Betty Legs Diamond Cabaret Show nightly Wednesday to Sunday.

Rumours

Talbot Square, Blackpool FY1 1NG
Tel. no 01253 293204
www.rumoursandhush.co.uk
rumoursandhush@btinternet.com

This sophisticated night spot is a wine bar, a nightclub and a party venue all in one. A recent refurbishment has brought a fresh look and an atmosphere that caters for a chic, diverse crowd of more discerning clubbers. Together with its funky counterpart Hush, they're redefining the club scene in Blackpool.

The Alabama

Liberty's Hotel, 1 Cocker Square, Blackpool FY1 1RX
Tel. no 01253 291155
www.thealabama.co.uk
info@thealabama.co.uk

A multi award winning cabaret venue hosted by the outrageous Leye D Johns. Featuring fun floor shows, with the beautiful Liberty Dancers and the best singers in the North West. When the show finishes at midnight the party keeps on going with a disco.

The Syndicate Superclub

130–140 Church Street, Blackpool
FY1 3PR
Tel. no 01253 753222
www.thesyndicate.com
info@thesyndicate.com

The Syndicate claims to be the biggest party in the UK, and with a capacity of 5000 over three floors they must be right! Whatever your taste in music you'll find something to please whilst you strut your stuff on the biggest revolving dancefloor in Europe. So get on your glad rags and your slap and get down there for some serious partying.

Level two at The Syndicate Superclub.

bournemouth

Buckets and spades at the ready – we're digging for UK gold. If you love long, sandy beaches, a dynamic holiday vibe and the sight of sun-drenched surfer boys wandering around, Bournemouth is an absolute treasure. With seven miles of award-winning beaches, it's time to don that bikini, girls!

Sailing (top), beach huts (middle), the Pier (bottom).

what to do

This city by the sea boasts soft, sandy beaches, great clubs, a vibrant young population and a real holiday atmosphere. It's Britain's no. 1 staycation resort.

In 2007, a certain bank surveyed the country and discovered that Bournemouth was the happiest place in the UK. Furthermore, we can reveal that it's not because they're all over 90, mad and living off the state, oh no. In fact, Bournemouth has a massive young population, thanks to the university, thousands of language students, the bay's increasing popularity with surfers and a growing media industry. That's not to say that you can't still get a nice cup of tea and a slice of cake.

Bournemouth started life as a health resort and it's still good for the soul, having well below average rainfall and a generally sunny climate.

All in all, if your hen do is to take place in the summer, it seems a pity not to go to Bournemouth. Some of the UK's finest sandy beaches, the pleasure gardens, the pier, a thriving club scene and thousands of people milling around looking for fun, is bound to make for a fantastic few days.

10 good reasons

1. sand, sea and surf
2. watersports
3. holiday atmosphere
4. Boscombe surf reef
5. the Italianate Gardens
6. hiring a beach hut
7. kayak racing
8. riding in the New Forest
9. mini golf
10. spa hotels

There's plenty of surfer eye candy, thanks to the new Boscombe surf reef.

sounds of the city

Hyper music The O2, formerly the Opera House, should definitely be able to provide a highlight night for your hen party. Acts that have graced the stage include the Yeah Yeah Yeahs, Ian Brown and Tinchy Stryder, and it's a stop on the NME Shockwaves tour. The venue is beautiful, with royal boxes, proscenium arch and art deco features still intact.

Deep honey The desire to meet surfers will be strong once you see those buff blondies wandering around, and one way to make it happen is to book yourselves in for a surfing lesson. It's hard work but superb fun, and while body boarding and getting a dunking might be the general standard, some of you are guaranteed to be able to stand up at the end of the day. Which is probably more than you'll be able to say at the end of the night. Surf Steps will tailor the lesson to your needs.

Slide show Polestars offer masses of brilliant hen party ideas for venues all over the country. Those that catch our eye in Bournemouth are cheerleading and the cocktail-mixing masterclass.

Both are great value and a real giggle, and who knows when cocktail making expertise could come in handy… later in your hotel room with a couple of tooth mugs and the mini bar, probably. As to the cheerleading, what with all that jumping around and shouting, we can't think of a better way to get the laughter flowing for a fantastic hen night.

She's like the wind Poole Harbour is one of the best places to learn to windsurf – like most men, it's shallow and windy! Book in for two three-hour lessons and you've got a full beginner's course and two fantastic afternoons to look forward to. You'll quickly progress from hardly being able to climb onto the board to cruising across the bay at speed with a big grin on your face. Contact Poole Windsurfing for info.

Salt water If you feel like pushing the boat out for your one and only hen party, keep it literal with a private luxury boat charter from Principal Power. You'll be sipping champagne on comfortable white leather seats and feeling posh until the skipper opens up the throttle,

If you feel the need for speed, hire a Zapcat with exhilaration.co.uk and zoom across the bay Bond girl style.

at which point it's time to down your drinks and enjoy slicing through the waves at top speed – there's nothing like it for making you want to scream whooooo hooooooooo! There's a selection of sleek power boats for charter, but we recommend the elegant Princess V48, with two seating areas, a bar, an electric barbeque and sun deck. And that's how you make dear old Bournemouth feel like St Tropez.

Twist and shout How better to admire Thomas Hardy country than by viewing it from every angle, over and over again? True, your mind may be on other things as you career down a steep Dorset incline in a giant bouncy ball – especially if they've shoved a mate and a bucket of water in with you. At £15 per ride for a group of ten+, Zorbing is one cheap thrill you'll never forget. Call Zorb South on 01929 426595.

Hellbound We've seen some sights, but Saturday night debauchery in a church? Jesus! Ladies, if you're looking for Bournemouth's best, most opulent

nightclub, it has to be V. This is a fairly new arrival on Bournemouth's scene, and has an impressive events diary including parties from Hed Kandy. You can book a VIP package where you'll queue jump and have a private booth with platters of sushi, or just get glammed up and mingle in with your very party-minded fellow heathens. Shame on you all.

Space cowboy Laserquest, located near all the shops and nightlife, is one of the best hen activities going. It's the perfect icebreaker – if some of your friends don't know each other, this will get rid of any shyness! By the time you've hunted each other through swirling fog, flashing lights and pitch blackness, mercilessly zapped each other with lasers and had your winner and loser certificates presented, you'll all be ready for a great night out.

Heaven Bournemouth used to be a health resort – a perfect excuse for a pamper while you're there. Try the Hallmark on the West Cliff – lovely stuff.

Zorb South is the place for thrillseekers.

'been there...'

I love Bournemouth! I used to go there every summer, and when it came to my hen do it was a no brainer to go back. I just love the atmosphere - everyone's up for a laugh. I just love going out to the bars at night and seeing what happens. If you're dressed up people always get talking to you and it's more fun in the clubs. We did a space theme.

where to stay

A popular tourist destination since the Victorians brought the railway to Bournemouth, it's a town with plenty of choice from seaside chic to rural charm.

hotels

Cremona B&B ££
61 St Michael's Road, West Cliff, Bournemouth BH2 5DP
Tel. no 01202 290035
www.cremona.co.uk
enquiries@cremona.co.uk

Situated in the centre of Bournemouth, close to the beach, shopping and nightlife, you'll always get a warm welcome here. The rooms are clean and comfortable with ensuite facilities, and the breakfasts are legendary.

Hallmark Hotel and Spa £££
Durley Chine Road, Bournemouth BH2 5JS
Tel. no 01202 751000
www.hallmarkhotels.co.uk/bournemouth
bournemouth.sales@hallmarkhotels.co.uk

This four-star hotel has recently been transformed at a cost of £1.8million into one of the finest boutique-style hotels in Bournemouth. It offers everything a group of girls needs on a pre-wedding celebration: light and airy relaxing rooms, health spa and gym, stylish brasserie serving fine wine, champagne and carefully prepared meals.

Mory House ££
31 Grand Avenue, Southbourne, Bournemouth BH6 3SY
Tel. no 01202 433553
www.moryhouse.co.uk
stay@moryhouse.co.uk

The modern spacious bedrooms at Mory House have a real seaside feel. They are all ensuite and feature TVs, DVD players and hairdryers in every room.

✳ shared room without breakfast
£ under £30
££ £30–£60
£££ over £60
pppn

Premier Inn Bournemouth Central £
Westover Road, Bournemouth BH1 2BZ
Tel. no 0870 423 6462
www.premierinn.com

With over 500 hotels in their group, the people at Premier know how to run a hotel! Bournemouth Central is close to 7 glorious miles of sandy beaches, the town centre and all the nightlife. Many of the rooms have balconies and a sea view and they all have a comfy bed.

The Cumberland Hotel ££
27 East Overcliff Drive, Bournemouth BH1 3AF
Tel. no 01202 290722
www.cumberlandbournemouth.co.uk

This 1930s iconic Art Deco hotel is full of character. The many original features are complemented with modern twists since a refurb in 2006. Well located, it's a great place to stay.

Relax in pure comfort at Hallmark Hotel Bournemouth.

self-catering

Bournecoast ££

26 Southbourne Grove, Bournemouth
BH6 3RA
Tel. no 01202 437 888
www.bournecoast.co.uk
info@bournecoast.co.uk

This local family-run holiday letting agent will fix you up with the perfect accommodation for your group. They have a huge range of properties in the Bournemouth area in a wide variety of sizes so they are perfectly placed to find you the ideal self-catering accommodation.

Poole Harbour Rental ££

Suite 44, Poole BH15 2BA
Tel. no 07778 586710
www.pooleharbourrental.com

Elegant and stylishly decorated, serviced self-catering rental accommodation, with individual character. The rooms are spacious, airy, light, warm and welcoming with all the essential luxury of a top-quality serviced apartment. The various properties are located around Poole Harbour.

* shared room without breakfast
£ under £30
££ £30–£60
£££ over £60
pppn

Riviera Holiday Apartments ££

Studland Road, Alum Chine,
Bournemouth BH4 8HZ
Tel. no 01202 763653
www.rivierabournemouth.co.uk
reservations@rivierabournemouth.co.uk

With indoor and outdoors pools, spa bath and sauna, these apartments offer a relaxing break and they're just 2km from the beach. Each apartment sleeps from two–seven people in simply furnished and well-equipped surroundings.

St George's Holiday Flats £

4 Cecil Road, Boscombe,
Bournemouth BH5 1DU
Tel. no 01202 303066

In a highly sought-after location, just a short walk to golden sandy beaches and the shopping area, these are well suited to those wanting to catch some rays on the beach. Parking is available and there is free Wi-Fi.

Wootton Mews Apartments ££

3 Wootton Gardens, Bournemouth
BH1 1PW
Tel. no 01202 556432

Wootton Mews Holiday Apartments are situated in the heart of the town, meaning that you will be within minutes of all the fun and exciting facilities that Bournemouth has to offer. You have a range of different sized apartments within a converted Victorian property. Parking permits are available to guests on request.

The spa at Hallmark Hotel and Spa.

❛ We had a fabulous apartment in Bournemouth with a sea view. It was great waking up in the morning to the sound of waves. ❜

where to eat and drink

bars & pubs

Aruba

Pier Approach, Bournemouth BH2 5AA
Tel. no 01202 554211
www.aruba-bournemouth.co.uk
info@aruba-bournemouth.co.uk

This exotic world bar brings a touch of the tropics to the Southern English coast. There is an extensive list of wines, beers and champagne sourced from every corner of the globe and both their innovative and classic cocktails are to die for.

At Bar So they don't just mix cocktails, they 'flair' them.

Bazaar

103 Commerical Road, The Triangle,
Bournemouth BH2 5RT
Tel. no 01202 241998
www.bazaarbar.co.uk
info@bazaarbar.co.uk

This intimate lounge bar is set over two floors. Downstairs has a pool table and outside deck. Upstairs you can expect to hear everything from breaks and dub reggae through to soulful house, US garage and hip hop, nu soul, funk and disco. Live singers and acoustic sessions are lined up for 2010.

Bar So

Exeter Road, Bournemouth BH2 5AG
Tel. no 01202 203050
www.bar-so.com
barso@royalexeterhotel.com

This stylish bar is the place to see and be seen in Bournemouth. With two levels and an extensive terrace, it has something to suit every mood. This place is serious about cocktails, even holding their own 'flair' and mixology competition in 2009, bringing bar tenders from around the world.

Bliss

1–15 St Peter's Road, Bournemouth
BH1 2JZ
Tel. no 01202 318693
www.bliss-bar.co.uk
bliss.bournemouth@
yellowhammerbars.com

Situated in the very heart of the town centre this is Bournemouth's premier style bar and clubroom. Chill out in the luxurious bar area where you can reserve a booth or VIP area or head downstairs to bump and grind the night away to the latest R'n'B, hip hop and Urban Music. What about cocktail masterclasses? Bliss has it all.

The Lounge

30 Exeter Road, Bournemouth BH2 5AR
Tel. no 01202 296394
www.theloungebournemouth.co.uk
info@theloungebournemouth.co.uk

The Lounge is a sleek and shiny bar with a chic clientele. There are plenty of drinks offers here to get your party started and resident DJ Sleek Ray plays a selection of classic and upfront party jams on Saturdays.

restaurants

Indian Lounge £
148 Christchurch Road, Bournemouth
BH1 1NL
Tel. no 01202 293355
www.indian-lounge.com
info@indian-lounge.com

Widely complimented for its delicious Indian food and attentive staff, you can't do better that Indian Lounge if you love a good curry. Unless of course you try Indian Ocean on West Cliff Road.

La Stalla Restaurant £
270 Wallisdown Road, Bournemouth
BH10 4HZ
Tel. no 01202 535642
www.lastalla.co.uk
enquiries@lastalla.co.uk

Everyone loves Italian and this restaurant welcomes groups of all sizes. Whatever your favourite, from the traditional pizzas and pasta dishes to steaks, poultry and fish, you'll find it all on the extensive menu here.

'real life'

Me and my friends went to Westpoint in West Cliff Road because we all love seafood. We weren't disappointed – the food was great and the wine even better!

Locally caught shellfish.

2 courses + half a bottle of wine

£ under £20
££ £20–£35
£££ over £35

Bournemouth has plenty of places for fine dining.

Nippon Inn £
124 Charminster Road
Bournemouth BH8 8UT
Tel. no 01202 258859
www.nipponinn.co.uk

If you like noodles or sushi washed down with a cold Kirin beer, this is the place for you.

Salsa Latin Bar Restaurant ££
82 Charminster Road, Bournemouth
BH8 8US
Tel. no 01202 789696
www.salsabar.co.uk

There's always a lively atmosphere in this warm and inviting Spanish tapas bar. Choose from a wide selection of classic tapas dishes or try something from the Mexican menu, if that's not your thing there's pizza and pasta too. Wash it all down with jugfuls of Sangria!

The Lazy Shark £–££
682 Christchurch Road, Bournemouth
BH7 6BT
Tel. no 01202 303417

This lively eatery in Boscombe is just a little bit different. It has a restaurant and separate sports bar. The modern European food is stunning and the service friendly and helpful. It's the ideal venue close to the new surf reef.

where to party

There are so many clubs and bars in
Bournemouth we can't possibly mention
them all, but the good thing is that
everywhere is within walking distance.

Bournemouth has a steamy nightlife scene.

Bumbles
45 Poole Hill, Bournemouth BH2 5PW
Tel. no 01202 557006
www.bumblesnightclub.co.uk

A Bournemouth institution, Bumbles is hen
party heaven. With Dreamboys International,
self confessed 'sexiest boys on the planet',
performing their sizzling routine there every
Saturday night, it must be high up on your
list. Choose from the Red Room (RnB) and
the Blue Room (Cheesy party tracks).

DNA
224–226 Old Christchurch Road,
Bournemouth BH1 1PE
Tel. no 01202 319362
www.dnabournemouth.co.uk
info@dnabournemouth.co.uk

DNA, or Daytime Nightime Anytime, is the

town's top RnB club.partying through the
night until 5am. If you've got some serious
stamina then DNA is the club for you.

Dusk till Dawn
205 Old Christchurch Road,
Bournemouth BH1 1JU
Tel. no 01202 551681
www.dusktilldawnclub.com
dusk@dusktilldawnclub.com

The club offers two floors of alternative
Dance Music with a state of the art sound
system. Dusk till Dawn's underground music
policy, quality sounds and opening hours
make it an exclusive club for serious music
heads on the South Coast. Don't expect
cheesy or charty stuff here, but do expect
plenty of drinks promos and a great
atmosphere.

The up-for-it crowd at The Old Fire Station.

Klute Lounge

20 Exeter Road, Bournemouth
BH2 5AQ
Tel. no 01202 252533

A restaurant, a bar and a club all wrapped up in one neat package of entertainment. You can book a VIP booth for your group or even a room if you have a lot of friends.

The Old Fire Station

36 Holdenhurst Road, Bournemouth
BH8 8AD
Tel. no 01202 963888
www.oldfirestation.co.uk

Half commercial club, half student union for Bournemouth University, The Old FireStation has been rocking Bournemouth for over 15 years. With guest DJs and live events there's plenty of noise in this listed ex-firestation.

"The club scene in Bournemouth is great. Everyone is really up for it and having fun. "

Toko Nightclub

33–39 St Peters Road, Bournemouth
BH1 2JZ
Tel. no 01202 318 952
www.toko-bar.co.uk
toko.bournemouth@yellowhammerbars.com

With room for over 1000 people, this is the place to make friends! Famous for its huge fish tanks and awesome party atmosphere it is a must see for any Bournemouth visitor. There are two floors offering very different experiences. The main room is dedicated to party, whereas the basement offers a more intimate clubbing experience for those who love to dance.

V Club

The Church, Exeter Road,
Bournemouth BH2 5AQ
www.vbournemouthrocks.com
promotions@vbournemouth.com

This is a truly opulent venue in a converted church with a fantastic balcony overlooking the dancefloor. With a fabulous sound and light show to match, a great line up of events and permanent drinks offers, this is a guaranteed good night out.

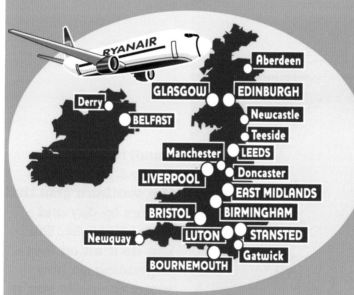

THE CHEAPEST WAY TO THE BEST STAG AND HEN PARTIES IN EUROPE

BUDAPEST   KAUNAS
PRAGUE   RIGA
GDANSK   KRAKOW
POZNAN   WROCLAW

FLIGHTS FROM SELECTED UK AIRPORT

RYANAIR

brighton

Small but perfectly formed, Brighton is the southern gem that shines by day and rocks by night. You can do it all on foot – depending on how many cocktails you've had of course – and the place is geared up for 24:7 fun.

Sign (top), the Pier (middle), the Royal Pavillion (bottom).

what to do

The residents love it. Londoners cruise down on sunny saturdays, and hen and stag parties descend every weekend. Leave your sanity at home and enjoy...

Since the Prince Regent established the mad Pavilion Palace as his den of debauchery in the 1820s, Brighton has been a byword for a good time.

So just what is it about this stretch of pebbly coast that makes it so different to Blackpool and other seaside towns around the UK?

All the fun of the fair!

The question needed proper research. And, frankly, we needed no second bidding to head down there. For your sake, dear reader, we spent a long, arduous weekend, shopping in the funky North Laine area, walking on the downs, drinking heavily in beachside bars and proper old pubs, wandering through the Lanes boutiques and eating in superb restaurants all over town, trying to work out what gives it that *je ne sais quoi*.

A few shots later, perched on the kitchen worktop of the random party we'd somehow ended up in, we came up with an unshakeable hypothesis. 'It's just an amazing town.'

Since Brighton aint cheap and brain cells are irreplaceable at our age, we hope you use this research wisely.

10 good reasons

1. loads of undie boutique
2. veggie restaurants
3. picnics on the Downs
4. beachside clubs
5. the buzz
6. straight-friendly gay scene
7. indie clothes shops
8. Tuaca (Italian liquer)
9. posh boutique hotels
10. cheap, central hostels

sounds of the city

Shake your tail feather You know what a bride needs to really take her mind off dresses, spray tans, mother-in-laws and caterers? 'Orbing', that's what. Replace petty worries with genuine fear for your life! Throwing yourself down a very steep hill inside a bouncy ball is both therapeutic and proof that you need therapy. It also gives you the chance to head to the lovely South Downs for a day of walks, picnics and craziness. Later on, you could follow up with cocktail making lessons at Roger Dodger the Fish (RDF), Preston Street. And if that little lot won't shake things up a bit, we don't know what will.

Underwater love If you find the English Channel an acceptable receptacle for a dip, then book a full day of watersports, including kayaking, windsurfing, ringo rides behind a speed boat and waterskiing, and finish with a BBQ dinner on the beach. Visit ViewBrighton.co.uk to find out more.

Rubberband girl The trampolines on the Palace Pier are fun, but Jumpzone bungy trampoline on the beach is, in our opinion, one of the most ridiculous things you can do. Therefore, it should not be missed. If you want something a bit edgier, the UK Bungee Club has several 'events' on Hove Lawns throughout the year. Book in and jump off. And since you're wearing a grin of hilarity already, a night at the excellent Komedia stand-up comedy club might round the day off nicely.

Welcome to the House of Fun
Wandering up the Palace Pier with a face full of unhealthy food is always lovely, as is the obligatory stop for pics of your mates faces grinning through the bawdy cut-outs next to the arcade. Seaside magic. And, when the man with the money belt shouted in bored tones, 'It's fun! It's exciting!', it was certainly enough to get our bums on seats at the Dolphin Derby for half an hour. It is fun and exciting, in case you're wondering. But not as fun as the dodgems, and not as exciting as the Crazy Mouse rollercoaster, which looks innocent but dangles you out over the sea in a most alarming manner. Eek, eek! The House of Horror is good for some girly screaming, too.

Jumpzone at the Palace Pier.

The wind beneath my wings

Getting your thermals on gets sexy when you're talking paragliding. Airworks of Glynde will enable you to 'soar like a bird' with tandem or taster flights. You sit securely on the lap of an instructor while he flies you around on a thermal breeze above Sussex.

Driving along in my automobile

Don't leave the driving to the stags. Getting kitted up and driving like a loon is what we ladies love best. Karting Nation's 800 metre track has a lap time and position display as well as tunnels and a split level track.

If you really want to get dirty, Adventure Connections does off-road 400cc buggies to have you bounding around at high speed on a mudslick. In total control and looking fab, naturally.

Luck be a lady Hove has one of the UK's best dog tracks, and the Saturday action starts at 5pm. If you want a more dressed-up do, perhaps a days' horseracing might be the thing. For later on, one of the Marina's swanky attractions is the Rendezvous Casino – high on glitz and the perfect opportunity to ditch the jeans and slink around in a sexy dress.

I bet you look good on the dancefloor

We don't know what you're looking for...but at least one club in Brighton is going to have it. The Honey Club has quality and cool, Casablanca has live funk, cheesy disco and laughs, and the Funky Buddha Lounge is a constant party. There are many other great places to go out dancin', so check out 'where to party' for the venues that say 'you'.

'been there...'

The first night we booked ourselves a karaoke party at Gars, which does fab Chinese food. You get a private room so things got pretty loud. Anyway, as you can imagine we were a big fragile next day so we just used the hotel pool and had a chill. Saturday night it was off to club Oceana for the Adonis Cabaret, which was soo cheesy but really good fun!

The Bohemian North Laine shops.

where to stay

If you want somewhere stylish, luxe or chic to stay, Brighton's the place. From boutique B&B to super cool self-catering, this funky town has it all...at a price!

hotels

Holiday Inn Brighton Seafront ££

137 Kings Road, Brighton BN1 2JF
Tel. no 01273 828250
www.hibrighton.com
reservations@hibrighton.com

As the name suggests, this hotel is well located opposite the beach. It has everything you would expect in a 4-star international hotel chain, including Wi-Fi and air conditioning. There are several lounges and bars to relax in and two restaurants. Check the website for special offers on room rates.

✳ shared room without breakfast

£ under £30
££ £30–£60
£££ over £60
pppn

Jurys Inn £

101 Stroudley Road, Brighton BN1 4GQ
Tel. no 01273 862121
brightonhotels.jurysinns.com

Join ranks with other hen and stag parties at this central hotel located near the train station. It's also walking distance to the centre and the seafront. With comfy rooms equipped with Wi-Fi, it's a good choice.

Kings Hotel ££

139–141 Kings Rd, Brighton BN1 2NA
Tel. no 01273 820854
www.kingshotelbrighton.co.uk
info@kingshotelbrighton.co.uk

Located right in the heart of Brighton and very close to the beach, the Kings Hotel is a magnificent Regency hotel converted from three former private residencies. The modern boutique style is clean and fresh; and the K bar, overlooking the sea, is a great place to start off your evening.

New Madeira Hotel ££

19–23 Marine Parade, Brighton BN2 1TL
Tel. no 01273 698331/0800 970 7634(free)
www.newmadeirahotel.com
info@newmadeirahotel.com

This seafront guesthouse offers a variety of rooms from budget to boutique (some with a jacuzzi bath) to suit your wallet. The period building has been fully modernised and the friendly staff will make your stay truly memorable.

West Beach Hotel ££

135 Kings Road, Brighton BN1 2HX
Tel. no 01273 323161
www.westbeachhotel.co.uk
rooms@westbeachhotel.co.uk

This hotel offers a little individuality. It boasts five quad rooms featuring four single beds perfect for a group booking. Twins and triples are also available, many with a sea view so make sure you put in your request.

Brighton beachfront.

self-catering

Best of Brighton Cottages £–£££
4 Laureens Walk, Nevill Road,
Rottingdean, Brighton BN2 7HG
Tel. no 01273 308779
www.bestofbrighton.co.uk
www.apartmentsinbrighton.com
enquiries@bestofbrighton.co.uk

Offering about 100 fully furnished
apartments, houses and cottages in
Brighton & Hove and the
surrounding countryside. Letting
periods start at three days and
properties are available in all
price ranges and sleep from
2–20 people.

Crown Gardens £–££
7 Gloucester Yard, 121–123
Gloucester Road, Brighton BN1 4AF
Tel. no 01273 608378
www.crown-gardens.co.uk
enquiries@crown-gardens.co.uk

The Brighton experts in finding
accommodation for groups, Crown Gardens'
friendly staff will provide you with the perfect
base for your party. They specialise in
centrally located apartments and cottages
close to Brighton's buzzing centre, ideal for
short lets.

Florence House Garden Annexe £
18 Florence Road, Brighton BN1 6DJ
Tel. no 01273 506624
www.brightonlets.net

This tranquil cottage is set in the garden of a
Victorian House just a mile from the seafront.
Sleeping up to nine people in five bedrooms,
it's ideal for a medium-sized group.

My Holiday Let £–££
6 Brunswick Place, Hove BN3 1EB
Tel. no 07976 923733
www.brightonholiday.com
catherine@myholidaylet.com

These luxury apartments are the self-catering
alternative to a boutique hotel. Just a stone's
throw from the beach, these gorgeous bow-
fronted regency apartments have a 5-star
rating and a Gold Award. Simply furnished,
they ooze understated style.

Palms Properties ££
25 Waterfront, Brighton Marina,
Brighton BN2 5WA
Tel. no 01273 626000
www.palmsproperties.co.uk
booking@palmsproperties.co.uk

Palms offer a wide range of accommodation
in Brighton Marina from waterside
studios to luxury penthouse
apartments. The four
apartments range from a
studio to three bedrooms,
all furnished to a high
standard.

✳ shared room without breakfast
£ under £30
££ £30–£60
£££ over £60
pppn

Queensbury Mews ££
15 Queensbury Mews
Brighton BN1 2FE
Tel. no 01273 270636
www.queensburycottage.co.uk
info@queensburycottage.co.uk.

This luxury townhouse is set right in the city
centre and close to the seafront, perfect for a
night on the town. Recently modernised and
refurbished, it is bright and airy with stylish
neutral decor.

Vida Retreats ££
5 Somerhill Rd, Hove BN3 1RP
Tel. no 01273 220358
www.vidaretreats.com

This is the ultimate luxury accommodation for
large groups. Lansdowne Regency Villa and
Somerhill Edwardian Mansion are 5 minutes
apart and sleep 22–30 in sumptuous style.

Brighton Marina.

where to eat and drink

Eat and drink from the global village in Brighton. There are food and beverages from all over the world here, all you need to do is find the time to try them.

bars & cafés

Browns Bar & Brasserie
3–4 Duke Street, Brighton BN1 1AH
Tel no. 01273 323501
www.browns-restaurants.co.uk

In the 40 years since Browns started it has become synomous with good food served in stylish surroundings. Here in Brighton that is as true as ever. Come for brunch, lunch, drinks, dinner or even afternoon tea.

Carluccio's
Unit 1 Jubilee Street, Brighton BN1 1GE
Tel. no 01273 690493
www.carluccios.com

For serious coffee aficionados Carluccio's has to be on the list. Pop in for a latte and biscotti while shopping, browse the gorgeous deli foods, or go for a blow-out lunch. You won't be disappointed, this is the art of eating Italian.

Koba
135 Western Road Brighton BN1 2LA
Tel no. 01273 720059
www.kobauk.com
info@kobauk.com

A little off the beaten track, you'll find this gem of a place. Its intimate and mysterious atmosphere draws you in and the cocktails make you stay! Enquire about mixology here.

Leo's Lounge
54–55 Meeting House Lane, Brighton BN1 1HB
Tel no. 01273 207040

This leopard print lined bar set in Brighon's trendy Lanes is the perfect place to start your evening off with cocktails or champagne.

Carluccio's Café.

Oxygen
63–65 West Street, Brighton BN1 2RA
Tel no. 01273 727378
www.oxygenbrighton.co.uk

This trendy bar has a 'shot-tail' (shooter cocktails) menu of over 40 concoctions plus regular cocktails on promotion in the early evening. The saloon bar theme makes this a wild card, but it will come up trumps.

Roger Dodger the Fish (RDF)
76 Preston Street, Brighton BN1 2HG
Tel no. 07761 166 300
www.rogerdodgerthefish.com
iinfo@rogerdodgerthefish.com

This place is legendary in Brighton for hen and stag parties. Claiming to be 'the sexiest bar in Brighton if not the world', the bar is split into a girls' area and a boys' area. The girls' area has sexy barmen, a princess and a pole (for dancing on...). You can arrange burlesque dance classes here, have a big screen movie showing and learn to make cocktails, or all three. There's nothing they won't do to entertain you on your hen night.

restaurants

El Mexicano £

7 New Road, Brighton BN1 1UF
Tel. no 01273 727766
www.elmexicano.co.uk
info@elmexicano.co.uk

Delicious authentic Mexican food and Spanish tapas all freshly prepared on the premises. Set in Brighton's 'theatreland' it's handy for pre- or post-theatre dining. A deposit is required for groups of eight or more and the maximum on Saturday is 14.

Gars ££

19 Prince Albert Street, Brighton BN1 1HF
Tel. no 01273 321321
www.gars.co.uk
info@gars.co.uk

In the heart of the Lanes, Gars offers a wide range of traditional Chinese food with a smattering of Thai and Japanese dishes for a taste of the Far East. The food is nicely complemented by the modern Asian decor featuring bamboo flooring and silk shades.

'real life'

Me and my chicks all went down to Brighton from London and had a great time wandering around the Lanes, just stopping for lunch at Jamie's Italian.

Retail therapy.

Old Orleans is hen party paradise.

Havana ££

32 Duke Street, Brighton BN1 1AG
Tel. no 01273 773 388
www.havana.uk.com
info@havana.uk.com

The laid back colonial style of this former theatre evokes the ambience of the Caribbean times past. An international menu, accompanied by fine wines and moody jazz, creates a leisurely evening out.

Jamie's Italian £££

11 Black Lion Street, Brighton BN1 1ND
Tel. no 01273 915480
www.jamieoliver.com

Jamie Oliver's passion for food is at the forefront of this new chain of restaurants. Simple, rustic Italian dishes all prepared with the best local and seasonal ingredients will make your mouth water. The all-Italian wine list offers something a bit different, too.

Old Orleans ££

13 Prince Albert Street, Brighton BN1 1HE
Tel. no 01273 747000
www.oldorleans.com
oldorleans.brighton@intertainuk.com

Experts in hosting hen and stag parties, Old Orleans can cater for any size of group. It's no surprise that the menu is mainly American incorporating favourites such as wings and nachos. You can also reserve an area in the bar at no cost.

where to party

The club scene in Brighton is buzzing with a unique vibe that people regularly travel miles for every weekend. For a truly memorable hen party Brighton's the place.

Audio

10 Marine Parade, Brighton BN2 1TL
Tel. no 01273 697775
www.audiobrighton.com

Set on two levels you have a choice of the downstairs bar or the Above Audio cocktail bar. There is also a terrace, which they bill as 'the classiest smoking area in Brighton'! This chilled out venue plays a mix of chart music and funky house downstairs and when the action wraps up about 2am, you can carry on partying in the upstairs club until 4am. There are no pretentions here, just honest fun.

Casablanca

3 Middle Street, Brighton BN1 1AL
Tel. no 01273 321817
www.casablancajazzclub.com
info@casablancajazzclub.com

Going since 1980, Casablanca is a mainstay of the Brighton scene. It prides itself on being a fun, independent environment, just a little bit different to the rest. On offer here are two floors with two different sounds: one playing live music, the other featuring a DJ. Saturday nights see a blend of live latino and the finest funk bands around playing to an up-for-it crowd who are there to enjoy the music.

Digital

187–193 Kings Rd Arches, Brighton, BN1 1NB
Tel. no 01273 227767
www.yourfutureisdigital.com
steve.joyce@yourfutureisdigital.com

This club is serious about music boasting some top-quality sound and light gear. On Saturday nights they feature 'Playroom', with sounds of house and electro along with an adult bouncy castle, ball pit, space hoppers, inflatables and giant games. This could be your last opportunity to revisit your childhood so revel in it.

It's always cocktail time in Brighton's lively scene.

Funky Buddha Lounge

169–170 Kings Rd Arches, Brighton
BN1 1NB
Tel. no 01273 725541
www.funkybuddhalounge.co.uk
info@funkybuddhalounge.co.uk

Housed in the subterranean arches of the
seafront, the Funky Buddha Lounge is the
city's premier style venue. Open till 4am this
venue won't sting you on the door or the bar.

Komedia

44–47 Gardner Street, Brighton BN1 1UN
Tel. no 0845 293 8480
www.komedia.co.uk
info@komedia.co.uk

Located in the trendy North Laine area of
Brighton, Komedia is famed for its award-
winning formula of great shows, fab food,
excellent drinks choice and welcoming
atmosphere. Whether you fancy laughing at
stand-up comedy, grooving with sultry
cabaret, kooky club nights...or all three...it's
the perfect venue for any Hen party!

Lucky Voice

8 Black Lion Street, Brighton BN1 1ND
Tel. no 01273 715770
www.luckyvoice.com
brighton@luckyvoice.com

If you're seeking a different yet classy hen
night idea, Lucky Voice has all you need.
They'll organise everything for you, give you a
private karaoke room, a dressing up box, ply
you with cocktails, teach you how to make
them and then let you sing your hearts out.
Sounds like fun!

Oceana

West Street, Brighton BN1 2RE
Tel. no 0845 296 8590
www.oceanaclubs.com/brighton
oceana-brighton@luminar.co.uk

This multi-million pound venue has seven
themed rooms and two VIP suites to choose
from. Chill in the Aspen Ski Lodge, dance
your heart out in the Icehouse, party the night
away in the New York Disco or relax in the
Parisian Boudoir. Who knows where you'll
end up?

Rendezvous Casino

Park Square, Brighton Marina, Brighton
BN2 5UF
Tel. no 01273 605602
www.rendezvouscasino.com

If you want some thrills on your last night of
freedom, head to the tables at Rendezvous.
There's a wide range of games on two floors
including roulette, blackjack, texas hold'em,
three card poker and let it ride.

Spend a night at the tables at Rendezvous Casino.

The Honey Club

214 Kings Rd Arches, Brighton BN1 1NB
Tel. no 01273 202807
www.thehoneyclub.co.uk
info@thehoneyclub.co.uk

Another vast multi-room venue including two
beachfront terraces. With a different music
genre in every room, there's something for
every musical taste here.

bristol & bath

Old fashioned charm, classic beauty and a funky social scene collide in the West Country's top city destinations. Opt for a relaxing wallow in mellow, luxurious Bath or have your cake and eat it in lush and lively Bristol.

Bristol Harbour (top), Bath's Pulteney Bridge (middle), Clifton Suspension Bridge, Bristol (bottom).

what to do

Whether you're looking for a spa, boat trips, floating nightclubs, arty cinema, boutique shopping, craft fairs or underground dancing, Somerset does it in unique style.

Taking your hen party to the wilds of Somerset is a good idea for two reasons: Bristol and Bath.

Bristol's got all the lively nightlife, big name shopping, harbourside bars, pack-'em-in cheap eateries and top restaurants you could possibly want from a modern cosmopolitan city. On top of all this is a liberal sprinkling of that arty, funky pixie dust that makes people come back again and again just to sample the very particular brand of laid-back cool that oozes from every nook and cranny of the city.

Meanwhile, down the road is one of Britain's most beautiful sights, Bath. For mellow trips down the river, for picnics in the park, for chilling out over bottles of wine and good food, this gorgeous Georgian city is simply unbeatable.

The new Komedia has given the Bath weekend a much-needed tweak of the funnybone, and there are decent little clubs, pubs and cocktail bars for small, civilised groups, as well as the odd large venue for pitcher glugging. If Bristol's arty, Bath's more hand crafted, but both of them have bags of style.

10 good reasons

1. good restaurant scenes
2. Bristol harbour bars
3. Clifton delis and boutiques
4. Bath's smart hotels
5. Bristol's value hotels
6. lovely countryside
7. historic and charming
8. Bristol Academy
9. small, quality clubs
10. proper old pubs

Find out what a roman pamper day was all about at the historic Roman Baths.

sounds of the cities

I've got a lovely bunch of coconuts
The Lido in Bristol doesn't look much from outside, and your guests might think it's a bit odd to have a swimming pool party at your age, but don't let that stop you. The pool and beach hut-style changing rooms ooze Victorian seaside charm, and the attractive restaurant over looking them serves good, modern food with a smile. Aside from the pool there's a sauna, steam room and hot tub. You can get some blissful body treatments, including the Ananda face massage, bio-energising body wrap and other sciencey sounding stuff, and retox with a nice drink at the poolside bar. Total winner.

Perfect day Meanwhile in Bath, spa is a well-practiced art and a traditional way to while away a few hours in this splendiferous Georgian city. Our recommended sunny day in Bath is this: Pitch up by train and head to the baths for a few hours of rooftop swimming, steaming and chilling. Have a genteel coffee and cake in the nearby Pump Rooms before trotting up the very filmic Great Pulteney Street and over to the Bathwick boating station.

Here, you can hire a variety of vessels including punts and large gondola type affairs. Now's the time to break out the champagne and strawberries, by the way. You'll eventually land at The Bathampton Mill, a lovely spot for an al fresco or sofa-bound boozy lunch. Suitably refreshed, the row back to Bath centre is mercifully downstream. If you want to stick around Bath then top class standup or dressed up cabaret nights at Komedia, with food from the River Cottage people, finishes off a perfect day in style.

God Save the Queen Thornbury Castle in South Gloucestershire was the marital home of Henry VIII and Ann Boleyn, but don't dwell on the matricidal detail. Book the group into the Tudor Hall for fabulous food in the company of freestanding suits of armour, creepy family portraits and decapitated animals for a truly authentic castle vibe. The Boyling House and Great Oven rooms next door can be turned into a casino and a bar for your event. Great for a big group of ladies who like to get off the beaten track and do something unique.

Take in the fantastic views from the rooftop pool at Bath's Thermae Spa.

Smash it up Flying Saucers in Clifton is a lovely, mellow few hours if there's nothing you like more than making stuff, having a chat with your mates and eating biscuits. You'll paint pottery, perhaps producing a set of bespoke tableware for the bride and groom to lovingly tuck away for best. There's never an occasion special enough for some things, is there?

Cold as ice Bath wasn't the first place we would have looked for an underground ice cave and yet, bucking the local inclination for all things thermal, Celsius welcomes you to its freezing lair. Huge padded jackets and gloves are supplied, and drinks are served in ice glasses. Next door is a buzzing club, serving up cheese, chart, house and dance at normal room temperature. Cool, yet hot. Not for those with sensitive teeth.

All hands on deck If Bristol's more your cuppa for a night out, then we recommend The Thekla – a club boat moored on the lovely Mud Dock. Some of the city's best nights happen aboard this much-loved vessel. Keep it simple (but good) by booking your group in for food and drinks on the top deck before the party gets going down below.

Red, red wine The chaps at the Tasting House in Larkhall, Bath are lovely and very knowledgeable in all things wine. Book your party in for a civilised evening tasting and appreciating fine wines on the sofas in their cosy little shop. With a glass of good champagne on arrival and a selection of delicious nibbles, it makes a gorgeous hen party for those who prefer a little civilisation while they get hammered. Hic.

'been there...'

We wanted to do a spa day, so we chose Bath. The new spa is modern but not really posh, it was so nice looking over the rooftops as we swam around in the sun. We went for lunch at Jamie's Italian, which is lush, then I had a treatment at Neal's Yard while the girls went shopping. We went to Opa and Po Na Nas later on. Bath is a really chilled out, beautiful city.

Start the evening off with a champagne reception at The Tasting House in Bath.

where to stay

For big city lights and the big chain hotels, where you know exactly what to expect, then Bristol's your bag. On the other hand, if you like a more unique feel, then stay in Bath.

hotels & hostels

Belushi's £
9 Green Street, Bath BA1 2JY
Tel. no 01225 481444
www.belushis.com/bath
party@belushis.com

This low cost hostel style accommodation in the centre of the city features dorm rooms with bunks. There is a lively Belushi bar restaurant on site and breakfast is included in the rate. Clean linen is provided, but you need to suppy your own towel.

Cabot Circus Hotel £
Bond Street South, Bristol BS1 3EN
Tel. no 0845 094 5588
www.futureinns.co.uk
reservations.bristol@futureinns.co.uk

Belonging to Future Inns, a small chain of three hotels, the Bristol outlet is attached to the shiny new shopping centre – Cabot Circus. With 149 ensuite rooms and Chophouse Restaurant and Bar, it has all the facilities you need in a central location.

Hotel Ibis Bristol Centre £££
Explore Lane, Harbourside, Bristol BS1 5TY
Tel. no 0117 989 7200
www.ibishotel.com

This international chain offers all the services and facilities you need to get a good night's sleep after some serious partying – comfy beds, ensuite shower rooms and more. There's also another branch of the hotel near Temple Meads station.

Harington's Hotel £££
8–10 Queen Street, Bath BA1 1HE
Tel. no 01225 461728
www.haringtonshotel.co.uk
post@haringtonshotel.co.uk

This bijou boutique hotel is right in the centre of Bath and just a couple of minutes walk from the Thermae Spa. Despite its central location it's in a quiet secluded street offering convenience and tranquility. The Harington also has apartments ideal for groups.

The Halcyon £££
2–3 South Parade Bath BA2 4AA
Tel. no 01225 331200
www.thehalcyon.com
info@thehalcyon.com

Bath's brand new boutique hotel offers pure luxury right in the heart of Bath. The standard rooms, all designed by an award-winning interiors expert, feature quality beds with sumptuous linen, 32" plasma TVs, walk-in showers and White Company products.

shared room without breakfast

£ under £30
££ £30–£60
£££ over £60
pppn

Belushi's, Bath.

self-catering

Bath Holiday Rentals ££
Regency House, 2 Wood Street,
Queen Square, Bath BA1 2JQ
Tel. no 01225 482 225
www.bathholidayrentals.com
alexa@bathholidayrentals.com

You'll get a warm and friendly service from this Bath-based company offering luxurious, short-term lets. The majority of properties are close to the heart of the city at some of the most prestigious addresses.

Premier Apartments, Bristol.

Bristol Serviced Lets ££
The Refinery, Jacob Street,
Bristol BS2 0HS
Tel. no 0871 226 1902
www.servicedlets.com

Serviced Lets Design Apartments has chosen the pick of the crop of Bristol's most stunning modern apartment developments both in the city centre and trendy Clifton. So whether you want Georgian splendour in Clifton or contemporary design near the harbour, this company has it all.

Geometric Serviced Apartments ££
Braggs Lane, Old Market,
Bristol BS2 0BE
Tel. no 0117 954 7490
www.geometricapartments.com
info@geometricapartments.com

These stylish contemporary apartments are furnished to the highest standards, featuring Bamboo teak flooring, designer bathrooms and chic Italian furniture. These one- and two-bedroomed apartments are the ultimate in boutique self-catering.

Laura's Townhouse Apartments ££
14 Beauford Square, Bath BA1 1HJ
Tel. no 01225 464238
www.laurastownhouseapartments.co.uk
laura@laurastownhouseapartments.co.uk

Laura's offers stunning townhouse and apartment self-catering accommodation in listed buildings in the heart of Bath. All tastefully furnished and with modern comforts of home, such as widescreen TV, DVD, Wi-Fi and Ipod dock. Properties sleep up to 12.

Premier Apartments ££
30–38 St Thomas Place, St Thomas Street, Redcliffe, Bristol BS1 6JZ
Tel. no 0117 954 4800
www.premierapartmentsbristol.com
info@premierapartmentsbristol.com

Located in Redcliffe, these apartments are 5 minutes walk from Temple Meads train station and the trendy Cabot Circus shopping centre. The 64 one- and two-bedroomed apartments are located within one building. Wi-Fi and LCD TVs are available in all apartments.

* shared room without breakfast
£ under £30
££ £30–£60
£££ over £60
pppn

Riverside Apartment £
Batheaston, Bath
Tel. no 01225 852226
www.riversapart.co.uk
sheilapex@questmusic.co.uk

At Riverside Apartment you get the best of both worlds, a beautiful rural setting on the River Avon only 10 minutes from the centre of Bath (by limo of course). Your friendly host will arrange pamper days, a recording studio party, catering and other services to order for a truly tailormade hen party.

The Residence £
Ormonde Lodge, Weston Road, Bath BA1 2XZ
Tel. no 01225 750180
www.theresidencebath.com
info@theresidencebath.com

Two splendid Georgian properties sleeping up to 15 people are available from this company. One is a 10 minute walk from the centre of Bath, the other just outside the city.

where to eat and drink

You're spoilt for choice in both Bath and
Bristol with a wealth of good quality, lively
bars and a choice of fine dining or large
budget eateries.

bars & pubs

Ha Ha Bar and Grill
The Tramshed, Beehive Yard,
Bath BA1 5BD
Tel. no 01225 421200
www.hahaonline.co.uk
haha.bath@bayrestaurantgroup.com

Situated just off Walcot Street, Bath's Boho
area, Ha Ha is a spacious bar and restaurant
with a large heated outdoor area, usable all
year round. You can reserve an exclusive
area for your party and select from the wine
list or sample something from the Grill.

Revolution
York Buildings, George Street,
Bath BA1 2EB
Tel. no 01225 336168
www.revolution-bars.co.uk/bath

This stunning venue, a former post office, is a
great place to spread out for a leisurely lunch
or party hard into the evening. With cocktail
lessons and chocolate fondues on offer, the
helpful management will put together a night
to remember. And you can dance on until late
with Bath's finest DJs. Revolution is also in St
Nicholas Street in the centre of Bristol.

Sub 13
4 Edgar Buildings, George Street,
Bath BA1 2EE
Tel. no 01225 466 667
www.sub13.net
drinks@sub13.net

This super chic underground bar is located at
the top of town close to Revolution. This
intimate bar with vaulted ceilings and cosy
booths, also has a large outdoor area.
There's always a party atmosphere here and
a very personal vibe.

The White Lion Bar
Avon Gorge Hotel, Sion Hill, Clifton,
Bristol BS8 4LD
Tel. no 0117 973 8955
www.theavongorge.com
events@theavongorge.com

The panoramic views of Clifton Suspension
bridge and the Avon Gorge from the terrace
at The White Lion are truly stunning. It's a
great place for a long lunch on a sunny day;
order a chilled glass of wine and a tasty dish
from the varied menu, sit back and take in
the view. The Avon Gorge Hotel, the setting
of The White Lion, is also an option for
accommodation if you want to base your hen
night in Clifton.

Try one of the splendid cocktails at Sub 13 in Bath.

cafés & restaurants

Aqua Italia ££
Welsh Back, Bristol BS1 4RR
Tel. no 0117 915 6060
www.aqua-restaurant.com
bristol@aqua-restaurant.com

With two outlets in Bristol and one in Bath, Aqua has perfected its formula of healthy, tasty and beautifully presented Italian cuisine. Enjoy Italian wines and cocktails here, as well as aperitivos, grappas and the best espresso coffees. Choose from the newly refurbished interior with marble bar and cosy corners or the waterfront terrace.

Jamie's Italian £££
10 Milsom Place, Bath BA1 1BZ
Tel. no 01225 510051
www.jamieoliver.com/italian/bath

Housed in an ecletic Georgian property right in the heart of Bath, this all day eatery is just what you'd expect from the phenomenon that is 'Jamie'. With hams, salamis and other mouth-watering ingredients hanging over the bar as you enter, you know from the start that this is going to be a true foodie experience.

Opa £££
14 North Parade, Bath BA2 4AJ
Tel. no 01225 317900
www.opabath.com

This Greek meze restaurant serves a wide range of authentic dishes and always has good fresh fish. The underground vaulted cellars next to the river transform into a lively club around 11pm and you can dance to a mix of cheesy disco and dance tunes until late in the evening.

**2 courses
+ half a bottle
of wine**

**£ under £20
££ £20–£35
£££ over £35**

Riverstation £££
The Grove, Harbourside, Bristol BS1 4RB
Tel. no 0117 914 4434
www.riverstation.co.uk
relax@riverstation.co.uk

This light and airy open-plan restaurant and bar-kitchen serves modern European food. Enjoy it on the open-air terrace!

Severnshed ££
The Grove, Harbourside, Bristol BS1 4RB
Tel. no 0117 925 1212
www.shedrestaurants.co.uk
severnshed@shed-restaurants.com

This former boathouse on the banks of the floating harbour offers a laid back yet luxurious dining experience. On Saturday nights DJs create a lively club atmosphere.

The Arch ££–£££
2–3 Queen Street, Bath BA1 1HE
Tel. no 01225 444403
www.thearchbath.co.uk

Enjoy a modern British menu featuring rustic and classic dishes at this flamboyant restaurant in the heart of Bath. Choose from casual, fine dining or set menu.

Watershed Café Bar £
1 Canon's Road, Harbourside,
Bristol BS1 5TX
Tel. no 0117 927 2082
www.watershed.co.uk
events@watershed.co.uk

This trendy arts centre and cinema on the harbour has a buzzing café bar popular with locals and visitors alike. Open from early in the morning to late at night, you can come here for breakfast, lunch or dinner. Grab a table on the balcony and enjoy watching the world go by on Bristol's bustling waterfront.

Hire a private dining room at The Arch in Bath.

where to party

They may be way out west, but both Bath and Bristol have a lively nightime scene. If you scratch the surface of the usual cheesy clubs, you'll find unique events and venues.

The fabulous Komedia in the exquisitely renovated Beau Nash Theatre.

Avon River Cruises £

Broad Quay, Bath BA1 1UB
Tel. no 0117 904 3671
www.avonrivercruises.co.uk
avonrivercruises@blueyonder.co.uk

The Silver Salmon is the most stylish cruiser on the River Avon and operates throughout the year. It's the ideal way to spend your hen party either in Bath from May to September or Bristol from October to April. You can charter the boat for dancing, live music or a sit down meal.

Blue Rooms

George Street, Bath BA1 2EB
Tel. no 01225 470040
www.bluerooms.net
info@bluerooms.net

This stylish bar and club serves an extraordinary range of spirits, claiming 'if you can't find it here it probably hasn't been invented'. Dance under the starlight ceiling until the wee small hours or book a VIP area for an exclusive experience.

Celsius

1–3 South Parade, Bath
Tel. no 01225 312800
www.celsiusicebar.co.uk
info@celsiusbar.co.uk

The Celsius Ice Bar is a snow and ice cave located in underground vaults in the centre of Bath. You get a hooded ice jacket and gloves to enter the freezing winter wonderland! Warm up with cool tunes in the club afterwards.

Komedia

22–23 Westgate Street, Bath BA1 1EP
Tel. no 0845 293 8480
www.komedia.co.uk/bath
info@komedia.co.uk

Based in the centre of Bath, Komedia is famed for its award-winning formula of great shows, fab food, excellent drinks' choice and welcoming atmosphere. With everything from hilarious stand-up comedy and the sassiest of sultry cabaret, to screenings of your favourite films – sing-a-long style – it's the perfect venue for any hen party!

Pero's Bridge taking you across the harbour into Bristol's humming nightlife scene.

Oceana
Harbourside, Bristol BS1 5UH
Tel. no 0845 293 2860
www.oceanaclubs.com
oceana-bristol@luminar.co.uk

The Oceana concept of seven themed rooms, including five bars and two unique clubs can be found in many UK cities. The Bristol superclub offers private booths and VIP areas plus Q jump packs.

Po Na Na
8–9 North Parade, Bath BA2 4AL
Tel. no 01225 424952
www.eclecticbars.co.uk/ponana
bathpnn@ponana.com

This Moroccan styled club in four underground caverns has lots of intimate seating booths for your party. Saturday nights see superstar DJ Ross Deviant playing an eclectic mix of quality anthems from a variety of genres.

Shake Rattle & Bowl at The Lanes
22 Nelson Street, Bristol BS1 2LD
Tel. no 0117 929 4861
www.shakerattleandbowl.com
letsdance@shakerattleandbowl.com

It's a club, a cinema, a bowling alley, a karaoke bar and a diner all wrapped into one exciting venue with a retro 50s theme. This is a monthly night so check the website for details. Bowling is available every night.

The Big Chill
15 Small Street, Bristol BS1 1DE
Tel. no 0117 930 4217
www.bigchill.net
sadie.f@bigchill.net

The ultimate laid back festival now has two bars to its name – Bristol and London. In the Bristol venue you can expect to find cool live music and resident DJs playing the best of the global music scene.

The Syndicate
15 Nelson Street, Bristol BS1 2JY
Tel. no 0117 945 0325
bristol.thesyndicate.com
bristol@thesyndicate.com

Bristol's biggest club features a variety of events on Saturdays from Foam Parties to Skool Discos. They also offer a variety of party packages with Q Jump entry and champagne that can be booked in advance. Check the website for details.

The Thekla
The Grove, Bristol BS1 4RB
Tel. no 0117 929 3301
www.theklabristol.co.uk
office@theklabristol.co.uk

A live music venue, a club and a bar all on board this boat moored at Mud Dock. Open seven nights a week the Thekla offers various nights featuring all music types from house to contemporary indie.

cardiff

Millenium Stadium (top), Mermaid Quay (middle), Cardiff Bay at night (bottom).

Cardiff has been busy. While the English have been smugly thinking they've got the British thing all sewn up, she's emerged as Europe's newest city beauty, with a fresh look and some surprisingly chic accessories.

what to do

It's official...the Welsh capital rocks!
Whether you want coastal cool, urban
sprawl, rural rambles or small town charm,
they've got it all in this bite-size city.

The English often neglect Wales due to its inconvenient position on that rocky outcrop in the west. Location, location, location – somebody should have told them. Still, as it's there it seems churlish not to explore. And that's just what adventurous hens are doing. You're not far over the Severn Bridge before you hit the Welsh capital city, which just might have everything you need for a classic hen weekend.

Cardiff is full of surprises. OK, we know about the Millennium Stadium and rugby, but how about the Millennium Centre and the rather chic Cardiff Bay? The club scene has earned nationwide recognition, but the shopping and live entertainment is growing up to be rather fabulous too.

Also, it's near some lovely beaches. But did you realise it practically backs on to the fabulous Brecon Beacons national park (breconbeacons.org)? You'll be hard pushed to find a city with so much to do on its doorstep, be it riding, surfing, quad biking or crazier things you won't find in many other UK spots, such as white-water rafting, gorge jumping and caving. It's worth the toll, honest.

Riding in the Brecon Beacons, near Llanthony Priory.

10 good reasons

1. friendly locals
2. good shopping
3. top gigs at The Point
4. club scene
5. it's near the sea
6. lots of outdoorsy stuff
7. up and coming eateries
8. it's practically abroad
9. The Live Lounge
10. Chapter Arts Centre

sounds of the city

Sittin' on the dock of the bay

Cardiff's dockers may be turning in their graves, but since the demise of the coal shipping trade, the kind of work that goes on around the old docklands is more along the lines of serving cappuccino to airy-fairy rich types like you and me. Hurrah! Cardiff Bay is now an impressive freshwater lake two miles from the city centre, and is fringed with an array of eateries, drinkeries, shopperies and ponceries.

Jump on the Baycar bendy-bus or the water bus from the city centre for an evening of culture at the Wales Millennium Centre (wmc.org.uk), where you can catch the likes of Jimmy Carr or Al Murray for comedy and shows such as Chicago and Strictly Come Dancing, as well as opera, ballet, contemporary dance and music, for the high browed. Just arriving at the WMC has a certain wowness, and the location is perfect for bayside chilling before the show.

Opportunities for adrenalin thrills in said bay include rowing, sailing, kayaking and power boating. A canoe slalom centre is also due to open in 2010. Visit adventurecardiff.com – this company can arrange a two-day multi-activity course for you, with water- and land-based thrills aplenty.

We're on a road to nowhere

If you yearn to get off the beaten track, take your mates for a weekend's camping in the picture-postcard Taff Valley, where you can choose from activities including gorge walking, quad biking, clay pigeon shooting, archery and raft building. It's hen party gold, farm-style – great fun as long as you like getting very, very muddy. A little further off the track, try shaggysheepwales.co.uk for action-packed weekends in Pembrokeshire. If you're a horsey type then head to Downs Side Riding Centre in Penarth. What better way to take in the scenery than from the saddle?

I will survive

What you need before a girl's night out is a salt scrub, a mineral soak and a good buffing – AKA coasteering. You'll climb around a cliff at sea level, leaping, swimming and clinging to dear life as the waves crash around you. Although you're safe in the hands of speciality organisers such as adventureswales.co.uk, it's still a challenge that feels like real survival. If that only whets your appetite, get the company to organise a full weekend of mayhem. They'll drop you into Cardiff for recovery drinks (and dancing if you've got the energy) in the evening.

Wales Millenium Centre dominates the skyline at the beautiful Cardiff Bay.

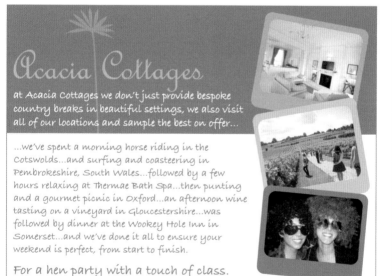

Here come the girls Alright, if you really want the marine hydro massage, not an Atlantic dunking, check out the 'Here come the girls' package at the swoon-inducing St David's Hotel and Spa. Accommodation, Welsh brekky and lunch in this hotel with views over Cardiff Bay would be good enough, but they throw in champagne, a juice bar, two treatments and use of the fabulous health suite. There's lovely!

Ooh la la la Shop, drink, eat, club. Exhausting, being 'It'. Still, if you think you're up to such Paris Hiltonesque action, how's about a nice amble around the famous arcades to shop for nick-nacks, accessories and…stuff. Lunch on Italian favourites at Zizzi, which is a little more glamorous than it's chain rivals but won't break the bank. Follow that with some proper

shopping in Queen Street, and then it's time for a little drinky in elegant 33 Windsor Place. Later, keep things at the artier end of partying with a trip to trendy Boudoir – all interior decor and beautiful people.

Murder on the dancefloor Cardiff's club scene is one good reason to go there. The city has some fantastic clubs and caters for all of you, from the giggly gaggle who don't get out much to the relentless fun bunnies who are out every weekend. Or, horror, a blend of both. Good news, Evolution has a room for cheesy pop and another for proper choons. Events at the club bring in world-class DJs such as Lisa Lashes.

If you don't want the big club vibe, then Clwb Ifor Bach might be the friendly crush of live music, decent DJs and fun-lovin' locals you're after.

Cardiff's arcades are great for boutique shops.

'been there…'

I had a group of 13 mates, all based around the South West. It was too much for me, so I got Wales Activity Breaks to sort it out. We did mad stuff like gorge walking as well as drinking a lot at night. The Glee comedy night was the best. Cardiff's fun at night but you should definitely get out and do activities in the Brecon Beacons in the day. It's gorgeous.

> **Me and my mates just love shopping and Cardiff was paradise for us, everything from the small boutiques to the international chains.**

where to stay

With a massive amount of regeneration around Cardiff Bay in recent years, the Welsh capital has been firmly put on the map and has the accommodation to suit.

hotels

Cardiff Bay Hotel £
Hemingway Road, Cardiff CF10 4AU
Tel. no 0845 094 5487
www.futureinns.co.uk/cardiff.htm
reservations.cardiff@futureinns.co.uk

Owned by the small West Country chain, Future Inns, this large hotel is just a few steps away from the vibrant nightlife of Cardiff Bay and is near the city centre. The ensuite bedrooms are comfortable and spacious with free internet access and local phone calls. There's also free parking which is a real bonus; all in all exceptional value for money.

shared room without breakfast

£ under £30
££ £30–£60
£££ over £60
pppn

Mercure Cardiff Lodge Hotel ££
Wharf Road, East Tyndall Street, Cardiff CF10 4BB
Tel. no 02920 894000
www.mercure.com
h6623@accor.com

This economy hotel is just minutes from the city centre and the waterfront. With contemporary styling throughout the 100 ensuite bedrooms, complete with power showers, this makes a good option.

NosDa @ The Riverbank £
53–59 Despenser Street, Riverside, Cardiff CF11 6AG
Tel. no 02920 378866
www.nosda.co.uk
info@nosda.co.uk

Uniquely situated on the banks of the River Taff and in the shadow of the Millennium Stadium, NosDa provides budget accommodation with ensuite private rooms and dormitory beds. Breakfast is included and there is a restaurant and late bar here.

Park Inn City Centre £–££
Mary Ann Street, Cardiff CF10 2JH
Tel. no 02920 341441
www.cardiff-city.parkinn.co.uk
info.cardiff-city@rezidorparkinn.com

Set right in the heart of the city, Park Inn has all the comforts you'd expect of an international chain. The funky RGB restaurant and bar serves modern food and great cocktails.

The St David's Hotel and Spa £££
Havannah Street, Cardiff CF10 5SD
Tel. no 02920 454045
www.thestdavidshotel.com
stdavids.reservations@principal-hayley.com

If you've got cash to splash, why not blow it here at the world famous luxury hotel and spa overlooking Cardiff Bay.

The River House Backpackers £
59 Fitzhamon, Embankment, Riverside, Cardiff CF11 6AN
Tel. no 02920 399810
www.riverhousebackpackers.com
info@riverhousebackpackers.com

Recently ranked as one of the top ten hostels in the world at the annual 'Hoscars' awards, this family-run hostel is just a few minutes walk from the central train and bus stations. The spotless rooms here are a mix of twins, female and mixed dorms. Breakfast included.

self-catering

A Space in the City ££
18 Harrowby Lane, Cardiff Bay
CF10 5GN
Tel. no 08452 60 70 50
www.aspaceinthecity.co.uk/
cardiff-leisure
info@aspaceinthecity.co.uk

With serviced apartments in 16 locations across Cardiff city centre and Cardiff Bay, there is a wealth of choice with this company. The apartments feature all the luxuries you would expect from a four or five star hotel with top quality interior decor, broadband and housekeeping. All the apartments have a fully equipped kitchen, living area and separate bedrooms. This luxurious accommodation option offers greater flexibility than a hotel and fantastic value for money.

Canal Barn Bunkhouse £
Ty Camlas, Brecon LD3 7HH
Tel. no 01874 625361
bunkhouse-brecon-beacons-
wales.co.uk/index.htm
enq-us@canal-barn.co.uk

If you want a party full of outdoor adventure in the beautiful Brecon Beacons National Park, then this could be the perfect base for you. With canoeing, caving, rock climbing, abseiling, hang gliding, gorge walking, rafting, quad biking and paintball on the doorstep and six cosy bedrooms with bunks, this is great value group accommodation.

Wild Spirit Tipis £
8 Beech Road, Pont-yr-Rhyl,
Bridgend CF32 8AJ
Tel. no 01656 871592
www.wildspiritbushcraft.co.uk
info@bushcraftcourses.co.uk

**shared room
without
breakfast**

**£ under £30
££ £30–£60
£££ over £60
pppn**

For an accommodation option with a difference, how about a few nights under canvas in a traditional Tipi? Lie back on reindeer skins, with a chilled glass of champagne in your hand in front of a roaring log fire and look up at the stars. Situated in a beautiful location, 10 minutes from one of the most beautiful coastlines in Wales, with the mystical Merthyr Mawr Castle looming behind.

For a unique alternative to regular camping – try a traditional Tipi.

where to eat and drink

bars

33 Windsor Place

33 Windsor Place, Cardiff CF10 3BZ
Tel. no 02920 383762
www.33windsorplace.co.uk
33windsorplace@sabrain.com

This slick city centre bar and restaurant is a stylish place to drink and dine. They also offer free use of the Windsor Room for private dining for groups of eight or more, where you can order from the full menu or create your own tailormade menus.

Revolution

9–11 Castle Street, Cardiff CF10 1BS
Tel. no 02920 236689
www.revolution-bars.co.uk/cardiff

The Cardiff bar has many faces, from the opulent and intimate to the modern utilitarian, with different moods for different times of the day, there's bound to be an area that suits you. With plenty of ideas for your party, Revolution will do all they can to give you a great send off. We recommend their cocktail masterclasses and the giant Nintendo Wii for a bit of friendly rivalry. Have a look at their facebook page 'Revolution Cardiff' for events listings.

The Funky Buddha Lounge

48 Charles Street, Cardiff CF10 2GP
Tel. no 02920 644311
www.thefunkybuddhalounge.com
info@thefunkybuddhalounge.com

Claiming to be the funkiest little bar in Cardiff, the Funky Buddha features live music, the hottest DJs, delicious world cuisine from Italy to the Far East via the US, decadent cocktails, premium European beers and a hand-picked wine list. Does a storming Sunday lunch too.

Millenium Quay is buzzing at night.

The Live Lounge

9 The Friary, Cardiff Bay,
Cardiff CF10 3FA
Tel. no 02920 397967
www.theliveloungecardiff.co.uk

A stylish and sophisticated live music bar offering great music, an expansive drinks menu and a buzzing atmosphere. The Live Lounge is the perfect venue, whether you're looking for a fabulous dining experience, to chat and watch live music or party on through until 4am, they have it all!

Tiger Tiger

The Friary, Greyfriars Road, Cardiff CF10 3QB
Tel. no 02920 391944
www.tigertiger-cardiff.co.uk
info@tigertiger-cardiff.co.uk

Located right in the centre of Cardiff, near the Millenium Centre and set over two floors. Tiger Tiger boasts a stylish restaurant, four bars and club. Tiger Tiger has a place for everyone to relax, from the stylish Round Room to the Moroccan influenced Medina, to the comfortable Restaurant. They also host Lucky Voice Karaoke in private rooms with 6000 songs at the touch of a button.

restaurants

Henry's Café Bar ££
Park Chambers, Park Place, Cardiff
CF10 3DN
Tel. no 02920 224672
www.henryscafebar.co.uk

This smart and spacious bar and restaurant serves a wide range of exciting cocktails, a good selection of wines and champagne. Choose from a wide range of grills, burgers and pasta from the reasonably priced menu. There's always a lively atmosphere here at the weekend when Henry's is open until 1am.

Old Orleans ££
18–19 Church Street, Cardiff CF10 1BG
Tel. no 02920 222078
www.oldorleans.com
oldorleans.cardiff@intertainuk.com

Cardiff's original cocktail bar is still the place to go for great cocktails and shooters, along with an extensive menu of Cajun and American food from the Deep South, cooked fresh on the grill. Parties of 12 plus can also be catered for in the private function room.

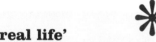

'real life'

Cardiff is surprisingly good for shopping. It has a really great mix of modern malls, like Capitol, and lovely old-fashioned arcades with independent shops.

The Capitol shopping centre.

2 courses + half a bottle of wine

£ under £20
££ £20–£35
£££ over £35

Champagne on ice – the essential hen night beverage.

Las Iguanas ££
8 Mill Lane, Cardiff CF10 1FL
Tel. no 02920 226 373
www.iguanas.co.uk/cardiff.asp
cardiff@iguanas.co.uk

The Latin American flavour of this well loved chain spreads beyond the menu to buzzing carnival atmosphere full of latino spirit. The excellent cocktails here will get you in the mood for partying and with happy hour until 7pm every day you may be tempted to have more than one!

Zizzi ££
27 High St, Cardiff CF10 1PU
Tel. no 02920 645110
www.zizzi.co.uk
info@zizzi.co.uk

Situated just 5 minutes away from the Millennium Stadium and Cardiff's shopping malls and arcades, Zizzi Cardiff is a great place to dine. The restaurant was once a bank and has an impressive interior with high ceilings, gentle lighting and plenty of space to cater for large parties. Tuck in to some excellent Italian food and wine in impressive and welcoming surroundings.

where to party

Whether you want to party in the city centre or in The Bay, there are plenty of options in Cardiff. Clubs of all sizes and for all musical persuasions are ready and waiting.

Clwb Ifor Bach
11 Womanby Street, Cardiff CF10 1BR
Tel. no 02920 232199
www.clwb.net
info@clwb.net

AKA 'The Welsh Club', this is a great live music venue playing true Welsh Indie and Rock music. A down-to-earth club with soul, rather than fancy decor and lighting, it's set on three floors. On a Saturday night you'll find dirty pop on the ground floor, a funky soul, RnB, house party in the middle and the Vinyl Vendettas with their mix of indie, rock'n'roll and classic on top.

Exit Nightclub
48 Charles Street, Cardiff CF10 2GF
Tel. no 02920 640102
www.exitclubcardiff.com
info@exitclubcardiff.com

Cardiff's longest running gay club welcomes all with an open mind. Playing cheesy party favourites on two floors, you'll blend in well with your leg warmers and tutus.

Lava Lounge
The Old Brewery Quarter, St Mary's Street, Cardiff
Tel. no 02920 382313
www.lavaloungecardiff.co.uk
cardiff@lavaloungecardiff.co.uk

Popular for its retro nights and being the only Sunday nightspot in Cardiff, Lava Lounge is a fun and lively club. With plenty of party promotions on offer and two large plasma screens showing sport this place is a magnet for hen and stag parties.

You only have one hen night – enjoy it!

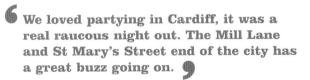

We loved partying in Cardiff, it was a real raucous night out. The Mill Lane and St Mary's Street end of the city has a great buzz going on.

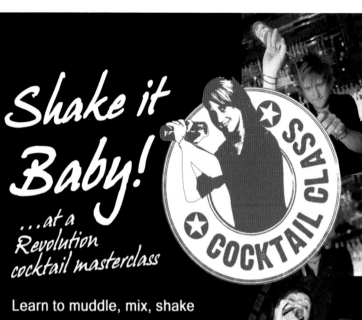

Cardiff has some of the best clubs in Wales.

Liquid & Life
Imperial Gate, St Mary's Street,
Cardiff CF10 1FA
Tel. no 02920 645464
www.liquidclubs.com
cardiff@liquidnightclub.co.uk

Liquid is Cardiff's ultimate dance and event venue. Playing all the best of funky house, electro, R'n'B and dance and featuring some of the world's best DJs, with state of the art sound and lighting systems, amazing visuals and an excellent outdoor area, Liquid & Life presents an unrivalled clubbing experience.

Oceana
Greyfriars Road, Cardiff CF10 3DP
Tel. no 0845 296 8588
www.oceanaclubs.com/cardiff
oceana-cardiff@luminar.co.uk

At Oceana they're experts in hen and stag parties. Just contact the party planners through the website for a range of party offers. The resident DJs here play a good range of old skool party classics and anthems.

The Glee Club
Mermaid Quay, Cardiff Bay,
Cardiff CF10 5BZ
Tel. no 0871 472 0400
www.glee.co.uk
duncan@glee.co.uk

Offering the best stand-up comedy in Cardiff every weekend, The Glee on Mermaid Quay has hosted names such as Jimmy Carr, Jack Dee, Alan Carr and Lee Evans. There are also live music events here, check the website for a list of gigs; Cerys Matthews is billed for 2010. Food is served most nights and there's 10% off if you pre-order.

The Point
Mount Stuart Square, Cardiff CF10 5EE
Tel. no 02920 460873

This popular intimate live music venue has played host to some of the country's biggest acts: The Stereophonics and Funeral for a Friend to name but two. Housed in a beautiful converted church, The Point has great acoustics. Despite being a little rough around the edges this venue has an authenticity of its own.

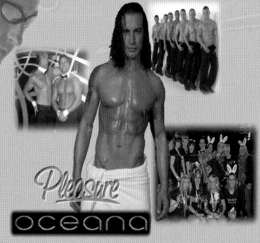

edinburgh

Ross Fountain (top), Fringe Festival (middle), Princes Street (bottom).

Famed for hogmanay and it's Fringe Festival, Edinburgh is a city that knows how to put on a party. For hens, it's a brilliant short break choice – culture, clubs and capital city vibes all rolled into one beautiful package.

what to do

She's a stunning city with a 1000-year-old heritage, sparkling cultural life and feisty character – so Scotland's capital is high on our list of top cities for your hen party.

Preparing for your trip to Edinburgh should probably involve a steadily rising drinking curve and an increase in stodge, because it would be criminal to wimp out on ceilidh dancing and whisky tots, not to mention the rib sticking puddings and hearty savouries that stay the effects of the occasional cool breeze around these parts.

It's also essential to gen up on events – check who's playing, where you can find a ceilidh and the opening hours of the Castle, Costume Haha fancy dress shop and other cultural essentials.

If you're going to hit town in August be prepared to get swept into the torrent of festival goers rushing through the city streets 24:7. It's fun but it's full on, and most pubs and hotels seriously inflate their prices. You'll need to book rooms well in advance if you want to do the Festival for your hen.

But Edinburgh is far from sleepy the rest of the year. Superb hen activities, nightclubs, shopping, bars, eateries and more await you.

10 good reasons

1. views over the city
2. mini highland games
3. capital city vibes
4. locally-sourced food
5. whisky tasting
6. the architecture
7. dancing at a pub ceilidh
8. watching the fireworks
9. shopping
10. Coco's chocolatier

Edinburgh Castle by night.

sounds of the city

All time love For views that make you catch your breath, head for Edinburgh Castle. Don't worry about naff displays and dusty pamphlets here, it's a genuinely interesting trip for about a tenner, and will give you that smug feeling that you've done something civilised. The rest of your historic tour will involve walking on the Royal Mile, which runs from the Castle in the west to the 15th-century Palace of Holyroodhouse in the east. En route you'll find various blue-plaque houses, churches and curiosities, so give yourselves time for a good old poke around. This is real, old Edinburgh. The controversial new parliament building will bring you back to the present with a slap, and then it will be time for a skinny latte and a double choc muffin or a slice of Dundee Cake, no doubt. Replenished and ready for a climb, head up to Arthur's Seat, the volcanic rock formation that towers over this end of the city. It's not for those with vertigo.

Feel so high There is another way to enjoy the stunning views of Edinburgh without ruining your Jimmy Choos and that's the Harvey Nicks Forth Floor Brasserie, from which you can take in gorgeous views of the Firth of Forth and the urban skyscape while you sip and nibble your way through suitably expensive refreshments.

Dream a little dream of me
Boobytrap Boutique is just one of many wallet-lightening retail gems in the classy West End area just off Princes Street. But it's not only shopping for curve-enhancing lingerie that's on offer here. Boobytrap does a fabulous champagne tea combined with burlesque dancing lessons from Edinburgh's own very fabulous Miss Lily White. Burlesque dance is all about embracing your feminine power and sexiness as a woman. Expressing these inner instincts with flirtatious moves using a feather boa, killer heels and satin gloves may almost be enough to take your mind off the spread of cakery laid out on linen cloths – just. That's correct ladies: champagne, sex and cake in a shop...and not a whingeing, innuendo-punting bloke in sight. It's the stuff that dreams are made of.

Harvey Nichols store, check out the 'Forth' floor.

'been there...'

Five of us got invited to stay in a mate's flat for the Fringe Festival, so I thought, perfect for the hen do. It was mental in Edinburgh – crowded, expensive and full-on! The shows we saw were mainly really good and I loved the city, but I wish I'd saved the hen do for another time – it felt a bit like having your birthday at Christmas! Climb up Arthur's Seat for the view!

For An Adrenaline Packed Race Experience

XTREME KARTING

Scottish TOURIST BOARD ★★★★★ ACTIVITY CENTRE

Scotland's ONLY 5 Star Karting Centre

Hen Packages Available

Hen Party Event Specialists!

Only 30 mins from Edinburgh

OPEN 7 DAYS

Mon – Fri   Midday to 10pm
Sat / Sun   10am to 10pm
Please call to check availability

Tel: 01324 579797
Web: www.xtremekarting.co.uk

Xtreme Karting, Unit J,
Lochlands Business Park,
Larbert, Falkirk FK5 3NS

Putting on the ritz More glamour's to be had with 'Vegas', a night that lounges in a few choice Edinburgh venues, including Ego and the art college, and asks you to dress up in 40s rat pack and Hollywood style for big band sounds, showgirls, funk and burlesque. It attracts a great, diverse crowd of clubbers and is a perfect excuse to really big up the vintage satin, costume jewellery and bouncy curls for a night of all-out flirting. If your bum looks big in that pencil skirt, wiggle it.

Scotland the brave Right, now it's time to stop fannying around and get your hands dirty. With caber tossing, farmer racing, haggis rolling and tug o war on the menu, the mini highland games, as organised by gobananas.co.uk, are a true test of your ladies' Celt spirit. Make sure you have Irn Bru with your porridge that morning – you could well meet another hen or stag party on the field, so competition is likely to get fierce. If that's not enough action for you, you can team it up with quad biking, archery or high ropes and make a day of it. All overseen by men in kilts, which is one of the major reasons for visiting Scotland, isn't it?

Food. glorious food Edinburgh's rather splendid boutique hotels and fine restaurants have made the city a snuggly romantic breaks favourite. But if you need somewhere that's good fun for a group to eat, drink and be merry, try the ornate Voodoo Rooms on West Register Street. There's a crowd-pleasing menu we can only describe as American-Italian-Scottish with an Asian zing. The cocktails are lush.

Meanwhile, when only Italian carbs will do after some arduous Princes Street shopping, it's got to be nearby Bar Roma. They take group bookings and serve up an extensive, fresh Italian menu as well as good pizzas, risottos and pasta dishes.

I'd like to teach the world to sing
Why not have a Pop Party at Groove Tunnel recording studio. Lay down professionally mixed tracks, and get your very own CD complete with a photo of your group on the front. Accessories are all provided and you can even have dance lessons with a professional choreographer, if you want the full X Factor experience. A package complete with bubbly and snacks, a copy of the CD and photograph each starts from £20 per pop star.

Have a Pop Party: the ultimate in karaoke, plus you get your own CD to take home with you.

where to stay

Thanks to the needs of The Fringe Festival, Edinburgh has more than a few places to rest your weary bones: from uni halls and apartments to five-star boutique hotels.

hotels

Cowgate Tourist Hotel £
96–112 Cowgate,
Edinburgh EH1 1JN
Tel. no 0131 226 2153
www.cowgatehostel.com
info@cowgatehostel.com

shared room without breakfast

£ under £30
££ £30–£60
£££ over £60
pppn

This hostel is clean and brightly painted, giving it a friendly, informal feeling that's perfect for a relaxed and slightly hedonistic few days in Edinburgh. Apartments have twin, four- or six-bedded rooms with a communal kitchen and TV area. Around you is the lovely Old Town, and the castle is just 2 minutes walk away.

Malmaison £££
1 Tower Place, Leith, Edinburgh EH6 7BZ
Tel. no 0131 468 5000
www.malmaison-edinburgh.com
edinburgh@malmaison.com

The original Malmaison is an impressive boutique hotel on the banks of the Forth in Leith. Complete with a turreted clock tower, it makes you feel like royalty when you check in. The suites are pretty fabulous: every one of the 100 rooms is individually styled. The Mal Bar has a reputation for serving up some of the best wine, cocktails and coffee in the city. There's also a great brasserie and private dining rooms.

Hotel Ceilidh-Donia ££
14–16 Marchhall Crescent,
Edinburgh EH16 5HL
Tel. no 0131 667 2743
www.hotelceilidh-donia.co.uk
reservations@hotelceilidh-donia.co.uk

This three-star Victorian hotel a mile from the centre has 17 comfortable, homely rooms with ensuite facilities. The bar and restaurant are smart and welcoming, and there is a lovely landscaped garden for sunny weather. A cosy, welcoming place and a popular choice.

Mercure Edinburgh Point Hotel ££
34 Bread Street, Edinburgh EH3 9AF
Tel. no 0131 221 5555
www.mercure.com
H6989@accor.com

This big, stylish hotel almost spans the gap between the great-value giant chain and the boutique, and has a fabulous view of the castle. Rooms are large and nicely styled with lovely ensuite bathrooms. The bar and restaurant are also suitably swish – all round, you get the feeling that you've got a bit of a bargain. The location is good too – you're in walking distance of all the major sights and attractions.

Travelodge £
33 St Mary's Street, Edinburgh EH1 1TA
Tel. no 0131 221 5555
Tel. no 0871 984 6137
www.travelodge.co.uk

It may be a big chain, but Travelodge Central is near everything and great value for money. There are several sister lodges available in Edinburgh if this one's booked up. Rooms are clean, smart and spacious, with plenty of facilities. Parking is available at a reasonable rate.

self-catering

Albany Street Apartments £

35b & 37b Albany Street, Edinburgh
EH1 3QN
Tel. no 0131 558 9007/07780 923 711
www.albanystreetedinburgh.com
clare@topparkapartments.com

There are plenty of stunning self-catering
apartments in Edinburgh, and these are no
exception. Beautifully spacious and light, with
polished wood floors and crisp linen, the
apartments are in a fabulous, safe
location near Princes Street. They
make a great place to relax
after a big night out or a day's
shopping – and the city
centre shops, eateries and
bars are all within easy
reach.

**shared room
without
breakfast**

£ under £30
££ £30–£60
£££ over £60
pppn

Edinburgh Festival Apartments £–£££

127 Rose Street, South Lane,
Edinburgh EH2 4BB
Tel. no 0131 220 7950
www.festivalapartments.com
info@festivalapartments.com

Apartments of all shapes and sizes are
offered in central areas including Holyrood,
The Royal Mile, Old Town and New Town.
Hen and stag parties are welcome, and
groups can be catered for all year round. The
apartments tend to have wow factor, but if
you're on a budget enquire about a hostel.
The rooms are spacious, you still get your
own kitchen area and there's a staffed bar
and restaurant.

Edlets ££

14 Albany Street, Edinburgh EH1 3QB
Tel. no 0131 510 0020
www.edlets.com

If you're worried about having too much
choice when you've seen the long list of
accommodation on the Edlets website, don't
fret. You need only fill in the online enquiry
form or make a call and you'll soon have one
of the team seeking out your ideal
accommodation. The flats are of a high
standard and towels and linen are provided.
Most have home comforts such as DVD
player, Wi-Fi, flatscreen TV and dishwasher.

No. 19 the apartment ££

19 Queen Street EH2 1JX
Tel. no 07762 229379/01334 828 697
www.no19theapartment.co.uk
belinda@no19theapartmentedinburgh.co.uk

Enquire about the flat or No. 32 the town
house, both of which have the interior design
and location that will secure wow factor for
your hen party. Gorgeous, feminine and
funky, the venues have the perfect
atmosphere and creature comforts to
allow a group of ten or more to chill
out and enjoy each other's
company. And the city centre's
attractions are right outside your
front door.

Queen Margaret University ££

Edinburgh EH21 6UU
Tel. no 0131 474 0000
www.qmu.ac.uk
capitalcampus@qmu.ac.uk

In Uni holidays you can book into halls of
residence to enjoy the cushy ensuite rooms
with shared living rooms and kitchens. You'll
stay in the lush green surrounds of
Musselburgh, a short train trip or 30 minute
bus ride from central Edinburgh. If it's too
much to contemplate getting up and making
eggs and bacon after a night on the town,
you can arrange to have breakfast included.

Festival Apartments offers some stylish choices.

where to eat and drink

From the glamourous, glittering Tigerlily's to the down-to-earth Monster Mash, Edinburgh caters for all your needs. But we love Rick's for the Scottish menu.

bars

Belushi's

9–13 Market Street, Edinburgh EH1 1DE
www.belushis.com

If you're looking for a big night of drinks, dancing and laughs, Belushi's is a great city-centre choice. This chain has bars in most of the UK's major party towns and knows how to make you feel welcome, whether you want to eat huge burgers and have a few casual drinks or hire the private room for your party.

Cargo

129 Fountainbridge,
Edinburgh EH3 9QG
Tel. no 0131 659 7880
cargo@festival-inns.co.uk

A cavernous waterside bar with funky lighting, a vibrant ambience and matching multi-coloured cocktails.

Dragonfly

52 West Port, Edinburgh EH1 2LD
Tel. no 0131 228 4543
info@dragonflycocktailbar.com

You can get a cocktail masterclass or just drink colourful concoctions in this popular and very stylish venue. Food is snacky, not substantial. Larger groups of hens may want a private room – ask about the Parlour Bar, where you can party in private and have canapés and drinks brought to you. The music goes on until 1am on the weekend, with DJs playing funk, soul and dance.

 We loved the 'Flirtinis' at Tigerlily's, yummy.

The cosy atmosphere at The Living Room.

The Living Room

113–115 George Street,
Edinburgh EH2 4JN
Tel. no 0131 226 0880
www.thelivingroom.co.uk

A classy bar any time of day, The Living Room's chocolate leather sofas and classic decor just beg you to relax for a few hours over a well chilled glass of wine or two. On weekdays you're likely to catch a talented pianist tinkling on the ivories, whilst on weekends the atmosphere gets more lively with DJs playing funky house. The odd touring live act also make an appearance. The menu is a good quality British and European crowd pleaser. The perfect place to spend a few hours.

Tigerlily's

125 George Street, Edinburgh EH2 4JN
Tel. no 0131 225 5005
www.tigerlilyedinburgh.co.uk

You could spend a lot of time in this chic boutique hotel bar. Glittering disco balls, cute little booths, fabulous original and classic cocktails and a champagne bar all make you feel like the kittens bits, and there's a restaurant and Lulu's nightclub attached too.

restaurants

Fishers £££
1 Shore, Leith, Edinburgh EH6 6QW
Tel. no 0131 554 5666
www.fishersbistros.co.uk
ask@fishersbistros.co.uk

Seafood lovers should book in at this very busy and popular waterside restaurant or its sister, Fishers in the City on Thistle Street.

La Favorita ££
325–331 Leith Walk
Edinburgh EH6 8SA
Tel. no 0131 554 2430
www.la-favorita.com

Not only is this Edinburgh's best pizza, it's also good value. The restaurant does delivery too, so if you've bagged yourself a nice apartment, why go out?

L'Amore ££
97/101 Fountainbridge, Edinburgh
EH3 9QG
Tel. no 0131 228 5069
www.lamoreditalia.co.uk

For food and laughs before you head off to one of the big clubs nearby, this unpretentious, family-run Italian gives you food and karaoke.

Monster Mash Café £
4 Forrest Road, Edinburgh EH1 2QN
Tel. no 0131 225 7069

The city's top spot for retro British favourites such as bangers and mash.

Rick's Boutique Hotel £££
55a Frederick Street, Edinburgh EH2 1HL
www.ricksedinburgh.co.uk

This gem of a boutique hotel is just a step away from the main shopping areas and the perfect place to show off some of your designer purchases. The Scottish food is fresh and beautifully executed at this very stylish and chic restaurant.

Stac Polly ££
38 St Marys Street, Edinburgh EH1 1SX
Tel. no 0131 557 5754
www.stacpolly.com
bookings@stacpolly.com

For fabulous modern Scottish food, try one of three Stac Polly restaurants in Edinburgh. Fine seasonal food, reasonably priced is served in relaxed, unpretentious surroundings. Private dining rooms are available.

2 courses + half a bottle of wine

£ under £20
££ £20–£35
£££ over £35

Tex Mex II ££
64 Thistle Street, Edinburgh
Tel. no 0131 260 9699
www.texmex2.com
fatdonny@texmex2.com

The interior is as fresh and colourful as the Tex Mex food and the cocktails look pretty good too. A restaurant with very high quality food served in a laid back atmosphere.

The Cambridge Bar £
20 Young Street, Edinburgh EH2 4JB
Tel. no 0131 226 2120
www.thecambridgebar.co.uk
info@thecambridgebar.co.uk

With a huge burger menu, including veggie options, low carb options and quite a few full monty diet busters, this is a great place for an informal lunch. Located close to all the New Town and West End attractions.

The dazzling interior at Tex Mex II.

where to party

Whether you want live entertainment, clubbing or comedy, you'll find plenty to whet your appetite in Edinburgh. Have yourselves a good old highland fling!

Cabaret Voltaire

36 Blair Street, Edinburgh EH1 1QR
Tel. no 0131 220 6176
www.thecabaretvoltaire.com
speakeasy@thecabaretvoltaire.com

This venue under the streets of Cowgate has an amazing events diary, from indie night, Sicknote, every Thursday to dance at Killer Kitsch on Sundays – both of which are free. On Saturdays you'll find the likes of house and techno night Ultragroove or the eclectic Dare! and some big name DJs. Additionally, this twin-roomed club hosts up to 30 live gigs per month.

City

1a Market Street, Edinburgh EH1 1DE
Tel. no 0131 226 9560
www.cityedinburgh.co.uk
edinburgh@citypeople.info

Offering free entry to hens and stags and various promotion nights including text for queue jump and the fabulous Broke! With cheap entry and drinks on Fridays, City has a lot going for it. The venue is very stylish, with swanky booths and seating areas as well as great lighting and a top sound system.

Club Ego

14 Picardy Place, Edinburgh EH1 3JT
Tel. no 0131 478 7434
www.clubego.co.uk

Nights at Ego include the decadent Burlesque 'Vegas' night, acts such as Mr Scruff, Judge Jules and Gil Scott Heron, popular gay night 'Vibe' and more. The venue started out as a dance hall and the main dancefloor still has the look of a huge, sparkly, ornate ballroom. So put your dancing shoes on and get the sequins out for a night at Club Ego.

Mata Hari club (top) and Kasbar (above), Espionage.

Espionage

4 India Buildings, Victoria Street, Edinburgh EH1 2EX
Tel. no 0131 477 7007
www.espionage007.co.uk
edinburgh@espionage007.co.uk

Make your way through the labyrinth of rooms at Espionage to discover five floors' worth of dancefloors, chill-out areas and bars including the Kasbar cocktail bar, the Pravda club on the mid level and the Mata Hari club in the basement. The events diary is full at this massively popular Edinburgh venue, so check out their website for more details.

There's more to the Edinburgh club scene than the Highland Fling.

Po Na Na
43b Frederick Street,
Edinburgh EH2 1EP
Tel. no 0131 226 2224
www.ponana.com
edinburghpnn@ponana.com

The Moroccan-themed Po Na Na remains a good-looking but relaxed little venue for a dance to good music, a vibrant atmosphere and rather nice chill-out areas where you can have a chat.

The Stand
4 India Buildings, Victoria Street,
Edinburgh EH1 2EX
Tel. no 0131 477 7007
www.thestand.co.uk
admin@thestand.co.uk

Scotland's homegrown stand-up comedy venue has acts on every night of the week – from total beginners to big names. On Sunday there's also a free lunchtime show to help you laugh your hangover into history. Food and drink are reasonably priced.

The Voodoo Rooms
19a West Register Street,
Edinburgh EH2 2AA
Tel. no 0131 556 7060
www.thevoodoorooms.com
info@thevoodoorooms.com

Fridays see a great line up, with comedy stand up until 9pm, then dancing to live music until 1am. Other nights see casino, bands and more, taking centre stage at this beautiful venue where you can enjoy a full menu, well stocked bar and the odd cocktail. Group bookings are welcome and may get a discount.

Why Not
14 George Street, Edinburgh EH2 2PF
Tel. no 0131 6248633

This little venue offers good value on drinks and entry, a mixed clientele, chart, dance and house music and the perfect location, under the famous Dome Bar in George Street, making it a popular place with hens who want to let their hair down.

glasgow

Mitchell Library (top), Kelvingrove Art Gallery (middle), Doulton Fountain (bottom).

Away from the shortcake and tartan heritage, Glasgow is the real Scotland. Don't expect anything less than real partying, real humour and a really good time in Scotland's most vibrant and most up-and-coming city.

what to do

Fast-paced, hard as nails, dry-humoured and partying like it's Armageddon, Glasgow is a city with personality, history, culture, the arts...and the most fabulous shopping.

If Edinburgh is Scotland's jewel, Glasgow's the rest of the outfit. The city has such a vibrant atmosphere and so much going on that a weekend can feel way too short. But with a little planning, Glasgow's a great short break city.

Although it has a long, rollercoaster of a history, much of that isn't really tourist fodder. Indeed, the city has done a great job over the past 20 years to smooth over its cracks and become a cultural hub rather than a troubled industrial town. So when you hit Glasgow, you won't so much be viewing historic buildings (although the architecture is lovely) as soaking up the here and now – the shops and galleries in the day and the clubs, live music venues, comedy and pubs at night.

And don't expect the cheesy tourist welcome in Glasgow. If you're out partying, you'll be included, but the red carpet won't get rolled out. The locals are famously intolerant of bullshit. So if you want to party hard, just do it.

Glasgow may not be the most obvious choice, but it's one of the best.

There's always a great party atmosphere in Glasgow.

10 good reasons

1. shopping
2. exploring Lomond's isles
3. the club scene
4. fun, feisty locals
5. picnics in the parks
6. handsome city centre
7. buzzing at night
8. good value bars
9. moseying in the West End
10. shopping

sounds of the city

Money can't buy it The shopping is amazing, but if you've not got the heart to dangle your cash in front of Calvin Klein, Jo Malone and the gang before remembering about the rent and making a hasty exit, then swerve Buchanon Street and head for the West End via the 'clockwork orange' subway. Here you'll find retail loveliness that amounts to something like Camden market meets Carnaby Street. With lots of boho charm and cobbledy streets, you'll be happy browsing.

Gay bar Scrub that, we mean day spa (day spa, day spa) Spa in the City on Vincent Street does a Luxury Beauty Experience with an aromatherapy facial, makeover, manicure and Toni & Guy blow dry, all washed down with a couple of glasses of bubbly. Perhaps the perfect end to a few hours' retail therapy in Buchanon Street and Princes Square, darling.

Cool scene If you do want to go to a gay bar, you're in the right town. The club and bar scene in Glasgow is kicking, Bennet's and Cafe Delmonica hailed as the best fun gay venues.

Groups with partying hard at the top of their night's agenda should head for The Tunnel – two big rooms and about 1000 people dancing in them every Friday and Saturday night. This club's about having fun, but the quality's there too with top resident and guest DJs.

Sub Club on Jamaica Street is hailed as one of the best clubs in the world. As it's full of cool meedja type people, you need to blend in or you won't get in, so leave the whistles and tiaras at home for Sub Club. This is the place to go if you're a small band of regular clubbers who are looking for Glasgow's best club scene.

Showdown Poledancing parties are hilarious – especially if you feign injury and watch from the bench! Complete failure to look remotely sexy is part of the fun: you won't and that's OK. At Heavenly Pole at the Play bar in Renfield Street you'll be shown how it's done then taught a lap dance and a few pole tricks. That should make Monday mornings on the Routemaster much more fun. A male stripper can be booked, if you want to give the bride-to-be a few blushes.

Get yourself scrubbed up, chilled out and feeling gorgeous at Spa in the City in Vincent Street.

Underneath the arches A venue you shouldn't miss, The Arches is a massive multi-arts venue that's best known as a clubber's paradise, with regular nights from Mr Scruff, Hed kandy, Octopussy and more, and massive parties. The Arches showcases new and groundbreaking theatre and art and the venue is also becoming renowned for putting on some fantastic gigs. Check the listings at thearches.co.uk because this place could provide your hen party highlight. It's an awesome night out.

Where's your head at? This and many other questions such as 'why do I always do this to myself?' may well be popping into your befuddled minds on Sunday morning. But Glasgow isn't known as the Dear Green Place for nothing. It's got no less than 70 parks in which to rest and recover. If the sun's shining, there's nothing better than lounging in the gorgeous botanical gardens on Great Western Road with a bag of deli goodies. If it's peeing down, head for the Willow Tea Rooms on Sauchiehall Street designed by Charles Rennie Mackintosh for fabulous brekky and culture in one tasty hit.

Gold One way to explore a city is to contact huntfun.co.uk and get them to send you on a treasure hunt. The hen party package can be personalised and the hunt will take you a couple of hours, unless people get lost, get a raging need to stop for a glass of wine or get distracted by the joys of shopping…. Let's call it four hours then.

'been there…'

I have to admit that I couldn't understand the accent until the very last day, but the Glaswegians seemed like really nice people anyway! The city centre's totally beautiful and people are right about the shops. We didn't budget for that though, so most of us stuck to eating and drinking a lot! We went dancing at The Arches and did mini highland games for daytime laughs – real quality.

A Huntfun treasure hunt is a great way to see the city and have a great laugh at the same time.

where to stay

If you must sleep when you're in Glasgow, it's easy to find central, stylish digs to match any budget in this up-and-coming destination for tourists.

hotels

Alamo Guest House ££
46 Gray Street, Kelvingrove Park,
Glasgow G3 7SE
Tel. no 0141 339 2395
www.alamoguesthouse.com
reservations@alamoguesthouse.com

This great value, family-run guesthouse looks over Kelvingrove Park and is an easy walk from all the attractions of the West End, City Centre and riverside. Just 2 minutes away are some of Glasgow's best bars and restaurants. Rooms are very smart and elegant, with excellent facilities and attention to detail.

Argyll Guest House £
Sauchiehall Street,
Glasgow G3 7TH
Tel. no 0141 357 5155
www.argyllguesthouseglasgow.co.uk
info@argyllguesthouseglasgow.co.uk

Just a few minutes' walk from the IMAX cinema and the vibrant night scene of Byres Road is this homely budget guesthouse. Rooms are ensuite and have Wi-Fi and TVs. A Scottish buffet breakfast is available at a small additional cost.

Devoncove Hotel £–££
931 Sauchiehall Street,
Glasgow G3 7TQ
Tel. no 0141 334 4000
www.devoncovehotel.com
info@devoncovehotel.com

A nicely decorated, smart hotel offering reasonable room rates and a complementary fitness suite. All rooms are ensuite and have

freeview TV and Wi-Fi access. Last minute deals may be available online. Parking is free, subject to availability.

Saint Judes Boutique Hotel £££
190 Bath Street, Glasgow
Tel. no 0141 352 8800
www.saintjudes.com
info@saintjudes.com

✳ shared room without breakfast

£ under £30
££ £30–£60
£££ over £60
pppn

Saint Judes is rather proud of its mixology skills, and offers cocktail masterclasses. In your individually designed room is a private martini bar with cocktail kit and recipe book, an iPod docking station, Hi-Fi, 24-hour room service and oodles of space and luxury. Why bother leaving the room? Well, if you do feel the need, Mama San Bar is one of the city's smoothest clubs, it's open until 3am and it's just downstairs.

The Sherbrooke Castle Hotel ££–£££
1 Sherbrooke Avenue, Pollokshields,
Glasgow G41 4PG
Tel. no 0141 427 4227
www.sherbrooke.co.uk
enquiries@sherbrooke.co.uk

This beautiful red sandstone 'castle' sits in its own landscaped grounds in a leafy suburb of Glasgow's southside. The city centre's attractions are just 10 minutes away, as is the Hampden Park stadium. You may be able to get a good deal on a few smart twin rooms, which hopefully will give you free reign to discover the delights of the Morrison's restaurant before you cosy up by an open fire in the lounge and have a few drinks.

self-catering

38 Bath Street £££

38 Bath Street, Glasgow G2 1HG
Tel. no 0845 222 38 38
www.38bathst.co.uk

At £80 each per night you can grab some two-bedroom apartments in this beautiful building and enjoy a seriously luxurious stay in Glasgow. Although the decor and opulence seem hotel-like (as do the maid service, reception and concierge), each flat has its own separate living room and well-equipped kitchen so the experience is actually very relaxed and homely – perfect if you're planning a night in.

* shared room without breakfast

£ under £30
££ £30–£60
£££ over £60
pppn

Bankell Farm Camping and Caravan Site £

Strathblane Road, Milngavie, Glasgow
G62 8LE
Tel. no 0141 956 1733
www.bankellfarm.co.uk
info@bankellfarm.co.uk

This family-run campsite is in the perfect spot to explore Glasgow, Loch Lomond and the West Highland Way, so if you're a walker and the sun's shining it could be a great choice.

Ben Lomond Lodge £

Rowardennan, Loch Lomond
Tel. no 07721 638091
www.benlomondlodge.co.uk

This lovely, modern lodge sleeps six and is perched on the bonnie banks of Loch Lomond – one of the UK's most beautiful spots. It's only 45 minutes' drive from Glasgow, but you'll feel like you're in the middle of nowhere when you're enjoying a few sunset drinks together on the deck. Boat hire, walking and golf are on tap and if you need to take the kids with you, what could be better than the wide open spaces?

City Apartments £

401 North Woodside Road, Glasgow
G20 6NN
Tel. no 0141 342 4060
www.mcquadehotels.com
city@mcquadehotels.com

The Scottish Tourist Board has awarded these apartments four stars, and when you arrive at your west end address and see the facilities on offer (including that hen party essential, the trouser press) you'll be surprised that this is actually a very budget-friendly option. The apartments are maintained as part of the Albion Hotel next door, so it's all clean and up together.

Drumboy Holiday Cottage £

Drumclog Strathaven, South
Lanarkshire ML10 6QJ
Tel. no 01357 440544/07766 347 896
www.drumboy-lodge.com
gillian@drumboy-lodge.com

Surround yourself and eight of your friends with beautiful countryside on a peaceful working farm in the Clyde Valley. The ideal spot for walking, horse riding or golf, the lodge is also within a 15-minute drive of retail centres, theme parks and boat trips to the Isles of Arran and Millport. Glasgow is about 27 miles away.

Unique Cottages £–£££

Monksford Road, Newtown St Boswells
TD6 0SB
Tel. no 01835 822277
www.unique-cottages.co.uk

Unique country holiday cottages in stunning locations all over Scotland can be found and booked through this company. Each property has been carefully selected to offer the best cottage holidays available in bonny Scotland.

where to eat and drink

There are so many good bars in Glasgow
that it's tempting to say, just hit the streets
and see where you end up. But here are
a few to get you started.

bars

Bar Soba

11 Mitchell Lane, Glasgow G1 3NU
Tel. no 0141 204 2404
www.barsoba.co.uk

If you like to try something a little different,
you might enjoy Soba's Thailand-inspired
cocktails, flavoured with chilli, lemongrass
and other fragrant treats. Live music and DJs
ensure the vibe is cool and upbeat, while the
two-floor venue is perfectly designed to let
groups party in style.

Cocktail time at The Sports Cafe Glasgow.

Madness Theatre of Fun

30 Bothwell Street, Glasgow G2 7EN
Tel. no 0141 204 5999
www.madnesstof.com
madnesstof@aol.com

If you want to get thrown into party mode this
is the place to go drinking. Live shows of all
descriptions, with tributes to Moulin Rouge,
Roy Chubby Brown, Michael Bublé and many
more acts, as well as Boogie Nights,
Glasgow's Got Talent and other regular
events mean that the place is far from
being dull.

The Bunker Bar

193–199 Bath Street, Glasgow G2 4HU
Tel. no 0141 229 1427
www.thebunkerbar.com
info@thebunkerbar.com

Dodge under the radar and head for the
Bunker Bar if you're looking for a pre-club bar
with atmosphere, cheap drinks, food promos
(largely it's pizza and pasta), regular DJs and
passes to the club next door. It makes life
sooo easy – and if you can't be bothered to
move after a few Woo Woos, Manhattans or
cther cocktaily delights, book your own cosy
booth and stay put until 2am.

The Loft

Ashton Lane, Hillhead,
Glasgow G12 8SJ
Tel. no 0845 166 6028
grosvenor@g1group.com

The Loft is a big and beautiful West End
venue with old films flickering on the walls
(it's in the roof of the Grosvenor Cinema),
trendy yet comfortable seating area and a
great atmosphere. Regular events, karaoke
booths, private dining rooms, drinks promos
and good value for money Italian food
complete the scene.

The Sports Cafe Glasgow

292–332 Sauchiehall Street,
Glasgow G2 3JA
Tel. no 0141 332 8000
www.thesportscafe.com/glasgow
glasgowfunctions@thesportscafe.com

The newly refurbished Glasgow Sports Cafe
is famous for its unforgettable hen and stag
parties. Hens can enjoy a huge range of
entertainment. Choose from Wii, race nights,
a DJ, a quiz, murder mystery, cocktail
lessons, salsa, burlesque or pole dance
classes and more. There's always a great
party atmosphere.

restaurants & cafés

It's fun all the way at Curryoke Club.

2 courses + half a bottle of wine

£ under £20
££ £20–£35
£££ over £35

Arta ££

The Old Cheesemarket, 62 Albion Street, Merchant City, Glasgow G1 1PA
Tel. no 0141 552 2101
www.arta.co.uk
arta@g1group.com

Lovely private dining rooms, live music and a nightclub are just a few things that make this Mediterranean restaurant a great choice for an evening out. Hen and stag parties are welcome, and you can book cocktail-making lessons, as well as a meal and club entry to make a real night of it. If you fancy something a bit different, the venue also hosts murder mystery nights, horror walks and seances!

Bibi's Cantina £–££

599 Dumbarton Road, Partick, Glasgow G11 6HY
Tel. no 0141 579 0179
www.bibiscantina.com

Mexican and American (Tex-Mex) food is served at this up and coming West End eatery. The place isn't huge, but the menu is definitely a crowd pleaser.

Curryoke Club ££

100 Stobcross Road, Glasgow G3 8QQ
Tel. no 0141 248 1485
www.curryoke.com
info@currykaraokeclub.com

Set up for fun-loving groups, this restaurant does its best to give you a night to remember, with good, plentiful Indian food, karaoke, dancing and the odd comedy night. Your table will be festooned with hen confetti, balloons and party hats, and it's almost guaranteed that you'll be sharing air time with other hen and stag parties.

Dragon-i ££–£££

311–313 Hope Street, Glasgow G2 3PT
Tel. no 0141 332 7728
www.dragon-i.co.uk
info@dragon-i.co.uk

This establishment has become famous throughout Scotland and is thought to be one of the UK's finest Chinese eateries. Dark

black-and-red decor, with stunning floral displays, make the venue ideal for a special occasion, too.

Rogano £££

11 Exchange Place, Glasgow G1 3AN
Tel. no 0141 248 4055
www.roganoglasgow.com
rogano@btconnect.com

This Glasgow institution was fitted out in 1936, when Cunard's Queen Mary was being built on the Clyde. It retains the 1930s decor and classic ambience, and is a gorgeous place to eat and drink, whether you choose upmarket bar snacks in the Oyster Bar, brasserie dishes in the Café or treat yourselves to a night of fine dining in the Restaurant, which majors on exquisite seafood and great French wines.

Tusk ££

18 Moss Side Road, Shawlands, Glasgow G41 3TN
Tel. no 0845 166 6017

Once you see this South Side venue, with its selection of opulent and inviting spaces, you won't want to leave – so it's just as well they lay on a whole party's worth of entertainment for you. Book a hen package of a beautiful three-course meal, cocktail lessons in a private bar and a bit of karaoke in your own booth, then let your hair down and dance 'til late in the club area.

where to party

You can party the night away at Curryoke Club.

Barrowlands Ballroom

244 Gallowgate, Glasgow G4 0TS
Tel. no 0141 552 4601
www.glasgow-barrowland.com

This has been voted the best venue in the UK for rock and indie gigs. From the Chemical Brothers to The Stiff Little Fingers, the Barrowlands has seen many legendary nights.

Boho

59 Dumbarton Road,
Glasgow G11 6PD
Tel. no 0141 357 6644
www.thebohoclub.co.uk

The Belvedere Booth is a great option for up to 20 guests. You get your own hostess and some complimentary vodka drinks, plus a space to call your own all night. Overlooking

the main venue from your opulent perch, you can pick your moment to go down and mingle with the rest of the crowd. The main venue itself is smart and feels more like a late night bar with a dancefloor than a classic nightclub.

King Tut's Wah Wah Hut

272 St. Vincent Street, Glasgow G2 5RL
Tel. no 0141 221 5279
www.kingtuts.co.uk

A regular stop on any up-and-coming band's first major tour, this hugely popular little venue has live music every night. In the daytime you can have a chilled out game of pool and play your favourite sounds on the juke box, get something to eat and sup down the venue's home brewed lager or a skinny latte if that's more your thing.

CURRYOKE CLUB
Party Animals Welcome

Attention Hens & Stags!
We've got all the Ingredients for The Perfect Party Night!

THE Curryoke Club sits on the banks of the River Clyde beside the Tall Ship and Scottish Exhibition Centre and is easliy accessible by road and rail. Our unique recipe of great food and fun, fun, fun has proved very popular and we have gained a reputation as the ultimate party venue for Hen and Stag Celebrations. Call our party planner for further details. Our food has been accredited by the exclusive Tourist Board **EatScotland**.

The Curryoke Club 100 Stobcross Road, Glasgow G3 8QQ

Scottish
TOURIST BOARD
EatScotland

RESERVATIONS 0141 248 1485 www.curryoke.com **Glasgow**
Scotland with style

O2 ABC Glasgow

300 Sauchiehall Street,
Glasgow G2 3JA
Tel. no 0141 332 2232
www.o2abcglasgow.co.uk
mail@o2abcglasgow.co.uk

Doing what O2 does well – big venue, big party nights and big gigs.

Sub Club

22 Jamaica Street, Glasgow G1 4QD
Tel. no 0141 248 4600
www.subclub.co.uk
info@subclub.co.uk

After 20 years plus of partying in Glasgow, the Sub Club still resides deep below number 22 Jamaica Street. Weekend in, weekend out, you can find the best of the city's music makers playing to the best people the city can muster on the best sound system for miles around.

The Arches

253 Argyle Street, Glasgow G2 8DL
Tel. no 0141 565 1000
www.thearches.co.uk

Another Glaswegian legend, just reopened after a refurb, this massive club under Glasgow Central Station continues to offer top name DJs and live acts to its loyal fans.

The Tunnel

84 Mitchell Street, Glasgow G4 3NA
Tel. no 0141 204 1000
www.tunnelglasgow.co.uk
tunnel@cplweb.com

Kicking the weekend off with a pop, R'n'B, hip hop and dance mash up and cocktail promos every Thursday, and keeping the hedonistic party animals happy until the early hours of Sunday, The Tunnel is an original 'superclub' and has been a major Glasgow venue that regularly hosts big names since it opened its doors in 1990.

Victoria's

98 Sauchiehall Street, Glasgow G2 3DE
Tel. no 0141 332 1444
www.victorias.tv
info@victorias.tv

If you're looking for risqué fun and frolics, check out Vicky's Secret, a night held on the first Saturday of each month, where male strippers The Hot Boyz take to the stage, along with 'filthy' comedy from Carrie Jones. The package for hens includes a two-course meal, disco and naughty party games. This fun and high-octane club also hosts The Sunday Club, Love Fridays and Saturday party night Infinity. Book a booth in advance for groups of six or more to get a real VIP experience at this classy club.

Fantastic light shows and cool scenes are easy to find in this lively city.

GoBananas

London
Edinburgh
Brighton
Newcastle
Cardiff
Loads More..

We've heard people get married just to try out one of our Weekends!

www.GoBananas.co.uk
0871 789 6200

leeds

This big, beautiful jewel of the North has a well-deserved reputation for being a fabulous night out. With world-class clubs, sophisticated bars and a funky, cosmopolitan vibe, could Leeds be your ideal hen destination?

Mill Square (top), City Square (middle), The Calls (bottom).

what to do

If you're wondering which city guarantees a great night out, look no further than Leeds. With some of the nation's best clubs and bars, the nightlife is electric.

On the one hand, it's good to know that Leeds was voted Britain's sexiest city last year. On the other, it's discouraging that Jeremy Paxman was named as one of its sexiest men. There's nowt so queer as folk, eh? Still, you'll notice that Leeds is packed with gorgeous 20–30 somethings. What more of an excuse do you need for getting seriously glammed up for your big night out? The shopping in Leeds is great, and you'll find all the big names as well as plenty of boutiques, and the city and its surrounds contains masses of spa, pamper and beauty places.

Once the slap, the heels and the LBD are on, it's off to the centre with your hens for a full-on night on the town. You can either keep yourselves to yourselves or get chatting to other groups and make the most of the friendly vibe in the city.

When the hangover's passed and you're all shopped out, there's still more to Leeds. All the major hen party organisers have activities based here, so you'll be able to book anything that takes your fancy. Also, if you and the girls like walking, riding or cycling, you can't beat the beautiful Yorkshire Dales.

The Corn Exchange shopping centre.

10 good reasons

1. clubbing in fancy dress
2. great cocktail bars
3. top shopping
4. party culture
5. riding in the Dales
6. sphering
7. luxurious spas
8. stylish boutique hotels
9. country cottages
10. friendly and fun

sounds of the city

School spirit Just the sight of the drinks menu at Smokestack on Lower Briggate makes us smile. These guys know their spirits and have a fine selection of brandies, vodkas, gins, bourbons and more, which they lovingly blend into some of the best cocktails on the planet. The bar's cool, dark and slick, with The Roost room upstairs playing funk and soul. Tucked away behind the Roost's bar you can take a Bartending Masterclass and learn how to mix up a storm in a martini glass. A buffet lunch is included, and you can choose how long your lessons last before you hand it all back to the experts and return to the front of the bar where you belong.

PYT Waterfall Spa at Brewery Wharf gives you the feeling of being in some countryside escape when you're actually slap bang in the middle of the city. This ladies-only pamper palace offers various packages, including an evening pass to the Thermal Spa Experience, with hydrotherapy spa pool, Norwegian tropicarium, aromatherapy steam room and other delights, including a relaxation boudoir

and an i-pod filled with mellow tunes to use. If you were feeling pre-wedding stress, wave it goodbye here.

New way home Meanwhile, if you're a Leeds local, or you're staying in a Yorkshire cottage – or even if you've slightly dented the budget on your hotel choice – why not bring the pampering to you? The Pamper Party will organise local beauty and massage therapists to visit you and the ladies and give you blissful treatments in the comfort of your very own boudoir. With a few bottles of fizz and some good music, you'll be in seventh heaven.

The lady is a tramp This is not one for ladylike hens we're afraid. But if you're lasses who love a challenge, read on. The Otley Run is an epic pub crawl down the Otley Road, usually done in fancy dress. First, eat a lot. Next, don your themed outfits and get yourselves to Headingley, where the crawl begins with three country-style locals, Woodies, the Three Horseshoes and the New Inn. Don't have more than a half in each. When we say this is an epic we mean it! A little further on is the

Ultimate relaxation at the Waterfall Spa.

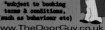

Taps, then it's two modern bars, Arc and Box. Still standing? OK, just keep following the other pissed muppets until you get to Strawberry Fields. Singing...

Make me smile Book a hilarious night at The Highlight on Albion Street – even the most up-tight of your chickens won't fail to find at least some of the jokes funny with fab comedians and a top compere. You'll get food and plenty of cocktails to drink, too.

Drinkin' again If you like beer, you mustn't miss the city's great North Bar. Plonk yourselves down on the long tables to sample a few lagers (they do serve other drinks) and enjoy the great music and fantastic atmosphere in this happy and well-loved drinking den. In March and October the party vibe really gets going with the annual beer fests.

Ride a white horse There is nothing better than horse riding to get you out exploring the Yorkshire Dales. If you're a mixed ability group or total beginners, opt for a residential weekend break at True Well Hall (01535 603292). You'll stay in a 16th century farmhouse or in self-catering cottages, and be given a steed to suit your ability. For the

evenings of nursing your aching thighs, there's an old village pub five minutes away. A truly relaxing girly retreat.

Deep kick Universal Dance Creations has a range of dance classes, but choose the can-can party workshop for brilliant hen party laughs, frilly hems and feather headdresses. Your teachers have danced at the Moulin Rouge, no less, and will go through the basic line kicks to more advanced moves with you. Ooh la la! Call 07961 579482.

'been there...'

I booked sphering with Into the Blue. OMG! Hilarious. I would never do it again, but I'm glad we did because nobody will ever forget my hen do! We had a fantastic couple of nights in Leeds, just in late night bars, chatting to stag groups and other hens. It's a brilliant place, Leeds, one of the best nights out anywhere. They just know how to party.

Learn to Can Can with Universal Dance Creations (www.universaldancecreations.com).

where to stay

Self-catering options, both in city apartments and Yorkshire cottages, are good value. But for those who like to be pampered, Leeds is choc full of great hotels.

hotels

Etap Hotel ££
2 The Gateway North,
Crown Point Road,
Leeds LS9 8BZ
Tel. no 0113 245 0725
www.etaphotel.com
H6002@accor.com

This modern hotel chain offers comfortable rooms, which can accommodate up to three people, with a shower, toilet and flatscreen TV. And the next day you help yourself at the great value for money breakfast buffet!

Holiday Inn Express ££
Amouries Drive, Leeds LS10 1LE
Tel. no 0870 890 0455
www.hiexpressleeds.co.uk
reservations.leeds@
holidayinnexpress.org.uk

This three-star hotel is located at Clarence Dock adjacent to the Armouries Museum. It has 130 stylish ensuite bedrooms offering comfort and a good value budget accommodation option. The hotel is 15 minutes walk from the vibrant city centre and the main train station.

Jurys Inn £
Brewery Place, Brewery Wharf,
Leeds LS10 1NE
Tel. no 0113 283 8800
leedshotels.jurysinns.com
jurysinnleeds@jurysinns.com

Just 5 minutes' walk from Leeds city centre and the train station, Jurys Inn enjoys a fantastic central location on the banks of the River Aire. The spacious and comfortable rooms are all ensuite and can accommodate three adults quite comfortably.

shared room without breakfast

£ under £30
££ £30–£60
£££ over £60
pppn

Novotel Leeds Centre ££
4 Whitehall Quay, Leeds
LS1 4HR
Tel. no 0113 242 6446
www.novotel.com
H3270@accor.com

Situated in the centre of Leeds, the hotel is close to shops and the main nightlife areas of Leeds. With Elements restaurant, bar, fitness suite, sauna, steam room and W-Fi, this hotel has all the facilities for a comfortable stay. The main railway station is just a few minutes walk away.

Radisson SAS Hotel ££
No 1 The Light, Leeds LS1 8TL
Tel. no 0113 236 6000
www.radissonblu.co.uk
info.leeds@radissonblu.com

Part of the retail and entertainment complex, The Light, this hotel is right in the heart of Leeds. Easily accessible from major motorway links, the hotel is just 5 minutes walk from the train station. Guests have access to the private Esporta Health and Fitness Club for a nominal fee.

Modern rooms at Holiday Inn Express.

self-catering

Currer Laithe Farm £
Moss Carr Road, Long Lee,
Keighly BD21 4SL
Tel. no 01535 604 387
www.currerlaithe.co.uk

This 16th century farmhouse is set in 200 acres of farmland overlooking the great sweep of the Aire Gap, Ilkley Moor and Ingleborough in the distance. It commands unparalleled views of walled pasture and moorland. An ideal base for any outdoor activities on the moors, this six-bedroomed unit sleeps 12–15 people in a fantastic stone building with beams and open log fires. There are also two additional cottages to rent if your group exceeds 15.

Harman Suites 1 & 2 £
48 St Martins Avenue, Leeds LS7 3LG
Tel. no 0871 702 0134

These detached ground floor chalet-style apartments offer good value for money close to the city centre. These self-catering units are well-furnished and fully equipped.

Nostell Priory Holiday Park £
Doncaster Road, Nostell,
Wakefield WF4 1QE
Tel. no 01924 863938
www.nostellprioryholidaypark.co.uk
park@nostellprioryholidaypark.co.uk

Self-catering holiday homes at Nostell Priory Caravan Park nestle in a forest glade within the expansive grounds of the National Trust's Nostell Priory Estate. The holiday homes are comprehensively equipped with cooker, fridge, TV and all home comforts. Electricity and gas is included in the tariff. The park is excellently situated as a base for good walking and exploring Yorkshire. The major towns of Leeds, Wakefield, Sheffield, Barnsley and Doncaster are all within easy driving distance.

✳ shared room without breakfast
£ under £30
££ £30–£60
£££ over £60
pppn

The Chambers ££
The Chambers, Riverside West,
Whitehall Road, Leeds LS1 4AW
Tel. no 0113 386 3300
www.morethanjustabed.com
stay@morethanjustabed.com

These sleek, stylish and sophisticated boutique serviced apartments are a haven of calm and five-star luxury. There is also a large room that can be hired out for a private dinner. Apartments are also available at Riverside West on the banks of the river Aire and at Park Place.

Westwood Lodge ££
Westwood Drive,
Ilkley LS29 9JF
Tel. no 01943 433430
www.westwoodlodge.co.uk
welcome@westwoodlodge.co.uk

Choose from four 'listed' cottages situated around the courtyard at Westwood Lodge. Orchard, Applebarn and Coach House Cottages each sleep up to six people. The Old Gallery is larger (sleeps up to 11) and is ideal for a group of friends.

Stunning scenery in the Yorkshire Dales.

LEEDS

Stag & Hen Do's
at the Leeds Marriott Hotel

Top 10 reasons why Leeds is the ideal location for you!

Just minutes away from the hotel you can walk to:

- Leeds train station just a 3 minute walk
- Leeds coach station just a 5 minute walk
- World class restaurants of all tastes inc.
Bar & Grill, Loch Fyne, Aagrah, Chaophraya
- Vibrant Bars & Nightclubs inc. The Living Room, Prohibition, Boutique, Oceana
- Fantastic shops with all high street names inc. Harvey Nicholls & Victoria Quarter
- Local Entertainment inc. casinos, go-karting, dance lessons, live music
- Luxurious spa treatments less than a minute walk at Russell Eaton Lifestyle Salon & Spa (Aveda)
- Just minutes away from major motorways M1, M62, M621
- On site leisure club with pool, Jacuzzi, steam room, sauna & gym
- Revive package bedding to re-charge in before taking on another dynamic day & all twin rooms feature two ultra comfortable double beds! With free upgrade for Hen or Stag subject to availability

Friday night stay from just £35 per person
Weekend 2 night stay from just £32.50 per person
(rates are based on 2 people sharing a room)

To make a booking or for more information call **0113 2366 366**
or visit **leedsmarriott.co.uk**
Limited availability, terms & conditions apply

where to eat and drink

Being a party kind of town, Leeds is heaving with pubs and bars, and there is no shortage of great restaurants for all tastes and breakfast cafes in which to recover.

bars

North Bar

24 New Briggate, Leeds LS1 6NU
Tel. no 0113 242 4540
www.northbar.com
info@northbar.com

With the finest selection of beers in the North of England and regular haunt of superstars, such as Sue Pollard, Sylvester McCoy and some of former band Hearsay, North is Leeds' coolest bar for lovers of great beer, music and art.

Revolution

41 Cookridge Street, Leeds LS2 3AW
Tel. no 0800 6300 860
www.revolution-bars.co.uk

The Millenium Square venue is cavern-like. This funky branch of the national Vodka bar chain has a cool patio overlooking the Square and an indoor courtyard for an inside-out experience. Revolution is also at Call Lane in the Exchange Quarter of the city. Recently refurbished, it forms part of the city's most fashionable drinking circuit.

A night out in Leeds has to start with cocktails.

Smokestack

159a Lower Briggate, Leeds LS1 6LY
Tel. no 0113 245 2222
www.myspace.com/smokestackleeds
info@smokestackleeds.co.uk

This dedicated music bar is the only place in Leeds playing funk and soul on a Saturday night. They also feature ska and northern soul on Fridays. You can do a bar-tending masterclass here and learn to make heavenly cocktails from Mojitos to Manhattans.

Strawberry Fields

104 Otley Road, Leeds LS16 5JG
Tel. no 0113 278 4393
www.strawbs.com
strawbsbar@yahoo.co.uk

The 13th bar on The Otley Run is a small, continental-style bar between the two Universities. Naturally it attracts a lot of students, but there's plenty fun to be had at this friendly bar. You can hire out the upstairs bar for a private do as well. And by the way The Otley Run is a mad pub crawl taking in about 20 pubs and bars.

The Arc

19 Ash Road, Leeds LS6 3JJ
Tel. no 0113 275 2223
www.arcinspirations.com
bookings@arcinspirations.com

This contemporary glass-fronted Headingley bar is a stylish place for drinking and eating. You can now book a private karaoke suite at The Arc for night of caterwauling!

restaurants

2 courses + half a bottle of wine

£ under £20
££ £20–£35
£££ over £35

The vast and fabulous Bibi's Italianissimo.

Bibi's Italianissimo ££–£££

Criterion Place (off Sovereign Street), Leeds LS1 4AG
Tel. no 0113 243 0905
www.bibisrestaurant.com
reservations@bibisrestaurant.com

This glamorous Art Deco styled restaurant and bar welcomes parties and offers an amazing dining experience. Executive chef Piero Vinci serves an extensive a la carte menu full of Mediterranean dishes plus traditional pizza and pastas using only the freshest, highest quality ingredients, sourced locally where possible.

Fig Mediterranean Grill ££

Alea Casino, 4 The Boulevard, Clarence Dock, Leeds LS10 1OPZ
Tel. no 0871963 8118
www.aleacasinos.com/alea/leeds
eventleeds@aleacasinos.com
Located next to the Royal Armouries inside the Alea Casino, the Fig Mediterranean Grill delivers a clean and simple grill menu that draws inspiration from the Med, cosmopolitan Leeds and the surrounding Yorkshire countryside.

Raja's Restaurant £–££

186 Roundhay Rd, Leeds LS8 5PL
Tel. no 0113 248 0411
www.rajasleeds.co.uk
bikrampalsingh@gmail.com

Rajas has gained a reputation as one of the finest Indian restaurants in Yorkshire, as well as the UK. The *Which? Good Food Guide* has recommended Rajas over the past few years and more recently, Raja's was voted one of the top ten Indian Restaurants in the UK by *The Times*. Raja's is located between the city centre and the outer residential areas of Leeds – Roundhay Road is the main road leading to the city from these areas. It will be worth the trip we can assure you.

Tiger Tiger ££–£££

The Light, 117 Albion St, Leeds LS2 8DY
Tel. no 0113 236 6999
www.tigertiger-leeds.co.uk
info@tigertiger-leeds.co.uk

The restaurant's cosmopolitan nature creates an upbeat and lively experience; a modern, relaxed and naturally stylish environment. The restaurant at Tiger Tiger, Leeds, is a new dining experience offering a taste of the east plus all the traditional favourites. Try delicious fusion dishes such as Tiger Tiger Katsu chicken curry and Stir fried Udon noodles or traditional favourites like Tiger Beer battered fish and chunky chips or char-grilled prime sirloin steak.

Viva Cuba ££

342 Kirkstall Road, Leeds LS4 2DS
Tel. no 0113 275 0888
www.vivacubaleeds.co.uk
info@vivacubaleeds.co.uk

Popular with locals and visitors alike, this latino restaurant serving delicious homemade tapas, authentic Cuban cocktails and Spanish and South American wines and beers gives great service in a warm vibrant atmosphere.

where to party

Every night is party night in this vibrant city.

Saturday night Voodoo@Halo has it all: regular celebrity PAs, huge themed events and massive giveaways. DJ Si Edwards and DJ Tango provide the music with a mix of funky house, electro, R'n'B, classics and more...this is clubbing in style.

Evolution

Cardigan Fields Leisure Complex, 9 Cardigan Fields Road, Leeds LS4 2DG
Tel. no 0113 263 2632

A little off the beaten track, Evolution has two rooms each offering a variety of music. It's also home to Sundissential North, which is a huge trance house event running most of the day and night.

Halo

Woodhouse Lane, Leeds LS2 9JT
Tel. no 0113 245 9263
halo@pbr.uk.com

This former church in the centre of Leeds is just up the road from all the main bars. Inside, the club is smart and modern, after a £5 million facelift, and the old church features give it loads of character. The original stained-glass windows, beams, wall features and high ceilings are still in place, which really set it apart from all the other clubs. The DJ plays from way up in the gods where the organ once was. The award-winning

Highlight Comedy Club

Bar Risa, The Cube, Albion Street, Leeds LS2 8ER
Tel. no 0113 247 1759
www.thehighlight.co.uk

Sit back and enjoy nearly two hours of top comedy with four acts, then boogie until the early hours after the show. Food and of course drinks are available and groups of 12 or more get a free celebration pack.

Halo resides in a converted church.

Club culture is king in Leeds (above and below right).

New York Disco, a Venetian Grand Ballroom complete with luxurious decor and a stunning chandelier, the seductive Parisian Boudoir, a chilled Aspen Ski Lodge with outside terrace, the First Port Bar, a Wakyama Tokyo Bar and Sydney Harbourside. There are also four exclusive VIP rooms perfect for your party each equipped with state-of-the-art plasma screen, waitress service, tailormade buffets and key card entry system. Oceana just loves themed nights and fancy dress, so you're definitely going to fit in here! However they have a policy ruling out sports wear, hoodies and full body paints...

Mint

8 Harrison Street, Leeds LS1 6PA
Tel. no 0113 244 3168
www.themintclub.com
info@themintclub.com

This stylish club offers a unique atmosphere and often plays host to the best DJs in the city. You'll love the unique decor complete with polo-mint inspired seating! The infamous unisex toilets provide an interesting, if at times inconvenient talking point and if you get too hot you can always chill in the open-air back room! With new state-of-the-art sound and light systems, Mint Club offers great nights to match its respected reputation.

Oceana

Merrion Centre, 6–18 Woodhouse Lane, Woodhouse, Leeds LS2 8LX
Tel. no 0113 243 8229
www.oceanaclubs.com/leeds
oceana-leeds@luminar.co.uk

Escape to Oceana and discover seven ways to one night out. Arrive early and leave late, explore the themed space and experience five bars and two distinct nightclubs, all under one roof. Inspired by worldwide destinations these include: a Studio 54 style

The Mezz Club

2 Waterloo House, Assembly Street, Leeds LS2 7DE
Tel. no 0113 243 9909

New kid on the block, The Mezz has brought a fresh perspective to clubbing in Leeds. It's a trendy club without being pretentious and it's the people who go there who really bring it to life. There are some interesting events taking place here, including Sinful Sessions – could be an opportunity to say goodbye to singledom in style and rather skimpy underwear...

The Space

The Basement Hirsts Yards, Duncan Street, Leeds LS1 6DQ
Tel. no 0113 246 1030

This cool and trendy basement club has regular DJ sets getting the dancefloor moving with the latest funky house and urban beats. A great selection of drinks and a vibrant and carefree atmosphere make The Space a popular choice for clubbers in Leeds. Awesome guest DJs include Paul Glasby, Andy Farley and loads more.

THE CHEAPEST WAY TO THE BEST STAG AND HEN PARTIES IN EUROPE

BUDAPEST   KAUNAS
PRAGUE   RIGA
GDANSK   KRAKOW
POZNAN   WROCLAW

Aberdeen
GLASGOW   EDINBURGH
Derry
BELFAST   Newcastle
Teeside
Manchester   LEEDS
LIVERPOOL   Doncaster
EAST MIDLANDS
BRISTOL   BIRMINGHAM
Newquay   LUTON   STANSTED
Gatwick
BOURNEMOUTH

FLIGHTS FROM SELECTED UK AIRPORT

RYANAIR

manchester

Manchester welcomes in its visitors with a certain smugness. Fabulous clubs, world-class eateries and more good bars than you can poke a twizzle stick at, on top of the footy, the shopping...it's the city that knows it's got it all.

Salford Quays (top), Trafford Centre (middle), cityscape (bottom).

what to do

It's a big, big city and Manchester is one of the UK's top places to party. Whether you're looking for sleekly groomed sophistication or grungy all-out fun, the answer is here.

First for football, second for media and commerce, third fave UK destination for foreign visitors, and taking every medal going for its music scene, you can't argue with the fact that Manchester's one of Britain's greatest centres. It's also absolutely huge, and has a massive young adult population – what with a big media industry, thousands of university students and graduates who won't leave. And that means the city is constantly trying to meet an insatiable demand for more bars, better clubs and world class eateries. All good news for hens coming to Manchester.

The Arndale is the largest city-centre mall in the UK with 240 of all the big-name retailers and fast food places you can think of. If you want clothes by small-name designers, go and have a rummage at Affleck's Palace, with 50 market-style stores. But it's the huge and elegant Trafford Centre, just out of town, that holds the crown for a classy afternoon's lunch and shopping.

And last but not least, Manchester girls are known for being well turned out – hair and beauty are big, so if you fancy a little pampering, look no further than here.

Combine thrills with chills at Alton Towers.

10 good reasons

1. massive club scene
2. good bars
3. shopping
4. spa and beauty places
5. Alton Towers
6. tubing at Chill Factor
7. West-end quality shows
8. range of accommodation
9. student nights and promos
10. nice weather for ducks

sounds of the city

Dammit, Janet When it comes to Rocky Horror, The Sound of Music or Joseph, there's only one thing you want to do and that's sing along. Sing-along-a nights are perfect for a hen party – you get a bit dressed up, get a bit drunk and watch the film, caterwauling along with lots of other people who have an equal disregard for what they look and sound like (although secretly, everyone does want the prize for the best fancy dress). Sing-along-a parties are constantly roaming around the UK and you'll often find one at the Manchester Opera House. Make those classic divas turn in their graves as you Timewarp, yodel or wail the night away.

Piece by piece If you don't fancy a film but you're not averse to a little singing with your supper, Bouzouki by Night is a fabulously fun night of Greek meze dishes and wine followed by Greek dancing lessons from the waiters and a spot of belly dancing. You can stay and dance the night away to disco classics, or make a sharp exit to your next venue if you've had enough feta for one night. Unfortunately they don't smash plates. From experience we can tell you that it's best not to introduce that feature yourself after a beverage or three.

Whole again Anyone for an enema? This and other detox, de-stress and disgusting-sounding but undoubtedly healthy activities may appeal to the hen who's having kittens over the pre-nuptial arrangements. And if they don't, then how about some fabulous massage, manicure, pedicure, facials and tanning to make you all feel like a million squids before your night out on the town? You can find all the health and beauty treatments your heart and other parts desire at the gorgeously calming Inner Sanctuary Retreat in the Northern Quarter. Look out for the Total Indulgence Packages, including Moody Cow and Hangover Recovery.

Rockin' robin The locals rate these as some of the best club nights in Manchester: Sankeys Saturdays, the Warehouse Project, Pure R'n'B Boutique, 5th Avenue for indie – but there are many many more. We say, for hen party laughs, burlesque, cheese and cabaret, it has to be The Birdcage. It's a totally unique concept of club and cabaret.

Get the basques and stockings out; it's time to Timewarp with Rocky Horror Sing-a-long-a.

Let it snow Not far from Old Trafford (which is of course worth a tour if you're a Man U fan) you'll find a little slice of Alpine life in the shape of the Chill Factor[e] – Manchester's indoor real snow centre. If you're looking to ski or snowboard, there is a wide range of lessons available for groups, or head for a session on the main slope. The 180m-indoor slope is the longest in the UK and is sure to give your group a thrill! If skiing or boarding isn't for you, then why not try Tubing (zooming down in a rubber tube) or the Luge (a 60m ice slide). As Manchester is generally devoid of snow and big mountains, this isn't exactly a way to explore the local culture, but it's a lot of fun.

It's raining men For all you active hens who like nothing more than a good soaking. Why not have a go at gorge scrambling...it's a bit like caving but with the roof off! Cling to slippery rocks and climb waterfalls while following streams, becks and gorges. The nice people at adventure21.co.uk say you can get as wet or stay as dry as you like. We say plunge pool jumping is all a part of the fun!

Five o'clock world 5–7pm is a weird time. Too early for dinner, too late to shop. But perfect for cocktails. For some of the city's best, trot round the back of House of Fraser on Deansgate and find Prohibition or Mojo. The latter plays classic rock and packs in a crowd at the weekend, while Prohibition has a friendly vibe, good music and makes for a relaxed few hours. If your night out is focused on the Northern Quarter, tucked away little gem Socio Rehab has some of the best cocktails in the UK and is hugely popular – so you have to get there early to avoid the queues. It's a hard life, isn't it? Be aware of dress codes for cocktail bars and clubs – it's a dressed up scene.

Happy Jealous, actually. The thought of you swanning off for golf, spa and luxury at the stunning Formby Hall makes us a bit sick. The packages are great value – a little golfing, using the utterly gorgeous, spick and span spa facilities, gliding up and down the pool, having beauty treatments, being wined, dined and then going to sleep in the elegant bedrooms – arrghh! When's our next hen do?

Apres-ski Chill Factor[e] stylie.

> ### 'been there...'
> We all loved Canal Street where all the gay bars and clubs are. We did a tour of Old Trafford as I'm a Man U fan, but I think I was the only one who really enjoyed that! In the evening we went to a bar off Deansgate, then back to the hotel to get into our hula outfits for Airport at Entourage. We got a Club Class booth and it was totally fab.... Manchester rocks.

where to stay

You'll find a warm welcome and great accommodation for good prices here. Stay within reach of all the bars and clubs, so that you don't have a huge spend on cabs.

hotels

Arora International ££

18–24 Princess Street,
Manchester M1 4LY
Tel. no 0161 236 8999
www.arorahotels.com
manchester@arorahotels.com

This four-star hotel is contemporary in design while retaining the character of the Grade II listed building. Set right in the heart of the city, it's close to all the attractions and the train station. The rooms feature all the facilities you will need and there is the Obsidian bar and restaurant on site.

Formby Hall Golf Resort and Spa £££

Southport Old Road, Formby L37 0AB
Tel. no 01704 875699
www.formbyhallgolfresort.co.uk
booking@formbyhallgolfresort.co.uk

If you want to get away from the city for some peace and tranquility, head west to the coast and experience some pure luxury at Formby Hall. Stylish and sophisticated, every detail has been meticulously thought about here.

The Hatters Hostel £

50 Newton Street, The Northern Quarter, Manchester M1 2EA
Tel. no 0161 236 9500
www.hattersgroup.com/manchester
manchester@hattersgroup.com
Located in the trendy bohemian Northern Quarter, Hatters offers a clean and comfortable stay in dorms or triple rooms for a very reasonable rate.

Hallmark Hotel ££

Stanley Road, Handforth, Wilmslow SK9 3LD
Tel. no 0161 437 0511
www.hallmarkhotels.co.uk
manchester.reservations@hallmark hotels.co.uk

Close to Manchester airport, this boutique-style hotel offers a lot of luxury for a relatively small price. Relax in the warmth of the decadent lounge bar or totally chill out in the health spa.

shared room without breakfast

£ under £30
££ £30–£60
£££ over £60
pppn

Elegant luxury at the Hallmark Hotel.

Stay Inn Hotel £

55 Blackfriars Road, Manchester M3 7DB
Tel. no 0161 907 2277
www.stayinn.co.uk
info@stayinn.co.uk

Less than a 10 minute walk to the city centre and handy for Old Trafford and the MEN Arena, this budget hotel offers unbelievable value. It even has free car parking, which is a big bonus. All the rooms are ensuite with TV and Wi-Fi, and there's a restaurant and bar.

The Mitre Hotel £

1–3 Cathedral Gates, Printworks, Manchester M3 1SW
Tel. no 0161 834 4128
www.themitrehotel.net
info@themitrehotel.net

This budget hotel is located in The Printworks – Manchester's huge entertainment complex right in the centre of the city – so you're right on the spot for all the bars, restaurants and clubs you could wish for. Being refurbished as we went to print.

self-catering

Burrs Activity Centre £

Woodhill Road, Bury
BL8 1DA
Tel. no 0161 764 9649
www.burrs.org.uk
burrs@btconnect.com

To take advantage of a wide range of outdoor activities available in Lancashire, base yourselves here in the Burrs Country Park. The bunkhouse comprises five rooms with two, four, six, ten and twelve beds. There's a fully equipped kitchen and dining area. Just bring your sleeping bag for an adventure!

City Warehouse Apartments ££

6–14 Great Ancoats Street, Manchester M4 1LJ
Tel. no 0161 236 3066
www.citywarehouseapartments.com
mail@citywarehouseapartments.com

These modern, stylish apartments are perfectly located in the heart of the Northern Quarter, minutes from Victoria Station and the Shudehill Interchange. All the fully furnished apartments have plasma TVs and DVD player.

Serviced City Pads ££

Tel. no 0844 335 8866
www.servicedcitypads.com
info@servicedcitypads.com

A range of quality apartments sleeping up to eight people are available in several central Manchester locations with this booking agent. If you want to splash out, they have plenty of apartments with wow factor.

Premier Apartments Manchester ££

64 Shudehill, Manchester M4 4AA
Tel. no 0161 827 3930
www.premierapartmentsmanchester.com
info@premierapartmentsmanchester.com

Well located for The Printworks, the Arndale Shopping Centre and both Victoria and Piccadilly train stations, there's also a metro link stop right opposite. There are 60 fully furnished apartments over four floors in this luxury block.

shared room without breakfast

£ under £30
££ £30–£60
£££ over £60
pppn

The Place ££

Ducie Street, Piccadilly, Manchester M1 2TP
Tel. no 0161 778 7500
www.theplacehotel.com
reservations@theplacehotel.com

This loft-style apartment hotel offers the flexibility of an apartment, with kitchen facilities and living room, plus the convenience of a hotel with restaurant and bar on site. Choose from one- or two-bedroom apartments all with Sky TV and Wi-Fi.

The bright lights of central Manchester.

where to eat and drink

Head to the Northern Quarter for a little boho atmosphere, stick with the familiar chains of the city centre or try something from a country you've never even heard of.

bars & pubs

Brannigans
27 Peter Street, Manchester M2 5QR
Tel. no 0161 835 9697
www.brannigansbars.com
brannigansmanchester@
cougarleisureltd.co.uk

Open until 3am on Saturday nights (Sunday morning), there's always a great party vibe at this lively bar. Their colourful lit dancefloor is a real centrepiece and when the DJ plays the place really comes to life. There are private areas and rooms available to book for your group – just go to the 'book a party' area of their website.

Mojo
19 Back Bridge Street,
Manchester M3 2PB
Tel. no 0161 839 5330
www.mojobar.co.uk

If you want to get away from the ubiquitous sounds of house and dance music, Mojo's is the place for you. Playing their individual blend of 'real music' and serving up fantastic cocktails, they offer a great night out for lovers of soul, R'n'B and rock'n'roll.

Prohibition
2–10 St Marys Street,
Manchester M3 2LB
Tel. no 0161 831 9326
www.prohibition.uk.com
info@prohibition.uk.com

The high ceilings and intricate wood carving on the bar give an immediate sense of the American Prohibition era, but don't worry they do sell alcohol and there's plenty of fun and good food to be had at this bar and grill.

We love the 70s dancefloor at Brannigans.

Revolution
Arch 7 Deansgate Locks, Manchester
M1 5LH
Tel. no 0161 839 7558
www.revolution-bars.co.uk

One of four Manchester Revolution venues, Deansgate Locks features a massive state-of-the-art basement club, four fantastic bars, dedicated restaurant and chilled-out lounge area. Whether you're relaxing in the lounge or dancing the night away in the club, you're guaranteed to have a great night in this warehouse style bar. There is loads of choice for a hen party here, just call the dedicated party planner line (see website) and they'll talk you through the options.

Socio Rehab
100–102 High Street, Manchester M4 1HP
Tel. no 0161 832 4529
www.sociorehab.com
info@sociorehab.com

If you need rehabilitating in a social environment, this is one place you should visit. If the cool tunes and sumptuous decor don't reel you in, the delicious cocktails certainly will.

restaurants

Evuna ££

277–279 Deansgate, Manchester
M3 4EW
Tel. no 0161 819 2752
www.evuna.com
enquiries@evuna.com

Sample some fine Spanish food and wine in the heart of Manchester. Choose from a wide range of tapas dishes or eat a la carte, alternatively try their signature dish of Sea Bass baked in rock salt and filleted at the table. You can also have a wine-tasting party here, where you can try some of the less well known, but delectable, Spanish wines.

Hard Rock Cafe ££

Exchange Square, Manchester M4 2BS
Tel. no 0161 831 6700
www.hardrock.com
david_atkinson@hardrock.com

It's a worldwide phenomenon, but here in Manchester there's an awe-inspiring collection of rock memorabilia. Choose a party menu for a great value night out, or learn to shake up your favourite cocktails with the resident mixologist.

'real life'

Learning to mix cocktails at the Hard Rock Cafe was great fun, but tasting what we'd concocted was even better!

The mixology bar at the Hard Rock Cafe.

The Hard Rock Cafe in The Printworks.

Ithaca £££

36 John Dalton Street, City Centre,
Manchester M2 6LE
Tel. no 0161 831 7409
www.ithacamanchester.com
pa@loveithaca.com

This elegant restaurant serving an eclectic mix of Japanese and Pan-Asian dishes has just been awarded the 2010 HILDA best restaurant in Manchester prize. So if you want a night of sparkling five-star luxury book into Ithaca.

Tiger Tiger ££

The Printworks, 27 Withy Grove,
Manchester M4 2BS
Tel. no 0161 385 8080
www.tigertiger-manch.co.uk
info@tigertiger-manch.co.uk

With a restaurant, six bars and a lively club, this is a great place to party. You could start here at lunch time and work your way through the bars – Tiger, Kaz, Raffles, Lounge and The Loft – to the restaurant with an amazing range of dishes and then on to the club for late-night dancing or to Lucky Voice for some serious caterwauling in the privacy of your own luxury private room.

where to party

Dancing and cabaret at The Birdcage, cocktails at Ithaca, karaoke at Tiger Tiger, comedy at Opus, clubbing at Pure, in The Printworks...just what do you fancy?

The relaxed and comfortable bar area at Pure nightclub.

Entourage

Unit 2a, The Printworks, 27 Withy Grove, Manchester M4 2BS
Tel. no 0161 839 1344
www.entouragemanchester.com
info@entouragemanchester.com

This 800-capacity venue makes up for in style and glamour what it may lack in size. The club is spread over two levels, with a dancefloor on the ground floor and private booths and VIP area on the balcony. There is a range of drinks packages that can be pre-ordered on the website and if one of those doesn't float your boat, you can tailormake your own and the club will happily supply.

Lucky Voice @ Tiger Tiger

The Printworks, Withy Grove, Manchester M4 2BS
Tel. no 0161 385 8080
www.tigertiger-manch.co.uk
info@tigertiger-manch.co.uk

Lucky Voice is thought by some to be the most liberating, heart-racing, life-affirming private karaoke experience on earth. Sing your heart out with your friends in the luxury of one of the exclusive private karaoke rooms available at Tiger Tiger. Choose from over 6000 songs to sing along to and order your drinks at the mere touch of a button.

Opus

The Printworks, Units 21–23, Withy Grove, Manchester M4 2BS
Tel. no 0161 834 2414
www.opusmanchester.com
faye@opusmanchester.com

As well as a three-room clubbing venue, Opus hosts the Comedy Lounge every Saturday night featuring some big names and all the up-and-coming stand-up comedians on 'the tour'. There's a variety of packages you can book with different food options, from burger and chips during the show to a three-course meal served in the O Bar before the show, or a hot and cold buffet served in the Chill room before the show. You can even get cocktail-making lessons to complete the night's entertainment.

Shake it Baby!

...at a Revolution cocktail masterclass

COCKTAIL CLASS

Learn to muddle, mix, shake and serve like a professional cocktail mixologist

90 minute session includes:

★ Flavoured vodka shots
★ History of cocktails
★ Bar tools, skills & games
★ Demo cocktail tasting
THEN get behind the bar and shake up some classic drinks!

other food, drink & table packages available

PRICES FROM ONLY £20pp

Book online today at...
www.revolution-bars.co.uk

REVOLUTION
manchester and nationwide

Lights and action at Pure in The Printworks.

Pure

Unit 11–12, The Printworks, 27 Withy
Grove, Manchester M4 2BS
Tel. no 0161 819 7770
www.pure.co.uk
info@puremanchester.com

Manchester's one and only superclub can
entertain 2700 clubbers in three different
rooms, plus an exclusive VIP experience is
on offer at The Island club for members only.
At the weekend crowd-pulling DJs play the
biggest tunes on state-of the-art sound
system accompanied by laser lightshows,
stilt walkers, fire breathers, podium dancers
and club visuals.
Friday and
Saturday nights
also feature a
comedy club
where you can get
your night off to
a hilarious start.

The Birdcage

Withy Grove, Manchester M4 3AQ
Tel. no 0161 832 1700
www.birdcagelive.com
info@birdcagelive.com

The number one hen party venue in
Manchester, The Birdcage offers an
entertaining mix of drag queens, showgirls,
male dancers and non-stop DJs that will
have you dancing in your seats. This
flamboyant mix of disco and cabaret is on
every Friday and Saturday night. Parties can
be booked in advance or you can pay on
the door!

The Birdcage will bring some old-fashioned glitz and glamour to your hen party.

newcastle

Angel of the North (top), Millenium Bridge (middle), Laing Art Gallery (bottom).

Newcastle is the UK's most popular stag party venue. Well, girls, we can't have you lagging behind, now can we? With the country's very best nightlife crammed into one lovely city, it's time to get yourselves to Toon.

what to do

Newcastle's nightlife is unparalleled in the UK and you'll be hard-pushed to find a town anywhere in Europe that can beat the party vibe here. It's hen party heaven. Why aye!

Newcastle has undergone a massive facelift in the past decade – while it was always known that Geordies liked to party, the city's caught up to provide the most incredible selection of pubs, bars, restaurants and clubs. Every taste is catered for, and it's usually easy on the bank balance. The locals may have a reputation for being hard, but that's really due to their ability to go out in sub-zero temperatures wearing almost nothing – you'll find a warm welcome in Newcastle and lots of hen and stag groups partying hard with you.

Apart from the nightlife, the shopping's great over in Gateshead at the Metro Centre, which has over 330 stores and 50 restaurants. The arts centre at Gateshead, the Quayside and the older parts of the city centre have all been revamped and made gorgeous, so it's a great area to look around in the daytime and is fast becoming one of Europe's established city break destinations. You'll find beautiful cafes, galleries and museums, if you're more into sporty action, then check out the horse and dog racing for authentic North-easterly fun.

10 good reasons

1. brilliant clubs
2. the Metro Centre
3. Newcastle Brown Ale
4. footy at St James' Park
5. decent pies
6. Collingwood Street bars
7. greyhound racing
8. the Gateshead arts centre
9. little old pubs
10. buzzing atmosphere

Newcastle's grand Grey Street.

sounds of the city

Natural woman Are you a Geordie lass who's feeling just a bit past all this clubbing malarkey? Or maybe you've booked accommodation for a couple of nights, but don't want to party both Friday and Saturday because you'd quite like to be alive on Sunday? Well, here's a top Newkey night in – it'll make you feel like you've taken a one way trip to heaven. Contact The Pamper Party (thepamperparty.co.uk) and they'll arrange for local beauty and massage therapists to visit and give you all treatments. Everyone chips in for shiatsu massage, manicure, reiki, henna tattoos and many more luxurious treats – a party with ultimate chill factor, especially if everyone brings a bottle of fizz or some nibbles along. This is one way to show your friends that you love them. And you know what that means don't you? Wedding presents...

It's oh so quiet Since we're on the topic of quiet nights in, The Silent Disco can certainly provide that, but you might find yourself in fits of laughter most of the time. Picture your mates, all headphoned up and dancing away in a silent room. You could all be dancing to the same tunes; on the other hand it could be Macarena v Queen chaos. The Silent Disco's been a massive hit in clubs, student unions and festivals all over the world (see silentdisco.com), and now you can hire the kit for your own party. Have a look at silentdiscokit.co.uk. If you're stuck for ideas as to where to host this epic night, check out The Cooperage for a party venue slap bang in the middle of the nightlife central, Quayside – perfect.

Diamonds are a girl's best friend If you want a quality night with a few choice friends, head for Central Station area, increasingly referred to as the Diamond Strip for its gorgeous eateries, bars and clubs. It starts with Revolution on the corner of Collingwood Street and reaches down to include the intimate Madame Koos and the very cool Bijoux. This area is dressed up WAG land, and not the place to pitch up in a novelty hat and order a pint with a straw. If the latter's more your bag then head for the Quayside and Bigg Market for unpretentious fun amid loads of other hens and stags – an unbeatable vibe, good value drinks and an array of bars and clubs to choose from. You know it makes sense.

Bring the pampering to you with a relaxing party at your house courtesy of ThePamperParty.co.uk.

Milkshake Time was when women weren't really supposed to enjoy sex. While we're all a bit more enlightened these days, most of us could still do with some guidance in the art of sweet lurve – and a good laugh at the male genitalia while we're at it. Cue Milky Moments (!!??) foreplay lessons, hosted by Tiger Tiger at The Gate. MMs' private hen parties will show you how to deal effectively with a large appendage, should one arise.

Spies Your mission: to crack codes, find out who's the genius in your group or take over the town, Monopoly style… with Wildgoose Treasure Hunts you can choose a challenge that will get your brains working and introduce some hilarious competition to your weekend in Newcastle. The huntthegoose.co.uk team can either be there on the day or send you a DIY pack, and you'll spend two–three hours somewhere in the city, finding clues, solving riddles and taking ridiculous photographs, all against the clock. It's the perfect excuse to wear Harry Potter specs or deerstalker hats, if you needed an excuse of course. And yes, you can get a package that ties in with a pub crawl…

The last laugh If you opt for a hilarious daytime activity, be it foreplay lessons, treasure hunting or any number of driving experiences you can get in Newcastle and Gateshead, keep the laughs coming all evening by booking the Hyena Comedy Café. The venue's right in the city centre and you can turn up for great comedians, food, drinks and dancing to keep the ladies happy until the wee small hours.

> ## 'been there…'
>
> **My memories of Newcastle are a bit hazy. We dumped our bags in the hotel and went out on a cocktail cruise from about 5 o'clock! The locals were dead friendly, we got chatting with quite a few randoms throughout the night, probably because we were dressed as show girls! The bars were fab – really lively and good value. It's a top place to go for your hen.**

With a Milky Moments party everyone get a badge with their alias for the evening!

where to stay

Feel like lady muck in your uber cool Tyneside hotel suite or stumble into your B&B in the early hours. Newcastle welcomes the girl-about-town, whatever her budget.

hotels and b&bs

Beamish Park Hotel ££
Beamish Park Hotel, Marley Hill, Newcastle Upon Tyne, NE16 5EG
Tel. no 01207 230666
www.beamish-park-hotel.co.uk
reception@beamish-park-hotel.co.uk

Situated in beautiful countryside, just one mile from Beamish and only 10 minutes' drive from Newcastle city centre, the Beamish Park is an independently owned hotel with 42 bedrooms. Adjacent to the hotel is a golf academy, including a nine-hole par three course, practice greens and bunkers and a 20 bay flood-lit golf driving range.

✳ shared room without breakfast
£ under £30
££ £30–£60
£££ over £60
pppn

Grainger Hotel B&B ££
1–3 Graingerville North, Westgate Road, Newcastle Upon Tyne NE4 6UJ
Tel. no 0191 298 3800
www.graingerhotel.co.uk
info@graingerhotel.co.uk

Grainger Hotel has easy access to the city centre and makes the perfect base to explore the North East of England. All the guest rooms and suites of this luxury bed and breakfast are tastefully decorated in an elegant style using rich fabrics and ornate furnishings. All rooms are equipped with satellite TV.

Roselodge House £
Benwell Lane, Benwell, Newcastle Upon Tyne NE15 6RU
Tel. no 0191 274 7388
www.roselodgehouse.com
jaz.sarwar@btinternet.com

Initially built as a Church, now an impressive B&B boasting 50 luxurious rooms. Sympathetically restored to retain the stunning Gothic architecture, The Roselodge provides comfortable beds at affordable prices. All rates include breakfast and complimentary toiletries. Just 10 minutes away from the city centre, they can accommodate large group bookings up to 30 people.

Royal Station Hotel ££
Neville Street, Newcastle Upon Tyne NE1 5DH
Tel. no 0191 232 0781
www.royalstationhotel.com
info@royalstationhotel.com

Conveniently located next to Central Station, the three-star Royal Station Hotel combines elegant Victorian architecture with up-to-date facilities. There are 144 spacious ensuite bedrooms and a leisure club with indoor swimming pool, jacuzzi, steam room and plunge pool as well as the popular Destination Bar.

The George Hotel £
88 Osbourne Road, Jesmond, Newcastle Upon Tyne NE2 2AP
Tel. no 0191 281 4442
www.georgehotel-newcastle.co.uk
info@georgehotel-newcastle.co.uk

This friendly hotel is modern and pleasant providing excellent value for money. Rooms are comfortable with ensuite facilities, triples and quads are available. For large group bookings enquire about special rates. The city centre is just a 10-minute taxi ride away and there's a rank right outside the hotel.

self-catering

Chapel House Apartments ££
Causey Row, Marley Hill, Newcastle
Upon Tyne NE16 5EJ
Tel. no 01207 290992
www.chapelhouseapartments.co.uk
chapelhouseapartments@hotmail.co.uk

These four studio apartments, part of a
converted chapel, overlook rolling
countryside just 8 miles from Newcastle
and 4 miles from the Metro Centre. Each
double studio has a fitted
kitchen/dining area, ensuite
bathroom with shower,
independent access and
parking directly outside.

Coastal Retreats ££
9 Causey St, Gosforth,
Newcastle-upon-Tyne
NE3 4DJ
Tel. no 0191 2851272
www.coastalretreats.co.uk
info@coastalretreats.co.uk

These five-star luxury self-catering cottages
feature professionally designed
contemporary interiors with gorgeous soft
furnishings and fully equipped kitchens.
Guests also enjoy Leisure Club membership
for the duration of their stay.

Eland Farm ££
Eland Green Farm, Ponteland
NE20 9UR
Tel. no 01661 822188
www.elandfarm.co.uk
clhs@eland-green.fsnet.co.uk

Just 9 miles north-west of Newcastle and set
in idyllic surroundings of 200 acres of grass
farm, Eland Farm provides self-catering
holiday homes to escape the hustle and
bustle of the big city. The farm offers breathtaking views of the Cheviot Hills whilst being
within walking distance of friendly pubs,
shops and restaurants. Recently converted
from a 250-year-old stable block, these
three-star cottages give the luxury of modern
interiors, but with bags of character.

Hedley Grange Holiday Cottages ££
Hedley West Farm, Hedley Lane,
Newcastle upon Tyne NE16 5EQ
Tel. no 01207 232959
www.hedleygrange.co.uk
info@hedleygrange.co.uk

These exclusive barn conversions, Swallows
and Woodpeckers, offer stylish, modern
accommodation in a perfect rural setting on
the border between Northumberland and
County Durham. They are set in a
secluded garden overlooking a
nine-hole golf course. Both have
fully fitted kitchens, gas central
heating, electric cooker, TV,
video, radio, fridge,
microwave, iron and use of
washer/dryer. Both
apartments have safe
parking and south-facing
furnished patios.

✳ shared room without breakfast
£ under £30
££ £30–£60
£££ over £60
pppn

Newton Hall and Cottages ££
Newton by the Sea, Nr Alnwick,
Northumberland NE66 3DZ
Tel. 01665 576239
www.newtonholidays.co.uk
info@newtonholidays.co.uk

This magnificent Georgian house has nine
bedrooms and loads of charm. It stands
majestically in 4 acres of beautiful grounds
with three accompanying cottages, and is the
perfect costal hideaway within minutes of
white sandy beaches. The Hall sleeps 18, but
can cater for parties as large as 35, if you
include the cottages, which are available
separately and sleep four–six people.There
are nine large double bedrooms in the main
house, a fitted kitchen, a dining room with a
large table and a drawing room with a full-
sized snooker table and a huge world map.
Facilities include five widescreen TVs, DVDs
and Sky, Wi-Fi and laundry. It is a wonderful
location from which to explore this gorgeous
part of Northumberland, designated an area
of outstanding natural beauty by the National
Trust. Newton Hall is less than an hour from
Newcastle and 90 minutes from Edinburgh.

where to eat and drink

bars

Bijoux

Mosley Street, Newcastle Upon Tyne
NE1 1DF
Tel. no 0191 260 2378
www.bijouxbar.co.uk
manager@bijouxbar.co.uk

Bijoux bar is the latest edition to the Diamond strip of Newcastle's Mosley Street and Collingwood Street. This intimate and glamorous little bar serves a selection a wines, world beers and fresh cocktails.

There's no shortage of places to enjoy fine wines.

Madame Koos

36 Collingwood Street,
Newcastle NE1 1JF
Tel. no 0191 261 8271
www.madamekoo.co.uk
info@madamekoo.co.uk

This Oriental-styled bar with colourful lanterns and Asian artefacts is a hidden gem just waiting for you to discover the party atmosphere there. The Sneaky Disco plays classic soul, disco, R'n'B, indie, rock and pop, plus all the cheesy choons you could wish for and they're proud of it!

Revolution

Barclays Bank Chambers, Collingwood Street, Newcastle upon Tyne NE1 1JF
Tel. no 0191 261 8901
www.revolution-bars.co.uk/newcastleut

Revolution Newcastle is a luxurious bank conversion with original 30-foot high ceilings, marble pillars and classic wood features. It has cemented itself in the Newcastle scene with a great reputation for fantastic music, a great atmosphere and excellent service. Food is served all day until 8pm with a delicious selection of homemade stone-baked pizza right through until 1am.

The Cooperage

32 The Close, Quayside, Newcastle
Upon Tyne NE11 3RF
Tel. no 0191 233 2940
www.cooperage1730.co.uk

One of the oldest buildings in the city, dating back to the 13th century, The Cooperage is full of olde worlde charm. With its reputation for excellent real ales, this pub draws huge crowds, especially at the weekend. Split into several bars and a nightclub, you'll find a lively mix of jazz, soul, funk and latin salsa on most nights at The Cooperage.

Tiger Tiger

The Gate, Newgate Street, Newcastle
Upon Tyne NE1 5RE
Tel. no 0191 235 7065
www.tigertiger-newcastle.co.uk
info@tigertiger-newcastle.co.uk

With six bars, a restaurant and a lively club, this is not a place to get bored! A range of different styles across the bars means there's something for everyone and at the weekend the music varies from chart anthems in Tiger and Raffles to the best of the 70s and 80s in Groovy and Ibiza house classics and 90s pop in the White Room.

restaurants

Apartment £££

28–32 Collingwood Street, Newcastle
Upon Tyne NE1 1JF
Tel. no 0191 281 9609
www.apartment-luxebar.com
info@apartment-luxebar.com

This seductive restaurant, bar and members'
club is styled like a Manhattan apartment with
warehouse-sized windows, exposed brick
and solid walnut. East meets West in the
varied and imaginative menu and comes
together to provide a chic and unrivalled
dining experience in this part of the UK.

Frankie and Benny's ££

John Dobson Street, Northumberland
Road Newcastle Upon Tyne NE1 8JF
Tel. no 0191 261 4328
www.frankieandbennys.com

This retro 50s style New York Italian
restaurant and bar always has a great
atmosphere for large group dining. They
even have an online party maker that will
invite the guests for you!

Hotel du Vin Bistro ££

Allan House, City Road, Newcastle
Upon Tyne NE1 2BE
Tel. no 0191 229 2200
www.hotelduvin.com/newcastle
reception.newcastle@hotelduvin.com

Once the home of the Tyne Tees Steam
Shipping Company, it is now a stylish
boutique hotel with classy bistro and bar. The
menu is rooted in classic European cuisine
with a contemporary edge. You'll find
sensibly priced seasonal dishes using locally
sourced produce where possible.

Rocco Bar Trattoria £

22 Leazes Park Road, Newcastle
Upon Tyne NE1 4PG
Tel. no 0191 232 5871
www.roccobar.co.uk
roccobar@live.co.uk

Formerly La Toscana, this new incarnation
continues to serve top-quality Italian cuisine.
Bar Rocco will create a tailormade party
menu for your hen party. Just contact them in
advance to discuss.

The seductive atmosphere at Apartment Luxebar.

Mandarin Restaurant ££

14–18 Stowell Street, Newcastle
Upon Tyne NE1 4XQ
Tel. no 0191 261 7960
www.mandarin-newcastle.com

For some seriously good Chinese and
Szechaun food, try Mandarin. You can
experience a Chinese feast with one of their
banquet menus, starting at less than £11 per
head, featuring favourites such as BBQ ribs,
Sweet and Sour Pork, Lemon Chicken and
King Prawns in Black Bean Sauce.

Starters & Puds £££

2–6 Shakespeare Street, Newcastle
upon Tyne NE1 6AQ
Tel. no 0191 233 2515
www.startersandpuds.co.uk
eat@startersandpuds.co.uk

Starters & Puds is an exciting new concept in
leisurely eating. They take the best of savoury
and sweet cuisine, mixing it with friendly yet
distinctive surroundings and adding in a
large helping of relaxed ambience. You can
choose several starter dishes like tapas and
share around the table. You'll find this recipe
for a successful eating experience right in
the heart of Newcastle, adjacent to the
Theatre Royal.

where to party

You may be slightly confused by the sheer choice of clubs and bars in which to party your last weekend of freedom away, but if you want fun, you're in the right city.

You can expect some steamy action in Newcastle's top nightspots.

Bambu

13 Grainger Quarter, Newcastle
Upon Tyne NE1 1UW
Tel. no 0191 261 5811
blubambu@pbr.uk.com

Formerly known as Blu Bambu, but now rebranded as Bambu, this is the ultimate party venue. Located in Bigg Market you'll always find a fun party zone occurring here. Find Bambu on facebook and write on the wall for guest list and Q jump entry.

Digital

Times Square, Newcastle
Upon Tyne NE1 4EP
Tel. no 0191 261 9755
www.yourfutureisdigital.com/newcastle
info@yourfutureisdigital.com

This is a club that is serious about its music and the speaker system is second to none. The weekend line up includes Wax:On – a mix of breakbeat, electro and hip hop – on Fridays, while the legendary house night, Shindig, is the main event on a Saturday.

Liquid & Envy

49 New Bridge Street West,
Newcastle Upon Tyne NE1 8AN
Tel. no 0191 261 2526
www.liquidclubs.com
newcastle@liquidclubs.com

With two large club rooms, a VIP area and outdoor area, Liquid & Envy has it all under one roof. Inside you'll find state-of-the-art sound and lighting systems and 360 degree plasma screens providing visuals whichever way you look. You'll find a mix of R'n'B and hip hop playing here on a Saturday night to a discerning clubbing crowd. For a more exclusive experience, pre-book tickets to the VIP area, also known as The Liquid Lounge, there are various party packages on offer, so give them a call and get your last night of freedom sorted in style.

> ❝ A night out in Newcastle is full of surprises. ❞

Nancy's Bordello

13 Argyle Street, Newcastle Upon Tyne
NE1 6PF
Tel. no 0191 260 2929
www.nancysbordello.com
info@nancysbordello.com

Newcastle's only World Music bar and club,
Nancy's is unique. A million miles away from
the corporate scene, at Nancy's you'll find a
melting pot of sounds and scenes bringing
you a remixed version of a nightclub. On a
Saturday night Salsa Viva rules with resident
DJ Coco Vega and guests featuring live
acoustic sessions with a variety of
performers. Dance the night away to the
sounds of salsa, merengue, bachata, cha
cha and latin house. Nancy's also serves up
some tasty food from all corners of the globe
so you have everything you need for an
international night out.

Sea

Neptune House, Quayside, Newcastle
Upon Tyne NE1 3ZQ
Tel. no 0191 230 1813
sea@pbr.uk.com

This stylish nightclub is full of glitz and
glamour and is a popular hang out of WAGS
and local celebs. Top DJs regularly play here
and if you want to chill out you can head to
The Viper Lounge for R'n'B. Alternatively, for a
more exclusive experience, try the VIP room.

Sea nightclub is the place to be seen.

*The light and airy bar at The Attic becomes cool and
seductive after dark.*

The Attic

25–27 Mosley Street, Newcastle
Upon Tyne NE1 1YF
Tel. no 0191 233 1396
theattic@pbr.uk.com

This recently refurbished 1000-capacity
nightclub has swiftly established itself with
the cool set in the city. Arranged on four
floors this funky club is a guaranteed
awesome night out.

World Headquarters Club

Curtis Mayfield House,Carliol Square,
East Pilgrim Street, Newcastle Upon
Tyne NE1 6UF
Tel. no 0191 281 3445
www.welovewhq.com
www.myspace.com/whq (MySpace)
info@welovewhq.com

World Headquarters is an independent club
and proud of it. Here you'll find something a
little bit different to the ubiquitous 'packages'
offered in many clubs. At this club you'll get
more of an underground experience driven
by good music, and it relies on word of
mouth to spread the message. It is laid out
over two floors: upstairs, with its booming
sound system and eye-catching murals, is
the main party scene, downstairs is a more
laid-back affair with comfy leather sofas, a
pool table and the finest selection of whisky
on offer in the city.

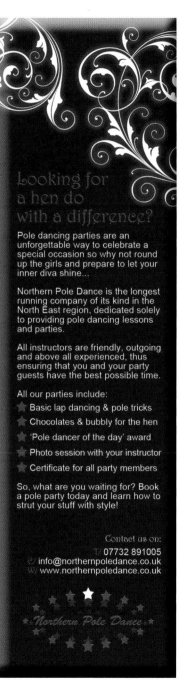

newquay

It may be a fishing port, but Newquay is up there with our biggest cities when it comes to partying. The town is alive all summer, thanks to surfers, a thriving nightlife and loads of people looking for fun in the sun.

Newquay Bay (top), the harbour (middle), Fistral Beach (bottom).

what to do

Enjoying the general vibe that there's more to life than the 9–5, Newquay is relaxed by day and kicking at night. It's fun all year round, but in the summer you can't beat it.

The UK's surfing capital is one of Britain's most popular hen party destinations – even if you've no intention of dipping your toe in the North Atlantic, the pretty harbour, coastal scenery, party atmosphere and considerable wetsuit-clad eye candy in these parts should tempt you.

And just to tip the balance, Newquay is all about extreme fun, so for hens who want activities – from horse riding on the beach to hovercraft driving – you'll love all the opportunities here for fun and adventure.

Three major annual festivals are now based in Newquay, and the visitor numbers each summer are growing. There's plenty of accommodation available, but you'll find the best deals out of high season. Winter wetsuits available for hire mean that you can brave the water any time of year!

It's not all sandy bunkhouses and tousled tresses. You can combine your activities with spa days and other hen faves such as poledancing lessons, and there are many beautiful hotels and self-catering properties in town.

Check out the board action down at the beach.

10 good reasons

1. watching the surfers
2. fun and relaxed nightlife
3. unsophisticated fun
4. lovely sandy beaches
5. fresh seafood
6. surfing lessons
7. ice cream
8. the Eden Project
9. beautiful scenery
10. Cornish pasties

sounds of the town

Hold me, thrill me, kiss me, kill me
Adventure Activities at Lusty Glaze beach offer various rock and sea adventures, and their hen packages are fantastic, especially the Extreme Experience, where you'll spend a morning coasteering or surfing, then after lunch scramble up a cliff assault course, walk a high wire over a chasm and take a high speed zip wire ride…all finished off with drinks on the beach. You can also book a Surf and Spa day or go for the I'm a Sealebrity challenge…believe us, the hen groups fare better than the stags when it comes to the Beach Tucker Trial.

What's goin' down A few miles inland from Newquay is the fantastic new Adrenalin Quarry. Here, you can scream very loudly as you travel at speed down the UK's longest zip wire. Deafen a friend on the twin zip or make it a solo mission as you step off the cliff and zoom over the lake below.

At the bottom of the quarry you can try your hand at hovercraft driving, giving it some serious welly on your solo adventure over land and lake. Just to make a full day of it, there's a karting centre at the quarry too, with Sodi GT2 karts and an 800m track. Kartworld do a great hen package with a proper, Grand Prix-style competition for groups of ten or more, as well as floodlit night karting. Have a look at the website: adrenalinquarry.co.uk

Soul surfing One thing Newquay's not short on is surf schools. If you want the best quality instruction on offer look no further than the Rip Curl ESF Surf School. They are a level 4 school (the highest standard in the UK) and are walking distance from two amazing beaches. With both surfing and bodyboarding on offer and a complimentary bottle of fizz for hen parties they are a great choice. Learn to pop up and ride that board, or alternatively just cling on tight and try not to drown – it's a brilliant laugh and you'll hire good quality kit that will keep you all warm, no matter what the weather's doing. Tuition is available all year round and you can book a package with accommodation either at Carnmarth Hotel or Bertie's Lodge within walking distance of the sea. Check prices at englishsurfschool.com.

Learn to surf with Rip Curl ESF Surf School.

'been there…'

We had the best time in Newquay. We piled into a minibus from London and headed down to the surf school. Two days of surfing lessons, bunk bed accommodation, fish and chips and a lot of drinking! It was fantastic. You don't care how you look, it's just about having fun and trying to stand up on that board. I didn't want to come home!

Knowing me, knowing you It's always good to be shown around an area by people who know and love it, which is exactly what you'll get if you book a hen party through Explore Southwest. This group of surfers, ex-travellers and beach bums have roamed the world and come back to Cornwall because they love it. They'll arrange accommodation, activities, clubs, bars and even eco-friendly transport to lovely Cornwall from any UK address see exploresouthwest.com.

A little less conversation What could be better than riding horses through the waves on a sunny morning in Cornwall? Newquay Riding Stables at Trenance will take you out on gorgeous steeds for a 1–2 hour trek, including that romantic canter along the beach. Cue slow mo and soft focus. If you want something with a little less chat time and a little more action, they do army mornings as part of adventure training. Intrigued? Find out more by contacting the company on 01637 872699. Make sure you do some inner thigh stretches first – you'll be walking like John Wayne if you don't.

I don't want to miss a thing This town is just wall to wall bars, surf shops, restaurants and clubs. Basically, it caters for a relaxed crowd who want to kick back after a day's surfing, so the atmosphere's happy and easy going – and fancy dress is much more common than smart casual round here. Have a simple bar crawl and enjoy the drinks promos, cheap eats and live music all over town.

For Big Nights Out choices include Sailors Club, Berties, Koola or Buzios…for a town this size the nightlife is amazing, so don't be tempted to collapse into bed after a day's surfing – partying hard is compulsory.

Gallop along the lovely beaches with Newquay Riding Stables.

where to stay

When the surf's down and the party's stumbled to a halt, sleep might be a plan. Newquay has masses of choice, but book early or you'll be kipping on the beach.

hotels

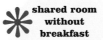

shared room without breakfast

£ under £30
££ £30–£60
£££ over £60
pppn

Bertie's Lodge £*
East Street, Newquay,
TR7 1DB
Tel. no 01637 870334
www.bertieslodge.co.uk
info@bertieslodge.co.uk

Berties Lodge is situated above Berties Pub and is an ideal location for any hen party. With a bar below and Berties nightclub on your doorstep plus great views of the beach, there is no better location. It's stylish budget accommodation with bunk beds and shared rooms. *Prices increase in high season.

Carnmarth Hotel ££
22 Headland Road, Newquay
Tel. no 01637 879571
www.carnmarth.com
enquiries@carnmarth.com

Overlooking the world famous Fistral Beach the Carnmarth is a sophisticated option. All the rooms have views of the sea or headland and some even have a private balcony. With the trendy C-bar on hand, it's a popular one.

Hotel Victoria ££
East Street, Newquay TR7 1DB
Tel. no 01637 872 255
www.hotel-victoria.co.uk
bookings@hotel-victoria.co.uk

The three-star Hotel Victoria is situated on the cliffs above the golden sands of Great Western beach with amazing views over Newquay Bay. It suits those seeking a higher class of accommodation with gym, indoor pool, spa and variety of rooms from doubles and twins to luxury suites. Book a surf package with the Rip Curl ESF Surf School.

Reef Island Surf Lodge £
30–32 Island Crescent,
Newquay TR7 1DZ
Tel. no 01637 879058
www.reefislandsurflodge.com
info@reefislandsurflodge.com

This funky retro 70s style surf lodge can accommodate large groups in a variety of rooms. They have secure storage for wetsuits and boards and on site is the Austin Powers style Reef Island bar. Book a package with Reef Surf School.

Tsunami Lodge £
84 Crantock Street, Newquay TR7 1JW
Tel. no 01637 872391
www.tsunami-lodge.co.uk
info@tsunami-lodge.co.uk

Small but perfectly formed this surf lodge offers four-person and six-person bunkrooms with ensuite shower rooms. The clean and comfortable surroundings make it a real home from home. Five minutes to the town centre and only a couple of minutes more to Fistral beach, Tsunami is very well located.

Hotel Victoria overlooking Newquay Bay.

self-catering

AbreakAway £
2 Higher Tower Road, Newquay TR7 1QL
Tel. no 07973 823083
www.abreakaway.co.uk
info@abreakaway.co.uk

A cross between serviced apartments and a hostel, this self-catering option could meet all your needs. Each self-contained apartment has bunk-bedded accommodation (apart from the penthouse with four single beds) with clean linen, an ensuite shower room, a kitchenette with microwave, fridge, crockery and cutlery. You will need to bring your own towels though. A few minutes' walk to Fistral beach and the centre, where all the night-time action takes place. You'll get your own key and there's no curfew!

Airborne Lodge £
98 Fore Street, Newquay TR7 1EY
Tel. no 01637 875648
www.airbornelodge.com
info@airbornelodge.com

This friendly and informal lodge is just five minutes' to the town centre and Fistral Beach. It has high quality twin and dorm rooms sleeping three–eight people. Bed linen is provided and there is a colour TV in every room. A large chillout lounge equipped with self-catering facilities and no curfew makes this a very relaxed place to stay.

Beachwalk Holiday House £
12 Belmont Place, Newquay TR7 1HG
Tel. no 07970 747109
www.beachwalkholidayhouse.co.uk
rich.holder@btopenworld.com
Just a few minutes walk from Fistral Beach, this pad sleeps eight in total luxury, with Playstation 3, iPod docking station, outside surf shower, gas barbecue and other surf break essentials. The minimum booking period is one week and make sure you book early for this popular rental.

Blue Bay Lodges £
Mawgan Porth Cornwall TR8 4DA
Tel. no 01637 860324

shared room without breakfast
£ under £30
££ £30–£60
£££ over £60
pppn

www.bluebaycornwall.co.uk
hotel@bluebaycornwall.co.uk

If you're looking for a bit of peace and tranquility away from the buzz of Newquay itself, this could be the place for you. There are four individual lodges sleeping up to eight people with stunning views of the Vale of Lanhern. All guests are welcome to use the nearby Blue Bay hotel restaurant, bar and facilities.

Smugglers Haven £
Porth, Newquay TR8 4AS
Tel. no 01637 852000
www.smugglershaven.co.uk
kelly.roberts@cranstar.co.uk

Rent a caravan, wheel up in your VW van or pitch your tent at Smugglers for a fun-filled stay. With a heated outdoor swimming pool and the Shakin' Shack Bar to get your party started, it's going to be rockin'.

The Shakin' Shack bar at Smugglers Haven.

Tolcarne Beach Surf Shacks £
Narrowcliff, Newquay TR7 2QN
Tel. no 01637 872489
www.tolcarnebeach.co.uk
info@tolcarnebeach.com

If you want to roll out of bed and into the sea, this is your place to stay. Right on the beach, each shack sleeps four in bunks with bed linen provided. There's a shared shower area and kitchenette on site and a tap outside your shack.

where to eat and drink

Book yer wenches into the Newquay Meadery, or head to the quayside for ultra fresh seafood, before diving into the party vibe that defines Newquay summer nights.

bars & pubs

Buzios
54–56 East Street, Newquay TR7 1BE
Tel. no 01637 870300
www.buziosbar.co.uk
info@buziosbar.co.uk

This award-winning contemporary style cafe bar, which incorporates a restaurant, a club and a pool hall, brings a slice of city sophistication to the North Cornish coast. It's set on three floors and is open 'til 4am in high season. You can also hire it out for your own private do.

Central Inn
11 Central Square, Newquay TR7 1EU
Tel. no 01637 873810
www.staustellbrewery.co.uk
thecentral@staustellbrewery.co.uk

As the name suggests, The Central is right in the heart of Newquay town centre. This lively and friendly pub has a large outdoor terrace, perfect for a sundowner and a spot of people watching after a hard day's surfing. There's a cocktail bar and you can eat here too; later on the DJs get started in the dance bar.

Red Square
11–17 Gover Lane, Newquay TR7 1ER
Tel. no 01637 878823
www.redsquare.co.uk
info@redsquareclub.co.uk

A bar and a club, Red Square boasts the largest Vodka menu in Newquay. So if you're a fan of the Russian tipple, this is the bar for you. They have everything from Absinthe (over 21s only – it's strong stuff!) to Creme Egg flavoured Vodka and about 60 others in between. Vodka lovers' paradise.

The cool bar area at Fistral Blu restaurant.

The Chy Bar & Kitchen
12 Beach Road, Newquay TR7 1ES
Tel. no 01637 873415
www.thekoola.com/the-chy-bar
the.koola@virgin.net

'Chy' is Cornish for 'home' and the relaxed atmosphere here will certainly give you a warm feeling. A cafe bar during the day, The Chy transforms into a lively cocktail bar later on with live DJs. The Kitchen serves modern British food and offers a party menu for larger groups. The homemade 100% pure British beef burger, The Chy Burger, is a smash hit.

Two Clomes
Quintrell Downs, Newquay TR8 4PD
Tel. no 01637 871163

Just outside Newquay, in the gorgeous Cornish countryside, is a real traditional pub serving great food at excellent value. If you want to get away from it all and sample some quality seafood with different specials every day then the Two Clomes is the one. They don't skimp on the portions here and are well known for their wines, so if you've got a good appetite, then come here and enjoy a chilled glass of wine in a quiet setting. If the sun shines on you, dine outside on the terrace.

restaurants

2 courses + half a bottle of wine

£ under £20
££ £20–£35
£££ over £35

Drinks on the balcony at Fistral Blu watching the sun set is the perfect way to start the evening off.

Fistral Blu ££

Fistral Beach, Headland Road,
Newquay TR7 1HY
Tel. no 01637 879444
www.fistral-blu.co.uk
info@fistral-blu.co.uk

With panoramic views of Fistral Beach, the Fistral Blu bar and bistro has a fabulous setting, perfect for watching the sun go down over the Atlantic. The varied menu with strong Mediterranean influences offers something to tantalise everyone's tastebuds.

New Harbour ££

South Quay Hill, Newquay Harbour,
Newquay TR7 1HT
Tel. no 01637 874062
www.new-harbour.com
info@new-harbour.com

Fresh, steamed mussels.

To sample some of the freshest locally caught seafood in a sophisticated environment, New Harbour is the place to book. With lobster, spider crab and fresh fish on the menu they are famous for their 'sexy fish and chips'. The emphasis here is on simple food cooked to perfection.

Newquay Meadery £

Marcus Hill, Newquay TR7 1BD
Tel. no 01637 873000
www.newquaymeadery.co.uk
info@newquaymeadery.co.uk

If you want to join up with other hen and stag parties on your last night of freedom then book into the Meadery for a night of medieval munching. The friendly hosts can offer you a party menu at a price per head to suit your group. We say let the feasting commence.

Senor Dicks £

East Street, Newquay TR7 1DB
Tel. no 01637 870350
www.senor-dicks.co.uk
info@senor-dicks.co.uk

Mexican food is always a popular choice and Senor Dicks serves up authentic Mexican recipes, not just hot hot hot food. Wash it all down with plenty of Mexican cerveza or the best Margaritas in Cornwall and you have a recipe for a night full of spice.

where to party

Get your fancy dress on and hit the town.
With multi-room clubs, small venues with
great DJs and live acts, and loads of bars
and clubs, it's a great place to party.

Radio One's Scott Mills at Berties.

Berties Club

East St, Newquay TR7 1DB,
Tel. no 01637 870369
www.bertiesclub.com
tony.townsend@bertiesclub.com

Anyone who's been to Newquay has been to
Berties. It claims to be Cornwall's largest
nightclub with a capacity of more than 2000.
It's a firm favourite of stag and hen parties
with many of the UK's biggest stars playing
the venue, from Radio One's Scott Mills to
world dance DJ Eddie Halliwell. Berties also
has exclusive VIP booths and a VIP room for
stags and hens to hire for the evening. It
even has its very own party bus, decked out
like a disco inside and free limo service
running from the town's bars.

Koola

12 Beach Road, Newquay TR7 1ES
Tel. no 01637 873415
www.thekoola.com
thekoola@virgin.net

If you're after live DJs and an electric
atmosphere, head to Koola – home of
underground music. The industrial-chic decor
of this intimate venue on three floors gives it
a really edgy feel only surpassed by the DJ
line-up. Past events include Ice-T, Groove
Rider, Judge Jules, The Kaiser Chiefs and the
list goes on. With audio delights from the
worlds of hip-hop, drum and bass, through
funk and beats to all types of house,
alternative rock & live bands, music
aficionados need look no further.

The pulsating dancefloor at Pure.

Pure

52 Tolcarne Road, Newquay TR7 2NQ
Tel. no 01637 850313
www.purenewquay.com
info@purenewquay.com

Formerly the legendary Tall Trees, Pure is a brand spanking new incarnation of the South West's no.1 superclub. With ultra cool decor and the best dance music around, Pure offers a quality night out. If there's eight or more of you, why not call ahead and book a table in the club's elegant VIP area: The Island. You'll get the full celeb treatment – priority entry, a table for the night and champagne on arrival. You can even book the Pure Party Bus to transport your group here from Bodmin, St Austell, Wadebridge, Truro, Falmouth and Penzance. Call Pure Transport on 01637 800150 for more details. Also ask about the new comedy club at Pure.

Sailors Club

Fore Street, Newquay
Tel. no 01637 872838
www.sailorsnightclub.com
info@sailorsnightclub.com

Playing commercial dance, hip hop and party anthems, the sailors is a popular destination for clubbers in Newquay. Whether you head straight for the dancefloor, hang out on the balcony above or go for a cheeky concoction in Sailors' legendary cocktail bar, there's

something to please everyone. With plenty of drinks on promotion and very friendly door tax. It's got to be on your map.

The Barracuda Bar

27–29 Cliff Road, Newquay TR7 2NE
Tel. no 01637 875800
www.barracudanewquay.com
newquay@barracudabars.co.uk

It's a bar, it's a club, it's a live music venue and it's massive! Arranged on three floors of fabulous fun, there are plenty of bars doing great drinks promotions, dancefloors, live music, food, pool, fruit machines...frankly, you could spend all day here!

The Beach Niteclub

1 Beach Road, Newquay TR7 1ES
Tel. no 01637 872194
www.beachclubnewquay.com
info@beachclubnewquay.com

With three floors, four bars and two DJs playing every Saturday, this is a club with plenty of choice. Located right in the centre of town and close to the Newquay Meadery and Fistral Blu restaurants, they can arrange hen night packages with both of these restaurants. Alternatively, you can pre-book entry to the club giving you fast track admission to this busy nightspot, so that you can get on with the serious business of partying.

HEN tastic

Specialists in
Hen Party
Merchandise

Free delivery
on all UK
orders

Visit our Online Shop at:

www.hentastic.com

oxford

It's one of those cities that makes you go 'ahh' when you arrive, thanks to the famous meadows and dreaming spires. But beauty's not just skin deep – Oxford is a vibrant, cosmopolitan, nerdy-yet-funky city with style.

Oxford skyline (top), Radcliffe Camera (middle), punts (bottom).

what to do

A beautiful city with lazy rivers, intelligent graffiti, great shops, superb little pubs and restaurants and an unusually high quotient of late night cocktail bars – we lurve Oxford.

Leave your cars at home (the traffic is horrendous) and make it a green weekend, hiring bikes, boating down the rivers and walking to shops, bars and cool little clubs in the city centre.

The student presence is huge. Young people of all nationalities with long scarves and big brains are in the bars, the bicycle lanes and clogging up the queues in H&M. Then there are all the lecturers and academics, clearly too intelligent to brush their hair, in the real ale pubs, delis and bookshops.

Visitors often worry that they will be asked difficult questions about their current reading habits or general knowledge, but relax, a lot of the scruffbags you see out and about are from the old poly, and thus no cleverer than anyone else.

The riverside pubs and boating stations come into their own in the summer. And though some think the Cotswold countryside around Oxford is twee, we reckon England doesn't get much lovelier.

10 good reasons

1. **riverside pubs**
2. **punting**
3. **cocktail culture**
4. **student promotions**
5. **friendly little clubs**
6. **arty crafty stuff**
7. **hiring bikes**
8. **really hard pub quizzes**
9. **thriving live music scene**
10. **exploring the Cotswolds**

Bikes are the transportation means of choice in Oxford.

sounds of the city

Keep young and beautiful If you feel too young to take golf seriously, take the Mickey with a nine-hole tour of Faringdon Golf Course. This gentle Par three is perfect for those of us who think that golf's basically a question of striding around in Pringle tank tops shouting 'fore' and receiving random applause. There's no need to book – just turn up with or without the Pringle and give it a go. Call 01367 243944.

Summertime You can't really go to Oxford in the summer without punting. Sorry, but there are rules. The River Cherwell, a major tributary of the Thames, wends its way past some of the best Cotswoldy pubs, including the locally loved Victoria Arms in Marston. There's just nothing more mellow than this, particularly if good food and a couple of glasses of Pimms are included. Start out at the Cherwell Boathouse, an idyllic spot and fabulous restaurant that's particularly renowned for its wines. Grab your punt, rowing boat or canoe after lunch (book a 'chauffeur' if you don't trust yourselves at the helm), and drift through impossibly pretty countryside for a few sunny hours.

Tall stories For a less horizontal river trip, Oxford River Cruises will pick hen parties up from various locations in Oxford and take you off for a Mad Hatter's tea party expedition, passing the college backs and meadows and through the scenery that inspired Alice in Wonderland. En route you'll eat cake and drink mysterious liquids labelled 'eat me' and 'drink me' a la Alice. Alternatively, take the picnic trip and disembark for a gourmet riverbank lunch. See oxfordrivercruises.com.

The closest thing to crazy Book your party into one of Oxford's coolest bars, Thirst, for the trendy decor, truly magnificent cocktails and the fact that this is where people come to drink and dance every night of the week. It's known as a haunt for those clubbers who still haven't had enough on a Sunday, possibly because it serves good bloody marys. In fact, Oxford's not short on really good cocktail places with a late licence, another of note being locally-loved Raoul's on Walton Street. Another little beauty is Baby Love, if you think you're cool enough and want to be up 'til 3am.

Pick up a punt at Cherwell Boathouse and head off down river.

Party Bar Risa on Hythe Bridge Street is a great place for a group to eat, drink and kick back, whether you're going upstairs to Jongleurs for the stand up comedy later on or opting for a night on the dancefloor at the classy Bridge nightclub nearby.

Jongleurs itself gets very dark, loud and packed – perfect for a night of rude jokes and stag and hen party debauchery, as after the comedians do their stand up routines the pished and giggling crowd takes to the dancefloor for a bit of a shuffle. It's the Jongleurs effect – you quaff away on those deceptively squash-like cocktails all night, but come midnight, somehow you're not walking straight. It's best to stay with your own kind – even if it does look like the night of the living dead – rather than try to get into another club at this point.

Fire it up If you're in the mood for making a mess, get a few bottles of wine and take the girls off to Unique Creations in Summertown. You'll paint your own ceramics, and you'll be amazed at how relaxing it is. Even if you've got the artistic skills of a hippo it doesn't matter – beauty is in the eye of the beholder so just give it to someone who loves you. Why not make hen party souvenirs for each other? Don't forget to book.

If you're after something a little hotter, why not head off to Banzai Events, near Bicester, for a day of full on outdoor-based activities, such as quad biking, rally driving, 4x4 off-roading, blind driving and reverse steer jeeps. Get competitive with a Jeep Gymkhana or a full on Grand Prix Day. Check it out at banzaievents.com.

Pretty Africa Many of Oxford's best drink and dance emporiums are located underground, Po Na Nas being no exception. With the exotic atmosphere of a Moroccan Souk, albeit one that serves poky cocktails, this is one of Oxford's most respected clubs, known for a great variety of music and a friendly crowd, as well as a bed to lie down on when it all gets a bit much.

Let off some steam in a rage buggy with Banzai.

where to stay

Take your pick from a city centre hotel within stumbling distance of the clubs, a good-value hostel or campsite, or a cute Cotswold cottage for your Oxford hen party.

hotels

Bicester Hotel £££

Chesterton, Bicester OX26 1TE
Tel. no 01869 241204
www.bicestercountryclub.com
reception2@bicesterhotelgolfandspa.com

This chic hotel, close to Blenheim Palace, has an 18-hole golf course and luxury spa all nestling in 134 acres of stunning Cotswold countryside. There are 52 deluxe bedrooms all with views over the fairways or into the designer courtyard. Free use of the gym, tennis courts and swimming pool is included with your stay. To eat, choose between Grays Restaurant and the less formal Brasserie.

Central Backpackers £

13 Park End Street, Oxford OX1 1HH
Tel. no 01865 242288
www.centralbackpackers.co.uk
oxford@centralbackpackers.co.uk

Oxford's premier hostel accommodation, named one of Europe's top hostels 2006–2008, is situated just 5 minutes walk from both the bus and train stations. This comfortable hostel has a high level of security with swipe card entry on all dorms and individual lockers. There's 24-hour access with no curfew and breakfast is included. There's even a BBQ on the roof terrace every Sunday.

Mercure Oxford Eastgate Hotel ££

73 High Street, Oxford OX1 4BE
Tel. no 01865 248332
www.mercure.com
H6668@accor.com

Originally a 17th century coaching inn, this four-star hotel has 63 ensuite rooms and the AA Rosette awarded for The High Table

'been there...'

We got a fab cottage just outside Burford. The first night we stocked up on wine and pizza and had a catch up. On Saturday we went and had a look round Oxford, did a bit of shopping and ate lunch at The Lamb and Flag. Saturday night was best – Pudding Pie came round and gave us this amazing cookery lesson in the cottage, with a three course meal...lush.

shared room without breakfast

£ under £30
££ £30–£60
£££ over £60
pppn

Brasserie and Bar. The hotel is ideally situated for visiting the colleges, punting on the river, shopping and all the nightlife on offer in the centre of the city. The hotel is easily accessible via M40.

Royal Oxford Hotel ££

Park End Street, Oxford OX1 1HR
Tel. no 01865 248432
www.royaloxfordhotel.co.uk
info@royaloxfordhotel.co.uk

The Royal Oxford Hotel is ideally located just 2 minutes walk from the heart of Oxford city centre, and within walking distance of the railway and bus stations. The ensuite rooms all feature free Wi-Fi, fresh fruit and bottled water. Café Coco restaurant is open from 8am–11pm at the weekend.

self-catering

Acacia Cottages ££

Tel. no 0800 234 6039
www.acaciacottages.co.uk
info@acaciacottages.co.uk

At Acacia Cottages they have hand-picked a selection of gorgeous Cotswold cottages for you to choose from. Not only that, but they will organise the whole weekend for you, drawing on their knowledge of the best local hen services and suppliers. So if you want something a bit different to the L-plate wearing ritual try Acacia.

shared room without breakfast

£ under £30
££ £30–£60
£££ over £60
pppn

One of Acacia's gorgeous Cotswold cottages.

Caswell House ££

Caswell Lane, Brize Norton OX18 3NJ
Tel. no 01993 701064
www.caswellhouse.co.uk
amanda@caswellhouse.co.uk

This beautiful historic 15th century manor house is set in the heart of 450 acres of Oxfordshire countryside and is surrounded by rural views with an ancient orchard, walled gardens and extensive lawns stretching down to the moat. Providing luxurious and spacious accommodation for up to 20 guests, Caswell House offers a relaxing, country house atmosphere in the heart of the Cotswolds.

Cherbridge Cottages ££

Hill Farm, Mill Lane, Marston, Oxford
OX3 0QG
Tel. no 07976 288329
www.cherbridgecottages.co.uk
enquiries@cherbridgecottages.co.uk

Cherbridge Cottage is part of a 1930s punting station providing contemporary self-catering holiday accommodation just 2 miles from Oxford. The property is set in large secluded gardens with extensive river frontage. Oxford is easily reached by car, cycle track or park-and-ride bus. A private punt and skiff are available to guests throughout the summer months.

Good Lake Barns ££

Church Farm, Shellingford,
Faringdon SN7 7QA
Tel. no 01367 710112
www.goodlakebarns.co.uk
info@goodlakebarns.co.uk

Shellingford is a charming small village in the picturesque Vale of the White Horse just 17 miles from Oxford. Goodlake Barns is a series of light and spacious self-catering cottages, sensitively converted and retaining much of the character and charm of the original stone barns, stables and outbuildings. There are three cottages sleeping four, six and eight as well as a studio that doubles as a fifth bedroom for the largest cottage. They are arranged around a courtyard on an organic dairy farm.

Kingfisher Barn ££

Rye Farm, Abingdon OX14 3NN
Tel. no 01235 537538
www.kingfisherbarn.com
info@kingfisherbarn.com

A few minutes from the River Thames in the heart of the most glorious countryside, you'll find Kingfisher Barn. Abingdon is just a 10-minute walk and Oxford is only 8 miles away. This self-catering accommodation is very well presented for a relaxing and comfortable stay. Stratford-upon-Avon, Blenheim Palace, Warwick Castle and of course the Cotswolds are all within easy driving distance.

where to eat and drink

Oxford has a lovely line in riverside pubs serving good British food and drink, but the city centre boasts some swanky bars and party-friendly restaurants too.

bars & pubs

Bar Risa

3–5 Hythe Bridge Street, Oxford
OX1 2EW
Tel. no 01865 722437
www.risa-oxford.co.uk
info@risa-oxford.co.uk

With two floors, two bars and an excellent outdoor terrace, Bar Risa has something for everyone. It's a great place to enjoy a lunchtime meal, an early evening cocktail or a club night. Food is served all day and all night here so you won't go hungry. There are frequent live events including Salsa dancing, Poker and bands; Jongleurs, the world class comedy club, also resides here.

Raoul's Bar

32 Walton Street, Oxford OX2 6AA
Tel. no 01865 553732
www.raoulsbar.co.uk
bartender@raoulsbar.com

Raoul's bar offers a wide range of award-winning cocktails featuring bartender Matt Marshall. Enjoy a cocktail making masterclass here, but make sure you book well in advance, these lessons get booked up very fast. Raoul's has a wonderful varied menu, so why not sample the food while you're there.

The Lamb and Flag

12 Saint Giles, Oxford OX1 3JS
Tel. no 01865 515787

Tucked away in a corner of Saint Giles, you have to look carefully not to miss it. The Lamb and Flag serves great-value traditional pub grub. This historic pub dates back to 1695 and, although it has been extensively remodelled over the years, the rear bars still have the character of an olde worlde pub.

Raoul's Bar in Walton Street.

Thirst

7–8 Park End Street, Oxford OX1 2HH,
Tel. no 01865 242 044
www.thirstbar.com
rob@thirstbar.com

A refuge for city slickers, students and just about anyone who finds out about it. There's something for everyone here. Spacious, lively, trendy cocktail bar, dead centre of Oxford's 'West End', with constant DJ action, Thirst also has a large and pleasant courtyard at rear. There are daily happy hours and even 'stupid hours'.

Victoria Arms

Mill Lane, Old Marston, Oxford
OX3 0PZ
Tel. no 01865 241382
www.victoriaarms.co.uk
victoriaarms@wadworth.co.uk

On the banks of the river Cherwell this country pub has a rural feel, yet it is just a short way from the dreaming spires of Oxford. With large gardens sweeping down to the river, it is a perfect spot in summer, especially if you arrive by punt. You may have seen this famous photogenic pub on Lewis or Inspector Morse!

restaurants

Cherwell Boathouse ££
50 Bardwell Road, Oxford OX2 6ST
Tel. no 01865 552746
www.cherwellboathouse.co.uk
info@cherwellboathouse.co.uk

Situated in the heart of Oxford on the banks of the Cherwell, The Boathouse is a place to relax and enjoy fine wine and fine French dining in a tranquil and picturesque setting. And if the sun shines, enjoy a meal on the fabulous terrace.

Kashmir Halal £
64 Cowley Road, Oxford OX4 1JB
Tel. no 01865 242941

If you're looking for a 'bring your own' (booze not food that is!) curry house, this is the best in Oxford. Kashmir Halal offers great value for excellent quality food. A brilliant choice for big groups, the Kashmir always has a bustling atmosphere and the service is efficient and friendly.

'real life'

We had a great night at The Living Room in the Oxford Castle redevelopment. We were really lucky with the weather and we sat out on the roof terrace which has amazing views. The food was all really well cooked and the cocktails to die for.

The Living Room, Oxford Castle.

2 courses + half a bottle of wine

£ under £20
££ £20–£35
£££ over £35

Who can resist pizza? Head to Mario's.

Mario's £
103 Cowley Road, Oxford OX4 1HU
Tel. no 01865 722955
www.mariooxford.co.uk
mariopizzeria@yahoo.co.uk

For an authentic Italian experience and food like 'mamma used to make' it has to be Mario's. With a great selection of traditional Italian dishes and friendly, attentive service makes this pizzeria trattoria a great place for a large group.

Portabello ££
7 South Parade, Oxford OX2 7JL
Tel. no 01865 559653
www.portabellorestaurant.co.uk
info@portabellorestaurant.co.uk

Dining at Portabello's is a relaxed casual affair whether inside or out on the terrace. Kick back with a chilled glass of Sauvignon and peruse the modern British menu featuring local and seasonal produce.

The Thai Orchid ££
58a St Clement's Street,
Oxford OX4 1AH
Tel. no 01865 798044
www.thaigroup.co.uk
thaiboathouse@btconnect.com

A local dining institution, The Orchid is great for parties. The authentic interior with teak furniture and tropical plants makes an atmospheric environment, but the star of the show here is the wonderful Thai food.

where to party

The lively student scene gives Oxford a great night time vibe, and you'll find a huge mix of live music, stand-up comedy, top cocktail joints and superb little nightclubs.

They'll be spinning the discs at Baby Love.

Baby Love
3 King Edward Street, Oxford OX1 4HS
Tel. no 01865 200011
www.baby-bar.co.uk
Easily Oxford's most eclectic music venue, Baby Love Bar is one of the safest, funkiest and varied venues for world-famous names in pop, house, drum'n'bass, indie and electro, to name but a few. With regulars including some of Oxford's serial party-goers, everybody's welcome to a guaranteed night of serious fun.

Clementine's
15 St Clement's Street,
Oxford OX4 1AB
Tel. no 01865 247214
Formerly the hip shakin' Club Latino, Clementine's is a two-floored bar of madness. Although long noisy queues are typical outside, once you're in the club the body-shaking bass will get your heart pumping. 'Fever' on a Saturday night features everyone's disco favourites.

Escape
9 High Street, Oxford OX1 4DB
Tel. no 01865 246766
www.escapeoxford.com
escape-oxford@hotmail.com

Escape boasts two floors playing a varied mix of music with a selection of guest DJs ensuring a stylish ambience to complete your night out. This luxurious and exclusive venue situated in the heart of Oxford's city centre combines a bar, restaurant and nightclub. It's a guaranteed good night out.

Lava & Ignite
Park End Street, Oxford OX1 1JD
Tel. no 01865 250 181
www.lavaignite.com
lava&ignite-oxford@luminar.co.uk

With four bars, three dancefloors, state-of-the-art sound and lighting systems, breathtaking visuals and unrivalled entertainment until 2am, Lava & Ignite presents a unique clubbing experience in Oxford.

Po Na Na

13 Magdalen Street, Oxford OX1 3AE
Tel. no 01865 249171
www.eclecticbars.co.uk/oxfordponana/
info@oxfordponana.com

Located in St.Giles at the heart of the
dreaming spires, Po Na Na Oxford is the
most vibrant cocktail bar and nightclub in this
very discerning city. The Souk-style decor
lends an off-beat sophistication and relaxed
atmosphere to every occasion, while the
warm ambience, and buzz from the trendy
regular clientele make Po Na Na the place to
party every weekend. The hottest resident
DJs playing credible music, teamed with
good service, provide the perfect mix.

The Bridge

6–9 Hythe Bridge Street,
Oxford OX1 2EW
Tel. no 01865 242 526
www.bridgeoxford.co.uk
phil@bridgeoxford.co.uk

This busy city centre club fills up early, so
don't be late. The Bridge is split into three
different parts: Anuba (the pre-club bar), the
main club and the lounge. Starting off at
Anuba gives you fast track admission to the
club and you can also hire this place for
private parties. The music at the club is

varied depending on what night you go.
Usually on the first floor there's hip hop and
R'n'B and the second floor plays dance
anthems. In the lounge the music is more
chilled with soulful sounds.

The Cellar

Frewin Court, Cornmarket St,
Oxford OX1 3HZ
Tel. no 01865 244761
www.cellarmusic.co.uk
Located right next to the Oxford Union's
Purple Turtle, this is a less cheesy option.
You can let your hair down and dance as if
no one is looking here. The staff are cool and
the music is always different and interesting.
This is a place for maximum fun.

The Old Fire Station

40 George Street, Oxford OX1 2AQ
Tel. no 01865 297182

The OFS is one of the top party destinations
in Oxford. A classic mix of 70s, 80s, 90s,
chart and cheese makes the weekends
partytastic – heaven for hen and stag parties.
The venue has a long bar with a great
selection of drinks and a good size
dancefloor. You can dance the night away to
all those cheesy choons you never admit to
liking and we won't tell anyone – honest!

Pucker up now girls!

york

Minster (top), Guildhall (middle), Clifford Tower (bottom).

York's the place to go if you're more interested in the paranormal than the paralytic – but with a large 20–40 year old population, the ghosts aren't the only ones with favourite haunts and high jinks on their nightly agenda.

what to do

York's crammed with curiosities, fun and vibrant…if you're looking for a real cultural city break rather than a could-be-anywhere bar crawl, you won't find a better place.

Famed for it's Viking, medieval and Roman history, not to mention the ghosts, you might think York's stuck in the past. Yet this stunning little city has a thriving nightlife and plethora of great places to eat and drink.

For hen parties, it's a sophisticated choice. The main attractions, shops, bars and pubs are all crammed into the labyrinthine streets, and encircled by the ancient city walls. It's the kind of town where you'll actually enjoy getting a bit lost, as it's full of curiosities and every street corner seems to have a

story, a saint or a visiting spirit (and we're not talking guest vodka). Sit by the river or take a boat trip; catch a major art exhibition or picnic by the old abbey ruins; have lunch in a Fossgate restaurant or cocktails and late night laughs at the Evil Eye…

The nightlife is not too twee or stuck in the past – thanks to the excellent university and a young population, York has a fantastic selection of swish bars, ancient pubs and top class eateries, as well as a few good places for dancin' later on.

The Shambles is all cobbled streets and Tudor houses.

10 good reasons

1. charm and charisma
2. cocktails at KoKo's
3. ancient pubs
4. quirky restaurants
5. Yorkminster
6. hiring a boat
7. historic and pretty
8. easy to walk around
9. ghost stories
10. lovely boutique hotels

sounds of the city

F.E.A.R. The world's first ghost tour was started up in York and is still going strong. Funny, chilling and gruesome in turns, the Original Ghost Walk guides walk and talk you around the oldest and spookiest parts of the city and generally aim to scare the bejeezus out of you. We loved it – grotesque tales of locked-up plague orphans, fascinating descriptions of Roman soldiers marching through a cellar, and many other horrible stories and legends bring the city and its past inhabitants to life. The nightly tours start at 8pm at the King's Arms by the river (take a look inside to see how often this place gets flooded, by the way).

You're history York is full of ancient sites, museums, galleries and other attractions. If you only look around two, make them York Minster and Clifford's Tower. The Minster is the largest Gothic cathedral in Europe, alongside Cologne's. The site dates from 627 CE, William the Conqueror was crowned here in 1066, it was trashed in the Reformation, burnt in 1984…. The history's fascinating, but the best thing about it is looking at the tiny gargoyles in the Chapterhouse. Reward yourselves for this cultural injection over the road at Café Concerto. It's the best café in the City – the cake is essential.

Clifford's Tower dates back to William the Conqueror. This small castle keep was where York's Jewish population fled in 1190 to escape violent persecution. They burned themselves to death rather than be captured by their tormentors. The tower's named after Robert Clifford, who was hanged there in 1322.

Take your mind off it with a trip round the nearby York Museum, which has an entire old street as part of its exhibition, or come back to the land of the living with an early bird dinner at the gorgeous 31 Castlegate restaurant. Book in advance, as it's popular.

Party hard Club Salvation, The Gallery and Ziggy's are top York venues for dancing after quaffing in the pubs. Club Salvation leads the way, with nightly DJs playing chart, dance and RnB music to party to. The Gallery is the place for cheese, flirting and fun.

The Majestic York Minster dominates the centre of the city.

Sometimes you just can't make it on your own If you and the ladies like cooking, there's no better way to spend a day (or evening) in York than at The Cooking Rooms. Take a class – from Spanish or Indian cuisine to chocolates or patisserie – or book for a private party and discuss the right menu for you. The people training you are all professional chefs (some are almost celebrity chefs), and by the end of your session you'll be fully skilled up, wined and dined. Even if you've burnt the salad and evaporated the soup, you'll still have a laugh over a wine or two.

Just looking Glam it up with a day at York Racecourse – which has some great hospitality facilities, including four 'dine and view' restaurants. You can book packages, including a box for parties of 16 or more. Rather!

Rock the house Baille Hill House, just outside the city walls, sleeps ten house-trained hens. The big kitchen diner is perfect for dinners together, and with six TVs, two hifis and a video and CD library you won't be bored if it rains. Why not have a civilised soiree in your new home from home – book an entertainer, caterers, hire a model for a life drawing lesson...?

The best entertainment of all, we think, for a stay-at-home hen party is a ThirtyFifty wine tasting night. You'll drink (no spitting out, please) fine wines or champagnes and sparkling wines all night. Learn what goes with what, how to sound knowledgeable about grapes and how to pretend you're not sozzled. Alternatively you can choose to have a chocolate and wine tasting session. They'll arrange a Butler in the Buff or some pampering, too, to really make a night of it. Call 0208 288 0314.

'been there...'

We did the tourist thing... York Minster, the museum, rowing on the Ouse and drinking in as many spooky old pubs as possible. We were staying in a hotel outside town, which is the only thing I'd change as we had to get cabs. I loved the shopping in York, it's such a nice place to wander around. The ghost walk was actually really good and not cheesy at all.

Move yer bloomin' arse! Why not dust off your hat and head to the races?

where to stay

Get thee to a nunnery! From a 17th century convent to Middlethorpe Hall, things can get pretty posh around here. But there's always the hostels for a budget option.

hotels and b&bs

Ace Hotel £–££

Micklegate House, 88–90 Micklegate, York YO1 6JX
Tel. no 01904 627720
www.ace-hotelyork.co.uk
reception@ace-hotelyork.co.uk

Located in the Mickelgate, the oldest part of York, and close to the railway station, this budget hotel is in a grand Georgian building with carved sweeping staircase, panelled rooms and Rococo ceiling. With its own games room, sauna and outside seating area this is a budget hotel with a difference. Choose from 14-bed to twin dorms to suit your wallet.

* shared room without breakfast

£ under £30
££ £30–£60
£££ over £60
pppn

Knavesmire Manor Hotel ££–£££

302 Tadcaster Road, York YO24 1HE
Tel. no 01904 702941
www.knavesmire.co.uk
enquire@knavesmire.co.uk

Once the home of the Rowntree family and now tastefully converted to a hotel with indoor swimming pool and quality restaurant. Situated close to York Racecourse, this family-run hotel offers friendly service to all guests and is less than 2 miles from the centre.

Middlethorpe Hall £££

Bishopthorpe Road York YO23 2GB
Tel. no 01904 641241
www.middlethorpe.com
booking@middlethorpe.com

Book into this exclusive country house hotel for a classy spa experience in the beautiful Yorkshire countryside. Stroll through 20 acres of parkland and escape from city life.

Newington Hotel ££

147 Mount Vale, York YO24 1DJ
Tel. no 01904 625173
www.thenewington.co.uk
info@thenewington.co.uk

Positioned on the Royal Approach, close to the racecourse, the Newington makes the perfect base for a visit to York. The modern ensuite bedrooms are comfortable and well equipped; and the indoor heated pool and sauna are the perfect place to relax at the end of the day. Prices include breakfast.

The Bar Convent ££

17 Blossom Street, York YO24 1AQ
Tel. no 01904 643238
www.bar-convent.org.uk
info@bar-convent.org.uk

This somewhat surprising option is a unique choice of B&B or self-catering accommodation. Although not all the rooms are ensuite, they are comfy and well presented.

Georgian grandeur at Ace Hotel.

self-catering

Allerthorpe Lakeland Park £

Allerthorpe Lakeland Park, Allerthorpe,
York YO42 4RL
Tel. no 01759 301444
www.allerthorpelakelandpark.co.uk
info@allerthorpelakelandpark.co.uk

This lakeside caravan and camping park also
has a luxury apartment for rent – Manderlay.
With 50 acres of grounds and lakes,
there is a variety of watersports on
offer here, including windsurfing,
powerboating, sailing, and
canoeing.

Baille Hill House ££

2 Bishopsgate Street,
York YO23 1JH
Tel. no 01845 597614
www.baillehillhouse.co.uk
enquiries@baillehillhouse.co.uk

This Georgian style self-catering cottage is
the only rental accommodation in the centre
of York catering for ten people. With pubs
and bars, restaurants and nightlife just 5
minutes walk away, it's so convenient.

Inyork Holidays ££

11 Walmgate, York, YO1 9TX
Tel. no 01904 632660
www.inyorkholidays.co.uk
agents@inyorkholidays.co.uk

This local accommodation agency brings
together a varied selection of self-catering
apartments and townhouses within easy
access of the city centre all with parking.

Merricote Cottages ££

Malton Road, Stockton on the Forest,
York YO32 9TL
Tel. no 01904 400256
www.merricote-holiday-cottages.co.uk
enquiries@merricote-holiday-
cottages.co.uk

Once a traditional working farm, Merricote
has been sympathetically converted to
provide eight superb cottages, each one with
individual character. Situated in 8 acres of
rural Yorkshire, 3 miles from the city centre,
Merricote is a great base to relax in and to
explore the surrounding area from.

**shared room
without
breakfast**

**£ under £30
££ £30–£60
£££ over £60
pppn**

The Riverside York ££

8a Peckitt Street, York
YO1 9SF
Tel. no 01904 623008
www.riverside-york.co.uk

This luxurious Victorian self-catering
townhouse provides a haven right in the
centre of the city. The spacious and elegantly
furnished rooms, overlooking the River
Ouse, are arranged on three floors.
Accommodating up to six people
and equipped with all the
modern comforts you require,
this will feel like home from
home.

York Holiday Homes ££

53 Goodramgate, York YO1
7LS
Tel. no 01904 641997
www.yorkholidayhomes.co.uk
enquiries@yorkholidayhomes.co.uk

Choose from 11 different properties all
centrally located just minutes away from the
sights and nightlife. The apartments
accommodate two–six guests, but up to 18
can be catered for in several together.

The City Walls.

where to eat and drink

bars & pubs

Evil Eye Lounge
42 Stonegate, York YO1 8AS
Tel. no 01904 640010
www.evileyelounge.com

It may look like an 'offie', but venture a little further and you'll find a bohemian bar and eatery serving Asian-style food. Famously a hang-out of Johnny Depp...

King's Arms
3 Kings Staith, York YO1 9SN
Tel. no 01904 659435

This is a proper pub serving quality beers and lagers with an unrivalled position right on the riverside. Frequent flooding has made the pub famous nationwide, but when the sun shines, there's no better location in York.

KoKo International Bar
31 Goodramgate, York YO1 7LS
Tel. no 01904 628344
vahe@kokobar.com

If you want good beer, exciting cocktails, excellent wine and champagne, a good atmosphere and interesting people, then this is the place to be! It's a beautiful listed building, believed to be an old monastery. Try KoKo's Ghost cocktail plus many more.

Pitcher and Piano
Coney Street, York YO1 9QL
Tel. no 01904 658580
www.pitcherandpiano.com

With a fantastic riverside location, The York Pitcher and Piano is a great place to enjoy an 'al fresco' drink or even a meal on the large balcony. There's always a vibrant atmosphere here in the evening and you can book a booth for 12–20 people.

The King's Arms pub on the riverside.

Revolution
Coney Street, York YO1 9NA
Tel. no 01904 676054
www.revolution-bars.co.uk/york

Revolution, home of Vodka, knows how to throw a party and has hosted some of the best hen parties. What could be better than getting all of your friends together for one big cocktail party? You can hire a room or book a table at Revolution and why not add on a cocktail masterclass to learn how to mash and shake your own fabulous blends. Then party on to the small hours.

The Living Room
Merchant Exchange, 1 Bridge Street, York YO1 6DD
Tel. no 01904 461000
www.thelivingroom.co.uk
york@thelivingroom.co.uk

With lovely views over the River Ouse, this cool, airy piano bar is an informal place to eat, drink and chill out. With a varied menu and wine list, and over 100 cocktails on offer, There's something to suit everyone here.

cafés & restaurants

31 Castlegate £££
31 Castlegate, York YO1 9RN
Tel. no 01904 621404
www.31castlegate.co.uk
nickjulius@31castlegate.co.uk

This elegant restaurant offers a true fine dining experience. Chef, Nick Julius, has created a menu of modern European dishes reflecting the knowledge and experience he gained working in places such as Marco Pierre White's L'Escargot. There is a private dining room available for parties of up to 20.

Bettys Café Tea Rooms ££
6–8 St Helen's Square, York YO1 8QP
Tel. no 01904 659142
www.bettys.co.uk

Inspired by the luxury liner, Queen Mary, in 1936, the York branch of Bettys is resplendent with huge curved windows, elegant wood panelling and ornate mirrors. Sample a hearty English breakfast, a traditional afternoon tea or a three-course meal with wine in Art Deco splendour.

Champagne afternoon tea at Bettys is a must.

Café Concerto ££
21 High Petergate, York YO1 7EN
Tel. no 01904 610478
www.cafeconcerto.biz
coffee@cafeconcerto.biz

Friendly and informal, the musically themed Café Concerto is right opposite York Minster. Serving everything from deli sandwiches for lunch to Swordfish steaks with cous cous on the evening menu, you'll find high quality food freshly prepared to an exceptional level.

Fiesta Mehicana ££
14 Clifford Street, York YO1 9RD
Tel. no 01904 610243
www.fiestamehicana.com
info@fiestamehicana.com

Groups of ten or more can order a party menu at this premier Mexican restaurant and sample a variety of authentic dishes, such as Nachos, Chimichangas, Burritos and Fajitas, for the excellent price of £15.95 a head. And if you're the organiser – you eat free!

La Tasca ££
21 Back Swinegate, York YO1 8AD
Tel. no 01904 521100
www.latasca.co.uk
latasca.york@bayrestaurantgroup.com

Share a tapas platter Spanish-style at this classic restaurant, but your fiesta won't be complete without a jug or two of Sangria!

'real life'

We had such a good time at The Living Room. Service was fantastic and the atmosphere was buzzing, so we stayed put all night!

The relaxed environment warms up later on!

where to party

Much of York's nightlife is centred on the riverside.

Club Salvation

3 George Hudson Street, York YO1 6JL
Tel. no 01904 635144
www.clubsalvation.co.uk
robyn@clubsalvation.co.uk

The relatively new kid on the block, Club Salvation is a two venue nightspot hosting big-named DJs and live PAs every month. The two rooms are distinctly different with a choice of music in each one. Open until 4.30am on Friday and Saturday nights and with VIP booths available for your private party, the helpful people at Salvation will even organise a limousine to deliver you to the door in style for your extra special night.

Fibbers

Stonebow House, The Stonebow,
York YO1 7NP
Tel. no 01904 641413
www.fibbers.co.uk
fibbers@fibbers.co.uk

The top live music venue in York, Fibbers is an intimate and steamy affair. If you want to get hot and sweaty with a load of other indie faithfuls, then this is the place for you. Fibbers also plays host to York's only alternative club night every Saturday – Distortion. So if you want to get away from the usual blend of laser lights and cocktails, give Fibbers a try.

Flares

6 Tanner Row, York YO1 6JB
Tel. no 01904 653283
www.flaresbars.com
info@flaresbars.com

Spread over three floors of this city centre venue, Flares brings you all your favourite 70s hits and disco floor-fillers. Get glammed up in some seriously loud gear and unfeasibly big hair and groove on down to the irresistible soundtrack. They love hen and stag parties at Flares, so contact the venue and find out about the cool party packages they can offer you. If you love ABBA, then Fridays at Flares are for you...it's Mamma Mia all the way.

Get some 70s action at Flares.

Hub Nightclub

53–55 Micklegate, York YO1 6LJ
Tel. no 01904 620602
www.ziggysnightclub.com
contact@ziggysnightclub.com

Currently undergoing a transformation from Ziggys to Hub, this is now the main venue for underground dance nights in York. So if you're into techno and electronic dance music, then this is the place for you. Check the website for more info on the DJs and the music they will be serving up, but expect plenty of heart-pumping beats and big sounds.

The Gallery

12 Clifford Street, York YO1 1RD
Tel. no 01904 647947
www.galleryclub.co.uk
gallery-york@luminar.co.uk

Owned by the ubiquitous Luminar Leisure, The Gallery offers the usual slick and shiny service you'd expect from a nationwide organisation. The very helpful party organisers here will put together a 'club pack' for you with lots of goodies to make your night extra special, all for a small fee of course.

Tru

3–5 Toft Green, York YO1 6JT
Tel. no 01904 620203
www.truyork.co.uk
tru-york@luminar.co.uk

Luminar have got their foot well and truly in the door in York. Tru is a four room venue within the city walls of historic York. You'll find the cream of the local talent DJing here and you can expect a pulsating dancefloor every weekend night grooving to all sorts of music from funky house to cheesy chart.

Vudu Lounge

37–39 Swinegate, York YO1 8AZ
Tel. no 01904 627627
www.vudulounge.co.uk
vudulounge@hotmail.co.uk

This classy cocktail bar has some of the best bartenders in York mixing some quality cocktails. DJ Jed plays here regularly, entertaining an R'n'B crowd 'til the early hours of the morning.

Drinks on the balcony overlooking the River Ouse.

THE CHEAPEST WAY TO THE BEST STAG AND HEN PARTIES IN EUROPE

BUDAPEST   KAUNAS
PRAGUE   RIGA
GDANSK   KRAKOW
POZNAN   WROCLAW

RYANAIR

Aberdeen
GLASGOW   EDINBURGH
Derry
BELFAST   Newcastle
            Teeside
Manchester LEEDS
LIVERPOOL   Doncaster
            EAST MIDLANDS
BRISTOL   BIRMINGHAM
Newquay   LUTON   STANSTED
            Gatwick
BOURNEMOUTH

FLIGHTS FROM SELECTED UK AIRPORT

RYANAIR

HEN PARTY WISH LIST:

- COCKTAILS with the girls!

- 5 Star Luxury hotels

- Shopping

- Pampering

- Fit blokes

- nightclub VIP ENTRY!

Why waste your time flicking through hundreds of hen companies?

Get access to 4500 hen products and plan your whole weekend with the henparty planner.
Invite all your friends and have a group vote of the favourite weekends you choose for them.
You and your friends can pay in interest free instalments of as little as £11 each!

- 100% satisfaction guarantee
- Inclusive insurance
- Do it all yourself - easy to use system
- Free access to award winning hen support specialists

Done in minutes with no need to speak to 'sales people' and you decide what weekends to let your friends choose from...

What are you waiting for...?

www.henparty.co.uk

picture credits

Bath Spa Media would like to thank the following for loan of pictures featured in this publication. The reference is given as page number followed by b (bottom), c (centre) l (left), r (right) or t (top) to indicate position where more than picture on the page.

5tl Karaoke Box; 5tr Pop Party; 5bl Riverside Apartment; 5br The Jungle NI; 9t&b Leisure Vouchers; 10tl Butlers in the Buff; 10tc Shaggy Sheep; 10tr Kempton Park; 10bl Piggi T-shirts; 10bc www.englishsurfschool.com; 10br Pop Party; 11tl Leisure Vouchers; 11c Adventure 21; 11tr Beas of Bloomsbury; 11bl Latin Salsa Belfast; 11bc Ascot; 11br Waterfall Spa, Leeds; 12t Leisure Vouchers; 12b Smugglers Haven, Newquay; 15 Pop Party; 18bl&br,19tl&tr Leisure Vouchers; 20 englishsurfschool.com; 23bl Leisure Vouchers; 24 Pop Party; 28tl istockphoto©Peter Heyworth; 28tr visitbath.com; 28cl istockphoto©Stuart Taylor; 28c istockphoto©Robert Mayne; 28cr Newcastle Gateshead Initiative; 28bl istockphoto©Craig Swatton; 28bc Cherwell Boathouse, Oxford; 28br visitbrighton.com; 29tl visitcardiff.com; 29tr istockphoto©weinaliphotography; 29cl visityork.com; 29c istockphoto©Alan Taylor; 29cr bournemouthtourism.co.uk; 29bl Destination Bristol; 29bc istockphoto©Adam Booth; 29bcr istockphoto; 29br www.visitnewquay.org; 30t istockphoto©Jason Keffert; 30c istockphoto©Alessandra Litta Modignani; 30b istockphoto©Craig Swatton; 31 Leisure Vouchers; 32 The Sanctuary; 34bl istockphoto© Dmitriy Shironosov; 34tr singalonga.net; 36 Ascot Racecourse; 37tl malelifephotographicmodel.com; 37br Create Boutique; 38bl Revolution Karting; 38tr schooldisco.com; 40 Grange Holborn Hotel; 41(all) Haymarket Hotel; 42t&b K West Hotel; 46 The Boundary; 48tl Buddha Bar; 48br Dirty Martinis; 49 On Anon; 52 Jewel Bar; 53 Karaoke Box; 54 Supperclub; 56t Belfast Visitor & Convention Bureau, 56c istockphoto©Robert Mayne; 56b istockphoto©Paul Kavanagh; 57l&r Belfast Visitor & Convention Bureau; 58 Latin Salsa; 60 Polercise party; 61 Rezidor Park Inns; 64 Botanic Inns; 65 Rezidor Park Inns; 66 Bambu Beach Club; 68 Belfast Visitor & Convention Bureau; 70t,c,b Marketing Birmingham, www.visitbirmingham.com; 71 istockphoto©weinaliphotography; 72 istockphoto©Lev Dolgatshjov; 74 Snow Dome, Tamworth; 76 City-Nites; 78 Marketing Birmingham, www.visitbirmingham.com; 79tr istockphoto©Joe Gough; 79bl Ha Ha Bar and Grill; 80 Pleasure Ladies Nights; 82 Sence Nightclub; 84t istockphoto©Adam Booth; 84c Leisure Vouchers; 84b istockphoto©Peter Heyworth; 85 Leisure Vouchers; 86 istockphoto©yang guo; 88 istockphoto©David Dawson; 89 Number One St Luke's Hotel; 90 istockphoto©Stuart Taylor; 92 Brannigans; 93tr West Coast Rock Café; 93bl istockphoto©Dmitriy Shironosov; 94 Funny Girls; 96 The Syndicate; 98tl Leisure Vouchers; 98c&b,99

bournemouthtourism.co.uk; 100 Leisure Vouchers; 102 Zorb South; 103&104 Hallmark Hotel Bournemouth; 106, 107bl, 108 bournemouthtourism.co.uk; 107tr istockphoto; 110 The Old Fire Station; 112t, c&b, 113, 114, 116, 117, 118, 119, 120, 121bl visitbrighton.com; 121tr Old Orleans Restaurant; 122 istockphoto©Anna Garmashova; 124 Rendezvous Casino; 126t istockphoto©Marek Slusarczyk; 126c istockphoto; 126b istockphoto; 127,128 www.visitbath.co.uk; 130 istockphoto©Cindy Singleton; 131 Belushis.com/bath; 134 Sub 13, Bath; 135 The Arch; 136 Komedia, Bath; 138 Destination Bristol; 140t,c&b visitcardiff.com; 141 breconbeacons.org©Nanette Hepburn; 142,144,148 &149bl visitcardiff.com; 149tr Leisure Vouchers; 150 istockphoto©Craig Swatton; 152 © DWP-Fotolia.com; 154t istockphoto©Douglas McGilviray; 154c Edinburgh Fringe Festival; 154b istockphoto; 155 istockphoto©Alan Taylor; 156 Harvey Nichols Edinburgh©Grant Smith 2005; 158 Pop Party; 160 Festival Apartments; 162 The Living Room; 163 Tex Mex II; 164t&b Espionage; 166 istockphoto©Dmitriy Shironosov; 168t,c&b Glasgow City Council; 169 Curryoke Club; 170 istockphoto©Miodrag Gajic; 172 Huntfun.co.uk; 176 Sports Café Glasgow; 177&178 Curryoke Club; 180 istockphoto; 182t,c&b, 183 Leeds City Council; 184 Waterfall Spa; 186 Universal Dance Creations; 187 Holiday Inn Express; 188,190,191,192&194 Leeds City Council; 196t istockphoto©Stuart Taylor; 196c&b Marketing Manchester; 197 Alton Towers; 198 singalonga.net; 200 The Chill Factore; 201 Hallmark Hotels; 202 Marketing Manchester; 204 Brannigans, Cougar Leisure; 205bl&tr Hard Rock Café; 206& 208t Pure Nightclub; 208b The Birdcage; 210t,c&b, 211 Newcastle Gateshead Initiative; 212 The Pamper Party; 214 Milky Moments; 218, 219 Newcastle Gateshead Initiative; 220 istockphoto; 222 The Attic; 224t Smuggler's Haven; 224c www.visitnewquay.org; 224b www.visitnewquay.org/Paul Watts; 225 www.visitnewquay.org; 226 englishsurfschool.com; 228 istockphoto©Arjan de Jager; 229 Hotel Victoria; 230 Smugglers Haven; 232&233t Fistral Blu; 233b istockphoto©Ryan Fox; 234 Berties Club; 236 Pure Newquay; 238t&c ©Kingpin Media Ltd; 238b Cherwell Boathouse; 239 istockphoto; 240 Cherwell Boathouse; 242 Banzai Events; 244 Acacia Cottages; 246 Raoul's Bar; 247bl The Living Room; 247tr istockphoto©Kai Zhang; 248 istockphoto; 250 istockphoto©Cat London; 252t,c&b, 253, 254, 256 visit york; 257 Ace Hotel; 258, 260 261tr Visit York; 261bl The Living Room; 262, 264 visit york.

'SOMETHING GORG

and a little **SOPHISTICATED...**
Pre-wedding celebrations for friends who desire a little more…

We know that the devil's in the detail and the detail's in the planning. Utilising our experience and hand picked database, the finest hotels, glamorous events and superior activities will be organised stress and hassle free, leaving you free to do whatever you do. Unique and original ideas for an exclusive pre-wedding party are just a call away. Let us take the strain while you enjoy the glory. Talk to us today for a friendly and professional approach to your big celebration. After all, fun is a serious business.

Something for nothing...
*Make an enquiry and you
will be entered into a free
prize draw to win a luxury
pamper experience.
No strings, no catches.
Details online.*

...OUS...

win a relaxation day for two

with www.exhilaration.co.uk

exhilaration

Send us five exciting photographs depicting the best moments of your hen party, along with captions to each picture, and you could win a fabulous day of pure relaxation for you and a friend.

The winner can use the prize at one of many locations across the UK. You'll get two treatments each, such as a soothing massage or invigorating facial, and full use of the fitness and leisure facilities. Fully trained professional staff will be on hand, so that you emerge feeling sleek and carefree!

For full details of the prize go to:
www.exhilaration.co.uk/experiences/Relaxation_Day_for_Two_140/

**Send your photo entry to: competition@cuttingedgeguides.com
Closing date for entries 31/12/10.**